The Peirce Seminar Papers
Essays in Semiotic Analysis

VOLUME V

2002

Berghahn Books
NEW YORK • OXFORD

Published in 2002 by
Berghahn Books

www.berghahnbooks.com

© 2002 Michael Shapiro

All rights reserved.
Except for the quotation of short passages
for the purposes of criticism and review, no part of this book
may be reproduced in any form or by any means, electronic or
mechanical, including photocopying, recording, or any information
storage and retrieval system now known or to be invented,
without written permission of the publisher.

Library of Congress control number: 2002025594

British Library Cataloguing in Publication Data

A catalogue record for this book is available from
the British Library.

Printed in the United States on acid-free paper

ISBN 1-57181-419-1 (hardback)
ISSN 1068-3771

VOLUME V 2002
The Peirce Seminar Papers

Editor's Introduction   v

Essays

Biopragmatism, Space/Time Cognition, and the Sense of Language
   Nils B. Thelin   1

The Biological Substrate of Icons, Indexes, and Symbols in Animal Communication: A Neurosemiotic Analysis of Vervet Monkey Alarm Calls
   João Queiroz and Sidarta Ribeiro   69

How 'Our Senses as Reasoning Machines' Prove That Our Perceptual Judgments Are True Representations of External Reality
   Dan Nesher   79

Aspects of a Neo-Peircean Linguistics: Language History as Linguistic Theory
   Michael Shapiro   108

Indication, Iconicity, Grammaticalization and the Categories
   Tony Jappy   126

The Sense of Language (as *Langage*) versus the Nonsense of Languages (as *Langues*): Iconicity versus Arbitrariness
   Joëlle Réthoré   152

Cognitive "Hot Spots" in the Russian Case System
   Laura A. Janda   165

Interrogation and Nonconfirmativity: A Peircean Approach to the Intersection between Expressive Past and Present
   Victor A. Friedman   189

Reading as Iconization
   Jørgen Dines Johansen   204

Editor
MICHAEL SHAPIRO
Brown University

Editorial Board
RAIMO ANTTILA
University of California, Los Angeles
DAN NESHER
University of Haifa
THOMAS L. SHORT
Titusville, New Jersey

Advisory Board
Jean Fisette (Université du Québec à Montréal)
Paul Friedrich (University of Chicago)
Michael C. Haley (University of Alaska Anchorage)
Robert Hatten (Indiana University)
Anthony Jappy (Université de Perpignan)
James J. Liszka (University of Alaska Anchorage)
Roland Posner (Technische Universität Berlin)
Joëlle Réthoré (Université de Perpignan)
Richard S. Robin (Mount Holyoke College)
Marianne Shapiro (New York, New York)

Editor's Introduction

The contributions appearing in this, the fifth volume of *The Peirce Seminar Papers*, have been selected from papers presented at the Colloque International, "Sémiotique peircienne: Etat des lieux/ Peircean Semiotics: The State of the Art," held 27–30 June 2001 at Canet-Plage en Roussillon, outside Perpignan, France. I wish to acknowledge with thanks the help of the organizers of the Colloquium, Tony Jappy and Joëlle Réthoré, in preparing this volume for publication. I am also happy to welcome them as new members of the Advisory Board, together with James Liszka.

Volume 5 also marks other changes in the composition of the Boards. Thomas Short has agreed to join Raimo Anttila and Dan Nesher on the Editorial Board. I note with sadness the death of Thomas Sebeok, who was among the founding members of the Advisory Board.

Finally, I must report with great regret the resignation of Michael Haley as Managing Editor. Mike served with admirable enthusiasm, assiduity, and skill since the series began in 1993. Indeed, *The Peirce Seminar Papers* would not exist but for his tireless labor in preparing camera-ready copy, and we are all very much in his debt. Fortunately, Mike remains on the masthead as a member of the Advisory Board.

M.S.

Nils B. Thelin

Biopragmatism, Space/Time Cognition, and the Sense of Language

> To my friend and colleague
> Andrzej Bogusławski
> on his 70th birthday

1. Teleology, Natural Selection, and Language Semiosis in a Pragmatic Framework

There are at least two ways in which questions about the *sense* of language can be said to refer. The first possibility is that we have in mind the overall communicative purpose of language, its teleology; the second—its mode of functioning in order to achieve this purpose, that is, its sense-making, or semiotic functionality. These two kinds of *sense*, as well as their interrelations, were essential to Michael Shapiro's guiding work on Peircean semiotics and language, unifying in a fundamental way 'the sense of grammar' and 'the sense of change' (see Shapiro 1983, 1991). The notions of teleology and semiosis have proved to be of utmost significance for our understanding not only of language but of human behavior in general. They may, therefore, be assumed also to form the basis for any theory of knowledge.

For significant discussions of the draft version of this essay (or parts of it) I am indebted in particular to Henning Andersen, Jesper Hoffmeyer, Robert Innis, Laura Janda, Tony Jappy, Dan Nesher, Joëlle Rethoré, Hansjacob Seiler, Michael Shapiro, and Colwyn Trevarthen. Any remaining inconsistencies or deficiencies are my responsibility.

Teleology thus tears down the walls between language and other forms of human behavior and also opens up a semiotic understanding of perception, emotion, cognition, and physical action. Truly explanatory models of language apparently cannot be achieved without attention to how man, on the basis of emotional primacy (cf. Trevarthen 1990a, 1990b, 1994; Damasio 1994; see below, section 15), perceives and cognizes the world, and acts in order to change or adapt to it. This cognitive-pragmatic view of language functionality is naturally linked to the idea of language as a biologically founded fact, associated uniquely with the human species, viz. as the result of *natural selection* on a teleological footing. Language, as an instrument of interaction through verbal communication, and intelligence (closely related to it) were the most powerful means of survival that evolution gave to mankind. The latter's corresponding biological adaptation by developing a speech apparatus and immense brain capacities allows us, no doubt, to include biology as the very foundation of cognitive-pragmatic models of language semiosis. This conception I intend to see conveyed by my notion of *biopragmatism*.

The latter notion is used here in a narrow, anthroposemiotic sense, but may, in a broader sense, be understood to integrate organically the domain of *biosemiotics* as the science of signs in all life forms (cf. J. von Uexküll 1920, 1940; Sebeok 1973, 1979, 1991, 2001; Sebeok and Umiker-Sebeok 1992; T. von Uexküll 1992; Hoffmeyer 1996, 1999; Kull 1999). This view emerges naturally from the idea that Peirce's pragmatically based semiotics represents "a logic of action by interpretation" (Parret 1983: 93, 105; cf. also Thelin 1994: 260). Since action is always performed and/or perceived/cognized according to a *telos* (i.e., intention, in a broad sense), and thus is interpretive by nature, it is uncertain whether action, as suggested by Deely (1990: 23), is at all conceivable outside semiosis—unless, of course, abstracted tacitly from the latter. The vital interconnection between action and semiosis is thus based on their joint dependence—apparently also on the cellular/molecular level—on interpretations by *subjects* according to their individual perspectives and corresponding goals. This understanding appears to harmonize with the modified role of natural selection as it has developed in post-Darwinian evolutionary theory (cf. Hoffmeyer 1996: 58; Kull 1999: 405; Swenson 1999: 574; see also T. von Uexküll 1992: 461ff.).

With these premises it appears consistent to assume the modified Darwinian principle of *variation and selection*, as the fundamental biological condition for collective survival (underlying the creation of order out of chaos and chance), to incarnate teleology in evolution ("Evolution is nothing more nor less than the working out of a definite end," CP 1.204), and thus to apply to the evolution not only of the human species but also of its characteristic linguistic and cognitive capacities. From this it does not follow that either evolution or the human species has in itself a purpose (cf. Short 1999: 126–29). Nor does it imply that teleology in language and thought is dictated in more direct ways by biological survival on levels other than the most basic ones. Space/time orientation (see below), interacting with change-of-state and cause-effect analysis, we may assume in essence to pertain by disposition to these levels. Although proceeding from a basically physical understanding of these matters, Peirce, as a matter of fact, made an equivalent observation on the cognitive nature of space/time: "The great utility and indispensableness of the conceptions of time, space, and force, even to the lowest intelligence, are such as to suggest that they are the results of natural selection" (CP 6.418).

The biological foundation of language semiosis is very much in line with Peirce's outspokenly evolutionary view of knowledge (and truth). His recognition of Darwin's theory of evolution is well known (CP 1.395, 7.269; cf. also Santaella Braga 1999: 6). So are his frequent references to natural selection in regard to the evolution of the mind (CP 6.417–18, 7.269), if not explicitly to language. A suggestive attempt to outline a corresponding 'evolutionary epistemology' in terms of instruction and selection was undertaken by Popper (1975: chap. 6).

In regard to language, this assumption was in a way anticipated by Wheeler's observation (1887; cited in Anttila 1972: 107; cf. Shapiro 1987: 165) that language change implies a tendency "to eliminate purposeless variety." This assumption harmonizes, more generally, with Wimsatt's understanding (1972: 13; cited in Shapiro 1987: 163) that selection "appears to be at the core of teleology and purposeful action whenever they occur," as well as with Short's view (1981: 380, note 3; cited in Shapiro 1987: 163; cf. also Short 1999: 120–29) that *a final cause is a principle of selection.* That is, we are entitled to infer that the variation-selection mechanism operates continuously in language and thought as well, subjecting them to a permanent evolutionary drift (Sapir 1921: chap. 7; Shapiro 1987). This is what makes Saussurian synchrony appear artificial in comparison to diachrony, i.e., to change as the natural state of linguistic affairs (Coseriu 1974: 178, 236; Shapiro 1991: 5).

Considerations of the biological foundations of language, suggested already by Eric Lenneberg (1967), would, along these lines, give further support to the correction of Saussurian structuralism by Shapiro from the standpoint of Peircean semiotics (Shapiro 1991: 20ff.). As a consequence of its explicit biological foundation (consider, as an eminent example, the neurobiological basis for space/time orientation discussed below), Peircean pragmatism, as the overall framework for semiosis, is understood to be consolidated further by the logical coherence offered by selection processes on different levels of semiosis (see below).

Within such a framework, cognition thus becomes an integrated part of a general theory of action (cf. Thelin 1985: 158), understood to include, accordingly, mental as well as physical action (without any Cartesian dualism, naturally). The way in which processes of thought are integrated with overall conditions of pragmatic—indeed, biopragmatic—nature is illustrated in a clarifying way by Peirce's central conception of *abduction* as the very logic of pragmatism, closely related to perception (CP 2.624, 6.522–35, 7.218–22).

2. Abduction and Perception, Perspectival Variety and Rule Selection

I must confess that I have over the years had some problem appreciating fully the merits of abduction as the logical procedure to which Peirce ascribed the pivotal role in human thought. In my cognitive-semantic practice, the procedures of *induction* and *deduction*, especially the latter's role according to Popper's hypothetical-deductive method (1959: 27–34; see below), alone appeared to warrant a reasonably exhaustive account of the logical processes involved. Today I am of another opinion. I would understand this new insight in such a way as to realize that the hierarchically highest level of thought—abduction—had (obviously) to a great extent been concealed from my consciousness.

That such a procedure had indeed to be recognized should become evident from the outcome of its working, but this I could see clearly only when I realized that abduction had to be elevated from its discrete and static role, as one (if also the dominant) of three different kinds of loosely interrelated inferences, to one integrated firmly, instead, in the logically coherent hierarchical process of semiosis. Then all of a sudden, I became aware that the cognitive-semantic binary oppositions I had frequently proposed as the backbone of my explanatory models were in fact the result of essentially abductive (hypothesis-forming) processes. However, the latter could not come from nowhere. Their logical primacy (according to Peirce) had to be understood, I realized, as a hierarchical-processual one, abduction being integrated in determinate ways by constant feedback with perception as well as the procedures of induction and deduction. In the light of this discovery, I also realized that Popper's model actually involved abduction, too, if only tacitly. It suppressed, however, the role of induction.

My intention here is to *reinterpret* in a functionally coherent model Peirce's logical analysis of the three inferential procedures. This decisively new model recognizes and develops further Peirce's implicit hierarchical-processual understanding and the primacy ascribed by him to abduction, but—being based on the crucial introduction of processual feedback, i.e., cyclicity—it differs in important respects from Peirce's proposals when it comes to the functional content and corresponding mutual order of the logical procedures (especially induction and deduction).

According to this model, there can be no abductive hypothesis formation without the input of sensory data being successively gathered, classified, experimented upon, and empirically systematized by induction into (tentative) rules, to be continuously tested, in turn, as to their (logical) consequences by deduction. Abduction, accordingly, is assumed to operate in a cyclical system as the superordinate *regulative and coordinating* procedure that, in order to form explanatory hypotheses about sensory data, first forwards the latter to induction for it to supply rules, then designates the testing of these rules by their application to data through deduction, compares the outcome of the hypotheses with the original data, and, finally, selects (accepts/dismisses) rules (for a more comprehensive account, see below).

Abductive hypotheses, in a circuit feedback fashion, thus both emerge from and determine *perception* and *mental/physical action*. Triggered by 'percepts' and inherent (through feedback) in 'perceptual judgements' (see below), they represent the questions ("A hypothesis ought, at first, to be entertained interrogatively," CP 6.524) that we ask when confronted with the world in order to rationalize (explain) it and act adequately ("To act intelligently and to see intelligently become at bottom one," CP 7.652).

In a processual feedback interpretation of this kind, Peirce's notion of abduction might, to my mind, finally reveal its true significance. "The first starting of a hypothesis and *the entertaining of it* [my emphasis] ... is an inferential step which I propose to call abduction" (CP 6.525). We are now able to understand more clearly the sensitivity of abductive hypotheses to new sensory data entering, through perception, the constant circuit process of empirical rule formation and logical testing and, possibly, changing these hypotheses and their corresponding rules—rules that had determined until now our mode of perception and our mode of action. By both triggering abduction and containing it, the processually caused dual nature of perception corresponds to Peirce's (CP 7.626ff.) distinction between 'percepts' and 'perceptual judgements', respectively (see figure 1 below).

Abduction, more generally, appears to reflect our permanent— I would assume, genetically predisposed—striving for order in a chaotic world, in particular, for logical coherence between old and new situations in terms of cause-effect relations. The latter enable us to manipulate or to adapt to this world by calculation. Abduction, therefore, may probably be viewed as representing a biologically motivated 'final' cause, the effect of which is achieved by way of selection from a variety of possible rules that are changing over time. The act of selection implied by abduction, to my mind, is crucial to our understanding of knowledge. Variety and choice are irreconcilable with absolute rules. Abduction, accordingly, appears to be the very locus in the cognitive processual system whereby the choice of hypothetical rules (explanations), the latter being determined by the individual experience systematized by induction, realizes a definite *perspective*. Variety in the above sense is thus perspectival by nature.

This amounts to saying that if we understand abductive hypotheses to *take creative part* in perception, then perception is always carried out from a definite perspective as well, viz. as an integrated part of these hypotheses. This inference appears most natural in regard to the perception of things from various *spatial* perspectives, but can be demonstrated to hold equally for the perception of events from various *temporal* perspectives (interacting with change-of-state and cause-effect analysis; see below). Abduction thus appears to confirm its central role in cognition ascribed to it by Peirce, namely, by the way it can be related logically to the decisive, empirically founded notion of perspective. This condition, in turn, gives support to the philosophical standpoint of *perspectivism* advocated (in agreement mainly with Nietzsche, Ortega y Gasset, and Popper; cf. Thelin 1999: 244, 271) in my theory of space/time cognition and its implications for epistemology (Thelin 1999, forthcoming a; see further below).

There is thus, as one common denominator, a primary biopragmatic motive ('final' cause; see discussion below, section 14) underlying all kinds of human (semiotic) behavior—and that is *the endeavor to establish order*, predicted, in turn, by the instinct for survival and reflected by the corresponding need for physical and mental *control* of things and events 'in space and time' (see below). This order is *relative* both by its nature as a strategy of adaptation to chaos and by its foundation in anthropocentric needs. All the way from this primary, biologically motivated human perspective, we can follow the role of perspective and its specification in the abductive processes of selection on every subsequent level of cognitive-pragmatic and linguistic processing—now as a permanent property of individual human behavior. Variation and specialization may be caused by chance or convention, but they might as well be predicted from specific perspectives on ordering chaos, determined by idiosyncratic personal, collective, ethnic, cultural-geographic, religious, and other conditions. In the round, perspective ought to play a more fundamental role in the construal of our world picture than hitherto assumed by semiotic theory.

In a discussion of these matters, Michael Shapiro (personal communication) made the constructive proposal to treat perspective as *condition on interpretation*—of lower rank than variation and selection. The problem is that if—according to this view—perspective is an 'efficient' cause and thus subordinate hierarchically to 'final' causes, then we would not apparently be able to explain how judgements involving 'final' causes—e.g., of what is necessary for survival—may differ precisely due to perspective, from culture to culture, from situation to situation, from person to person. The dynamic solution to this problem is apparently to understand perspective to operate freely through all levels of cognitive-pragmatic and linguistic processing according to my earlier interpretation of abduction, i.e., to be permanently actualized by the latter superordinate regulative and coordinating procedure of semiosis. Perspective as a condition on interpretation could indeed be understood then to be implied by *conditions on selection* from an inductively derived perspectival variety of rules in the way that this is implied by abduction on every single level of semiosis (all the way back to biological 'final' causes). The abductively governed logical procedures underlying semiosis of perception and mental/physical action may thus be simulated by the system of hierarchical-processual feedback relations schematized in figure 1.

Figure 1 can be understood as follows: By way of 'perceptual judgements' (see below), the *input sensory data* (the 'percepts') trigger *abduction*, which adopts these data as a *'case'* and starts searching for its explanation. This can be understood such that abduction in a regulative-coordinating manner first checks previous *experiential data* in the rule component to see whether the *'case data'* are stored and are assigned a *'rule'* already. If this is so, rule access is immediate. If the case data are not stored, abduction invokes *induction* to supply a rule. In this instance, rule access demands more or less extensive inductive operations, engaging the entire circuit system a number of times. Abduction in this procedure submits a (tentative) rule together with the case data to *deduction* in order to test the outcome of the rule's application to data. This outcome (the *'result'*), which I call *hypothetical data*, reenters the system together with the rule. Abduction compares the hypothetical data with the original case data and, if they tally, accepts the rule. If not, the circuit procedure continues as long as rule formation is improved or new sensory data turn up. The feedback presence of abduction in perception is represented by 'perceptual judgements', which I interpret as automatized hypotheses about sensory data (i.e., cognitive judgements about 'percepts') enabled by immediate ('short cut') access to the rule component. If the abductive procedure in general may be understood as fallible, 'perceptual judgements' should be so to a relatively higher degree. However, related to an abductive procedure applied to specific data and successively leading to the establishment of an adequate rule, 'perceptual judgements' should accordingly be characterized by a decreasing degree of fallibility. Both kinds of action, the mental (i.e., cognition) as well as the physical, are understood to be determined by 'perceptual judgements' mediating between sensory perception and mental action, and thus disposing of case data and a rule of behavior. Physical action is optional. The latter is monitored directly by perception and cognition in a feedback fashion. Mental action, if realized (properly) by physical action, is assumed to be monitored merely indirectly, while in other cases, directly by *metacognition*. If done consciously, the latter is usually referred to as 'introspection'. Since perceptualization (by way of 'imagization') appears to be indispensable also to such conscious metacognitive monitoring, we may assume the involvement here of *metaperception* as well. (For further explication of the model, see section 4 below.)

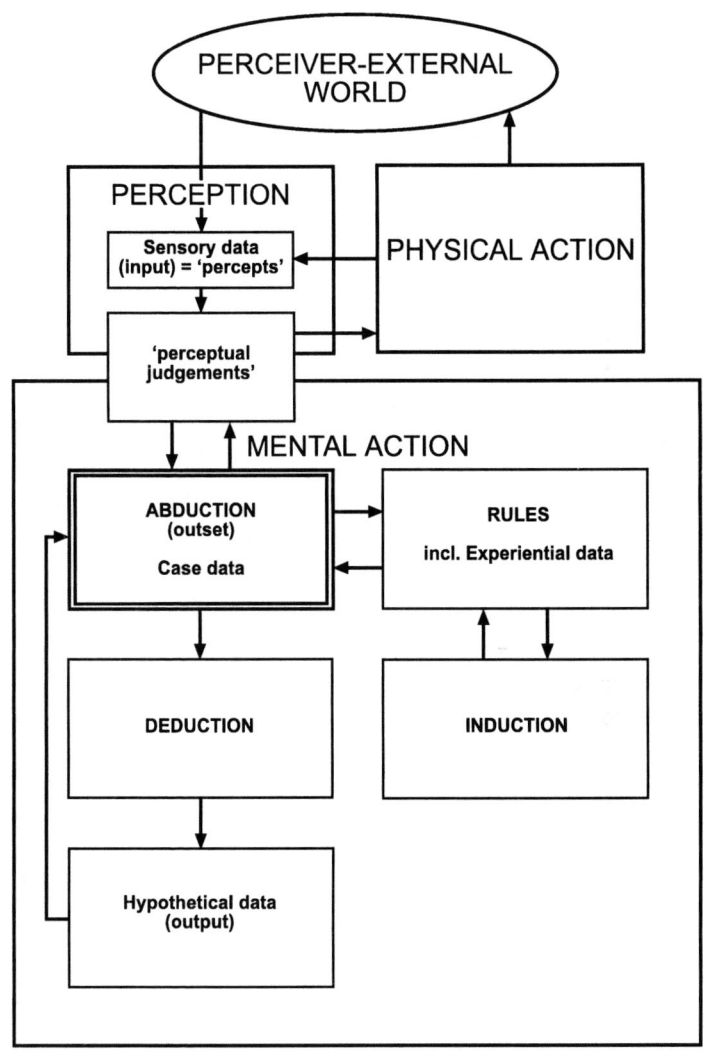

FIGURE 1 Logical-Cognitive Processing in Perception and Action

3. Circuit Feedback Processing, Neurobiology, and Continuity

The idea of circuit feedback processing was actually suggested already in Thelin (1985: 156, 160, 165ff.), for the correlation of perceptual and cognitive-pragmatic conditions with semantic structure. The interrelations between perception and cognition were also discussed there (162ff.) in terms reconcilable with the present interpretation of abduction and Peirce's distinction between 'percepts' and 'perceptual judgements'. The model proposed was applied to the linguistic category of aspect, and thus focused on the perception and cognitive organization of motion/events (in terms of temporal perspective; see below) within a general theory of action.

This approach has, as far as I can judge, been supported by subsequent developments in neurobiology. In his fundamental work on consciousness, Gerald Edelman (1989: 54ff.), within his general conception of 'neural Darwinism', suggested his equivalent idea of 'global mapping', a hierarchical-processual model characterized by extensive *reentry connections*, i.e., what I refer to as 'processual feedback'. Edelman's neurobiological model is intended to simulate the correlation of perception and ongoing motion, but can, to my mind, be generalized to include long-term memory and corresponding cognitive-pragmatic strategies involved in perception (of action) as well. Peirce's understanding of the interrelations between perception and action, quoted above, is thus echoed by Edelman's view that "the concept of global mapping takes account of the fact that perception depends upon and leads to action," and "the results of continual motor activity are ... an essential part of perceptual categorization." If we understand "the results of continual motor activity" to be projectable (by the inclusion of long-term memory) onto action as accumulated experience, then we see clearly the equivalence between the neurobiological model and the logical-cognitive one suggested above. This interpretation appears to emerge naturally from Edelman's opinion (139) that "*distinctions among the various kinds of functions of these mappings provide major bases for the development of concepts and conceptual categorization* [my emphasis]."

One of Edelman's interesting findings (119–39) is that spatial/temporal control of motion is apparently not handled alone by the cerebral cortex, but in interaction with the cortical appendages that are responsible in different ways for *succession*. These appendages, "the organs of succession," are the cerebellum, the hippocampus, and the basal ganglia. The concepts of space and time may indeed involve control of succession in actions performed and perceived as an essential component, but they are obviously more than that. Whereas the neurobiological correlates of space and time are still largely concealed from observation, cognitive-linguistic studies of these categories have, as we shall see, already arrived at a number of hypotheses qualified to suggest the search for their neurobiological correlates. One promising basis for future neurobiological evidence for such cognitive-linguistic models of space/time orientation is the idea that perception of events emerges from *continuity* (as a precondition, in fact, for succession).

It is certainly no coincidence that Edelman (33) together with his colleague George Reeke (personal communication) stumbled precisely on spatio-temporal continuity as one hypothetical requirement for "any representation of [the physical] world." This very idea was, in more general terms, anticipated by Peirce (CP 6.169) in the form of his central conception of *synechism*, which insisted upon "the necessity of hypotheses involving true continuity." Peirce never succeeded in penetrating the proper role of continuity in space/time cognition (cf. Thelin 1999: 289–97). However, he probably would have done so had he consistently applied his own idea of *diagrammatic patterning* (CP 1.383, 2.778) to the chaotic world observed. Then he might have realized that continuity is the consequence of our making chaos manageable by assigning *divisibility* to it. Things and events accordingly *become discernible in divisible continuity by way of discontinuation*, i.e., by spatial and temporal analysis proper (cf. Thelin 1999: 302; see below).

This discontinuation of the observed world is referred to by the Gestalt distinctions *figure vs. ground* and *parts vs. wholes*, and is reflected in aspectology by the situation-perspectival distinction *foreground vs. background* and the event-perspectival distinction *totality vs. partiality* (cf. Thelin 1978 and subsequent works on aspectology; see also below). The parallel between these observations and the assumptions made in neurobiological precincts becomes still more evident if we consider that along with continuity Edelman included "a property Reeke calls *zoomability* [my emphasis] as well as a set of requirements having to do with consistency between parts of the world." 'Zoomability' most naturally corresponds to my notion of divisibility as assigned to chaos, just as the related 'requirements' correspond to the system of cognitive rules, which in the case of events handle temporal (spatial/temporal) perspectivization as part of the overall discontinuation involved in change-of-state and cause-effect analysis. For a reinterpretation of Gestalt perception in the light of spatial/temporal perspective, see section 8 below.

Edelman (33) also makes the insightful observation that continuity is "inconsistent with a fundamental *symbolic* representation of the world considered as an *initial* neural transform." This view harmonizes with my suggestion below (cf. also Thelin forthcoming a, b) that we understand divisibility (divisible continuity) as correlated to fundamental neurobiological *rhythmization*, applied initially by attention and perception to chaos, and consider space/time analysis to cause subsequent discontinuity by way of binary cognitive choices of indexical nature, subordinate to symbolization in a primordial semiotic sense (cf. Thelin 1994).

4. Andersen's Conception of Cyclicity, and the Working of the Coherent Model

It is noteworthy that the need for a functional model of the circuit feedback type was, more generally, indicated already by Henning Andersen (1973). In his early treatment of the roles of abduction and deduction in phonological change (still today, as far as I can judge, the most important contribution to this field of research since Peirce introduced his notion of abduction), Andersen discerned the "cyclical application of induction and abduction, by which a grammar is built up [as] a goal-directed process" (op. cit.: 776). Inspired by Miller et al.'s (1960: 29ff., 32–37) TOTE model (Test-Operate-Test-Exit), and identifying Test with induction and Operate with abduction, Andersen arrived at a hierarchical-processual understanding of the components involved that differs somewhat from the one I am suggesting. The cycle, accordingly, is conceived by Andersen to start off with induction and continue with abduction, a process cyclically continued "until induction provides no further cause for abduction, and the Exit phase is reached."

If we overlook the fact that input sensory data are not formalized in this model and, what is perhaps more important, that abduction, accordingly, is not related explicitly to perception, with which it, according to Peirce, is most closely connected (as underlying hypotheses; cf. the two-way connection in my model above), the TOTE model causes another difficulty: the procedure of deduction, in Andersen's interpretation of it, is distinguished from the induction-abduction-induction cycle and represents a separate "part of grammar formation" (777), integrated only secondarily with the former by hierarchical superordination. Deduction is understood to "include induction," or rather, the entire induction-abduction-induction cycle. The TOTE model is used also for deduction, but reinterpreted so that Test is now deduction and Operate is the entire original cycle. This amounts to the hierarchical subordination of induction-abduction-induction to deduction, formalized as T(TOTE)TE, i.e., 'deduction(induction-abduction-induction-exit)deduction-exit'. This picture, to my mind, does not convey as clearly as we might expect Andersen's (and Peirce's) fertile understanding of the role of abduction as "unique ... vis-à-vis the other modes of inference."

The reason for this problematic situation, I believe, is inherent in the original TOTE model. First of all, its notion 'Test' is infelicitous since it (as we see from Andersen's interpretation) can, apparently, be associated both with testing through deduction, which should be logical by nature, and testing understood, as it were, to be performed empirically by induction (cf. Andersen, op. cit.: 776). In the latter case, however, I believe this is rather a metaphorical trap in which we (together with Peirce; cf. CP 6.526ff., 7.202ff.) may fall if we overlook the fact that the task of induction is basically to form and supply rules for abduction's hypothesis-formation, i.e., to gather, classify, experiment upon, and systematize data into rules, propelled *continuously* by abduction to testing through deduction. In other words, we may—if we are not aware of this continuous engagement of deduction (or detach it from the procedures of abduction and induction)—transfer its function of testing metaphorically to induction, where it essentially does not belong. From this interpretation would follow that the original TOTE model, indeed, represents rather 'deduction-abduction-deduction-exit'.

This hypothetical consequence is surprising, of course. Where is induction, and can the entire cycle really start off with deduction? The answer to the first question is that induction, as the procedure implied by (subordinate to) abduction, under the circumstances would most naturally have to be included as part of Operate. The answer to the second question is that this, according to my above model, could not be the case. However, this is actually what is suggested by the complex T(TOTE)TE structure and, as it appears, by Andersen's formulation (775; cf. also Itkonen 1999: 160, 163) that "abduction proceeds from an observed *result* [my emphasis]," predicted by deduction. This is obviously another metaphorical trap into which we may all easily fall if we do not consider explicitly input sensory data as the trigger of the entire cyclical process, and of abduction above all. Abduction, in my understanding (see also Andersen's explicitly constructive view, 776), does not proceed primarily from a result but from the *hypothesis* that *data are the result of* (can be explained by) *a rule*—as the effect of a cause. Induction supplies such a rule, and deduction tests it by applying it to data. The output is the 'result', i.e., hypothetical data, which, by reentering the system together with the rule, can be compared to the original case data memorized at the outset of abduction (in this secondary sense, Andersen's formulation in any case applies). If this confrontation falsifies the rule, abduction starts an entire, new circuit process over again. If the rule is confirmed, however, data have been explained satisfactorily, and the rule is stored in the memory of the rule component as adequate (and immediately accessible) for future application to corresponding data. That is, similar to the abductive outset, rules presuppose memory, as does the storage of experiential data to which the rules require access. The procedure can be understood like this: Abduction in the case of a confirmed rule stores the given data and assigns to them a given rule. In the case of a falsified rule, abduction once again forwards case data to induction. With access to old and new experiential data, induction forms a new rule that abduction subjects to deductive testing, and so forth.

The rule component can be compared to a huge and complex data base in which rules are ordered according to their *conditions on selection*, i.e., with integrated access to experiential data. This implies a structuring of rules into the various components of human behavior with their specific systems of rules interrelated through underlying general rules for perception and mental/physical action. One such system of rules regulates linguistic behavior. From this system rules are selected according to the matching of case data with experiential data, decomposed by a processual hierarchy of cognitive-pragmatic binary choices (cf. below the derivation of temporal, or rather compound spatial/temporal, perspective and its implementation by aspect, section 13). Encoding proceeds from the top to the bottom of the hierarchy, decoding, in the reverse direction; but the hierarchy is open to processual feedback so that changes can take place by abduction, invoking induction-deduction in cases of rule innovation. To assume generally that linguistic encoding implies deduction and decoding abduction (cf. Andersen, 777) appears problematic, since both encoding and decoding involve perception and abductive hypotheses and, consequently, deductive testing (not necessarily induction, if change is not immediately involved). Decoding, in other words, can be understood as an attempt to verify hypotheses about hypotheses or interpretations of interpretations, performed from the perspectives of the encoder and the decoder, respectively (cf. Thelin 1985: 161).

5. The Modified Role of Abduction in Language Change

In a fixed set of rules, such as those of chess, we see the outcome of a process of rule formation that is terminated. There can be hardly any changes in the rules here due to tendencies toward a variety in their application of the kind we can see in the innovation of rules over time in other games, such as football, for example. In language, being—through its symbiosis with thought—the active filter of most human activities, such tendencies are rooted in every single human being (cf. Short 1999: 149–54) and his/her individual needs and wishes, as we see them expressed by a huge number of choices at the various hierarchical levels of life (biological, emotional, rational, social, economical, ideological, aesthetic, etc.). Within collective systems of rules, individuals perceive, feel, think, speak, and act from the standpoint of their own interpretations of the world. Within the communicative needs of the collective, language accordingly serves the individual perspective. On this basis we may assume that we think and apparently also speak by applying rules in an individual way, the decisive point being that the output is adequate, that our individual behavior is communicable and interpretable. Variety in rules and rule application is the constant state of affairs with which language has to live. This is the basis for language change. Variety of rules means selection of rules, and selection of rules means a possible change of rules.

According to my model (above) there are roughly three possibilities involved in language change: abduction (a) selects inconsistently one of two (or more) established (adequate) rules but successively gives preference to one of them and dismisses the other(s), (b) selects a rule that applies to data inconsistently and therefore either invokes induction to supply a new (adequate) one (to replace it, or in transitory addition to it), or (c) simply dismisses that rule. In all three cases of change, abduction (as the regulative-selective procedure) and deduction are involved, but only in case (b) is induction involved. A distinction between abductive and deductive change (as suggested by Andersen, op. cit.) does not follow from the model I am suggesting. According to it, all changes are abductive in the sense that they start with and are monitored by abduction. They also are all deductive in the sense that they involve deductive testing. Changes may be said to involve induction only to the extent that they imply the formation of new rules (triggered by new data). Changes in transitory rules (Andersen's 'adaptive' rules; the changes he characterizes as 'deductive') would be no exceptions. They lose their applicability gradually by the preference abduction through selection gives to the more economical structural change. As Peirce observed: "[T]he leading consideration in abduction is the question of economy" (cited in Hookway 1985: 226).

These remarks do not in the least affect Andersen's exemplary account of the linguistic facts, nor—in essence—his theoretical interpretation. They rather amount to the suggestion (made possible by the coherent circuit feedback model) that we make a more rigid demarcation of the procedures within his basically cyclical conception of their functioning and thereby assign to abduction its proper role as superordinate regulating and coordinating device. Deduction, according to this understanding, is strictly limited to the logical testing (by application to case data) of the rules selected exclusively by abduction. I am aware that this processual reinterpretation of abduction (and the correlated functional roles of induction and deduction) may appear alien to those not accustomed to the idea of cyclicity, but my feeling is that this alone allows us to abandon the traditional discrete-static treatment of abduction as one of three kinds of inference, and to discern more clearly the nature of the prominent role ascribed to it by Peirce, within coherent models correlatable with neurobiological processing (see sections 3 and 11).

My attempt here to simulate in a hierarchical-processual feedback model the logical procedures involved in abduction by integrating it firmly with perception and the procedures of induction and deduction appears well founded. With its aid I believe it is possible to dispel much of the confusion arising from earlier attempts to relate the three modes of inference to each other on the basis of incoherent or insufficiently coherent treatments. Andersen's work (based on Peirce's original ideas) in this respect implied an important paradigmatic change toward a coherent treatment without which my present suggestions would have appeared inconsistent.

6. Itkonen's Discrete Model

Therefore, I am unable fully to appreciate the criticism directed toward Andersen's basic interpretation of abduction by Esa Itkonen (1999: 160–61). I would assume that we are concerned here rather with a misunderstanding due to Itkonen's non-penetration of the very idea of cyclicity underlying Andersen's proposals. This appears to emerge from the former's processually incoherent treatment of the three modes of inference. Itkonen clearly sees that "abduction is not at all on an equal footing with induction and deduction" (161) but does not get beyond an individual characterization of the three processes involved. Since he does not incorporate the idea of hierarchical-processual integration in his approach, Itkonen is unaware that it is the consequences of the latter that he is treating when he defines abduction as "a composite process" (whereas induction and deduction, according to him, are "single" processes). The closest he comes to a hierarchical understanding is when he states that "abduction always contains deduction" and "abduction ... is triggered by a (perceived) fact in need of explanation."

I see no reason in Andersen's model to support Itkonen's view that, according to it, abduction is "an inference pertaining *only* to antecedent conditions" (161). This view appears to emerge from Itkonen's difficulties to conceive of hypothesis-formation as a cyclical process, assigning, according to my suggestion, to abduction two main tasks: (a) the regulative-coordinating one (or, 'entertaining' one, according to Peirce), and (b) the selectional one. Abduction, therefore, by necessity involves (according to [a]) "antecedent conditions," viz. as partaking of 'case data' (see above) to which rules are applied; and it involves (according to [b]), by way of selection (acceptance/dismissal), the continuous establishment of these rules (rule systems) developed from successively strengthened hypotheses.

If Andersen, according to Itkonen (161), "is able to maintain his interpretation only by incongruously *identifying* the 'law' with the abductive inference," this would then rather be an argument in favor of Andersen's model, since the selection of (hypothetical) rules ('laws') remains the essential task of 'abductive inference'. This certainly does not amount to saying that rules are *identical* with the process of abduction. As demonstrated above, this is an idea alien to the cyclical understanding of abduction. Itkonen arrives at this conclusion because he applies his discrete, i.e., incoherent, model to the assumptions of the coherent, i.e., cyclical, one. By neglecting the changing character of data (cf. above the distinctive functions of 'sensory data', 'case data', 'experiential data', and 'hypothetical data', respectively), he conceives of abduction as a process starting and ending in identical data. This approach presumes a system of fixed rules and fixed data, which contradicts, in turn, Itkonen's view that 'laws' are the *result* of abduction, i.e., if this is meant to imply that rules emerge as the result of a hypothetical-selectional formation process, involving new ('case') data and, correspondingly, induction as well. By including deduction but leaving induction outside the realm of abductive regulation, Itkonen's model clearly applies only to rules established already as adequate for fixed data (conditions on selection).

7. The Problem of Hierarchical-Processual Ordering

There is, as we have seen, one major issue connected with the coherent model. This is the problem of *ordering*, implied by the hierarchical-processual (and cyclical) reinterpretation of the logical procedures of abduction, induction and deduction, i.e., when understood no longer as three independent modes of inference but as interdependent successive steps of logical processing (underlying perception and mental/physical action). The implicit foundation for the latter idea (and its further elaboration demonstrated by my above proposals) was laid by Peirce himself (see especially CP 7.202–7). The feature of cyclicity, suggested by Andersen and reflected by the mechanism of circuit feedback in my model, is an innovation, however, and one of considerable importance for our judgements about ordering (see further below).

There is, to my knowledge, only one further analysis that develops Peirce's dynamic understanding of the three logical procedures along similar lines, and, accordingly, actualizes the problem of ordering. That is the recent and very important study of learning and abduction by Dan Nesher (2001a; cf. also Nesher 2001b). Independently of my approach, Nesher thus explicates and elaborates Peirce's ideas in a fashion reconcilable in essence with the above model. Nesher (2001a: 32ff.) formulates "the pragmaticist method of inquiry and discovery" as "the dynamic repetition of *the ordered sequence of operations* of the trio abduction, deduction, and induction." Nesher thus adopts and makes explicit the hierarchical-processual understanding implied by Peirce's original treatment (CP 7.202ff.). The notion of repetition might even indicate Nesher's inclusion of *cyclicity* as additional constitutive component in his model, but no such component is, as far as I can discover, foreseen by him explicitly (had it been, it might have influenced his view on ordering; see below).

When it comes to ordering, Nesher is very clear: "According to Peirce, only the trio sequence of abduction, deduction, and induction (in that order) comprehends the logical method of inquiry, and only its entire operation can be understood as an empirical proof." This is the view adopted by Nesher on the basis of Peirce's (CP 5.171) analysis of the three procedures: "Abduction is the process of forming an explanatory hypothesis ... induction does nothing but determine a value, and deduction merely evolves the necessary consequences of a pure hypothesis ... [abduction's] only justification is that from its suggestion deduction can draw a prediction which can be tested by induction...."

From the latter explication it is evident that the ordering suggested by Peirce and accepted by Nesher for his further exploration is: abduction>deduction>induction. Now, this ordering differs from the one suggested by my model: abduction> induction> deduction(>abduction>induction>deduction ...). Why?

In order to explain this incongruity, let us proceed from abduction as the unanimously accepted hierarchically superordinate procedure of hypothesis formation, i.e., asking questions the answers to which are tested as to their ability to explain observed data. Our understanding of 'testing' here is crucial. As we can see, it is applied by Peirce (and Nesher) solely to induction, and it is here a process of (quantitative) evaluation. In order to understand properly the essence of the procedures involved, we must become aware now of the fact that their permanent objects are the observed data. If we understand abduction thus to represent (after 'perceptual judgements') the first reaction to observed data, and this reaction takes the shape of a question as a provisional hypothesis, what happens next? According to Peirce (and Nesher), deduction should now first draw a prediction from this hypothesis, to be tested subsequently by induction. But how can we, in the first place, draw a prediction from a hypothesis both invoked by and applied to one and the same set of data? And by what means? There is an important link missing here that has to be made explicit. In reality, it is not a hypothesis that is applied to data but a *rule* invoked as explanation of data by a hypothesis that is so applied. And rules (or habits) are supplied by induction, whose task it is to gather and classify experiential data and systematize them, through experimentation, into (tentative) rules for abduction that will then select (accept/dismiss) them through deductive (logical) testing. This amounts to saying that there is (after the very first abductive question) no abduction without appeal to rules supplied by induction, and there is no logical testing through deduction without its applying these rules to data.

In other words, the hierarchical-processual order of the logical procedures should rather be the one foreseen by the traditional view of induction as proceeding from particularities to generalities, i.e., from singular data to classes and rules (or habits), tested, in turn, on new data through deduction. This condition (reflected also by the simple, unambiguous input>output order of the 'black box' model) is apparently what Andersen had in mind when understanding deduction to "include induction" (see section 4 above), i.e., according to my view, as its hierarchical-processual precondition. The present interpretation appears to explain how the function of 'testing' can be ascribed metaphorically to induction, viz. as due to non-penetration of the condition that induction—not only for rule formation by experimentation but also for provisional classification as well—requires the continuous engagement of logical-deductive testing of rules and class features, respectively—specifically by way of circuit feedback simulating neural reentry processes capable of incomprehensible operational velocity.

Without the explicit inclusion of cyclicity and a corresponding mechanism of circuit feedback in our model, logical ordering is problematic, since hierarchical processing alone forces us to make an absolute choice between two procedures, whereas cyclicity allows for their relative order. That is to say, besides their basic internal order (discussed so far) the procedures may precede or succeed each other according to which procedure is actually activated. Finally, if we focus explicitly on rule formation, the solution of the problem appears to suggest itself. If it is true that rule formation (monitored by superordinate abduction) cannot take place without continuous deductive testing, but equally true that there can be no rule formation at all without induction, then this assigns to induction basic hierarchical-processual superiority vis-à-vis deduction. However, cyclicity allows for deduction to precede induction 'in the process', for example, in cases in which abduction judges deductive testing to have failed and invokes induction to supply a new rule. Furthermore, deduction may succeed abduction immediately in those cases in which there is no need for induction to be involved. As a matter of fact, the engagement of induction already in "new abductive discovery operations" is acknowledged also by Nesher (2001a: 33), notwithstanding his basic order of abduction > deduction > induction. A similar incongruity is reflected by Peirce's (CP 6.526) additional introduction of 'abductory induction'. This transitional concept, which in reality challenges Peirce's rather absolute understanding of hierarchical-processual order, is naturally made superfluous by the explicitly coherent model simulating thought processes by way not only of hierarchy but also of cyclicity and corresponding circuit feedback.

8. Toward a Reinterpretation of Gestalt Perception

By proceeding from biological rhythmization (for a more detailed account, see section 11 below) as the very basis for attention and perception and assuming its resulting assignment of *diagrammatic divisibility* (zoomability, focusability) and *continuity* to chaos to be a prerequisite for discerning things and events by discontinuation, i.e., *partitioning*, we are, as it will appear, in a position to confront in a clarifying way the Gestalt distinctions *figure* vs. *ground* and *parts* vs. *wholes* with the aspectual distinctions *foreground* vs. *background* and *totality* vs. *partiality*, respectively. Such a confrontation, done in order to explore the obvious but still vague relationship between the two kinds of basically perspectival selection, appears reasonable irrespective of the former being applied traditionally both to things and events, the latter, normally only to events. (For a more detailed account of aspect distinctions, see section 12 below.)

It should be noted that whereas the foreground-background distinction was obviously inspired by Gestalt psychology and introduced in aspectology rather late (cf. Grimes 1975; Reinhart 1984; Chvany 1985, 1990), the totality-partiality distinction in aspectology appeared independently and not at one time. The concept of totality was proposed already in the first half of the twentieth century in the form of a privative opposition totality vs. non-totality (cf. Thelin 1978: 31, 1990a: 30ff.). This opposition was only later, in agreement with my proposal (Thelin 1978: 31ff.), replaced by the equipollent opposition totality vs. partiality. My present comparison appears not only to confirm empirically, as we shall see, the latter development, but also to motivate the introduction already at the perceptual-sensory level of a more general distinction between 'totality' and 'partiality' (see below), superordinate not only to the two aspectual but also the two Gestalt distinctions and realized, accordingly, at lower levels by Gestalt part-whole and aspectual totality-partiality, respectively. It therefore also allows for a reinterpretation of the two Gestalt distinctions and, more particularly, a clarification of their hitherto fuzzy interrelations.

I would like to propose that we discern and perceive things and events by way of *hierarchical-successive chunk-wise selection* from the divisible/diagrammatized perceptual field. Perception involves abductive hypotheses underlying such partitioning selection and interacting cyclically with the analysis of sensory data, attained, apparently, by some kind of scanning procedure. Hierarchical-successive selection functions in agreement with *the principle of least effort*, i.e., it proceeds to smaller chunks only to the extent it is needed. The selection of objects is performed according to their discernible relevance in the present situation on the basis of previous experience. This together results roughly in a strategy adapting (a) the perceptual-sensory principle of 'selecting-as-big-chunks-as-possible' (i.e., restricting the effort and degree of zooming) to (b) the perceptual-cognitive principle of 'selecting-chunks-I-recognize-from-previous-experience', i.e., Gestalt perception or 'pattern-matching' (cf. Thelin 1985: 163), by way of constant feedback. In reality, the classical laws of Gestalt perception (cf. Köhler 1929; Koffka 1935), i.e., the laws of closeness, similarity, etc., may be understood to take a mediate position and thus be implied by both principles. According to the theory, Gestalt laws are not dependent on previous experience but cooperate with it in perception. They can, therefore, still be viewed as cognitive by nature.

Objects in the perceptual field not selected for the actual chunk are left outside its focus, in what Gestalt psychology has conceived of as 'ground'. The chunk of focus has been understood, correspondingly, to constitute 'figure'. It is important to realize, thus, that also the figure-ground distinction, according to the present interpretation, is a result of superordinate hierarchical-successive chunk-wise selection, reflected by what in Gestalt psychology was referred to vaguely, i.e., without the indication of a hierarchical-processual relationship between the two distinctions, as the part-whole distinction. When *gestalts*, as wholes, were understood to be characterized, among other things, by being divided into figure and ground, one obviously overlooked that they are the result not only of cognitive dispositions (according to principle [b]), but also of hierarchical-successive partitioning or division of continuity (according to principle [a]). This interpretation harmonizes with the view expressed by Michael Shapiro in a discussion of *metonymy* in *gestalts* (personal communication; see below), in particular, regarding the latter's reliance on part-whole relations in encompassing in a hierarchical fashion figure and ground. My proposal indeed treats such part-whole relations in a broader hierarchical-processual perspective, tracing them back (and thus promoting them) to their application to biologically motivated divisible continuity as the very foundation of attention and perception.

The flexible hierarchical-successive understanding of selection in perception thus allows us to think of attention, in the form of biological rhythmization (see further section 11 below), as being directed, if motivated, toward ever smaller chunks of the divisible/diagrammatized perceptual field. It also apparently agrees with the well-known sensory primacy of two-dimensional spatial vision as demonstrated by the elementary chunk-wise selection between *focus* and *non-focus*. Three-dimensional spatial (spatial/temporal) selection between figure and ground (foreground and background) may accordingly be assumed to have evolved secondarily as a perceptual-cognitive strategy emerging from the need for observer-related calculations of distance by way of a primarily scalar distinction, *close-remote*. The phylogenetic origin of the latter distinction in cognitive-pragmatic conditions appears to be evidenced by the way—in the binary aspectual (compound spatial/temporal) distinction foreground vs. background—foreground represents state-changing events of immediate causal relevance for the observer while background represents events merely of mediate causal relevance.

What we may infer from these reflections is that the traditionally most prominent Gestalt distinction figure vs. ground apparently must be subordinate to—indeed, derived by—not only superordinate partitioning but also the traditionally less prominent Gestalt part-whole distinction. That is, figure is always a part selected from a whole, the rest of which is left for the ground. We may, according to this hierarchical interpretation, further infer that a *gestalt*, as a whole, is also a part of a greater whole, i.e., a figure, leaving the rest of this whole for the ground. In a corresponding way, the fact that *gestalts* have been understood to be divided into figure and ground is a consequence of their comprising not just parts but hierarchies of parts, as figures ascribed on intrinsic superordinate levels the function of wholes, i.e., in effect, subordinate *gestalts*. We might accordingly imagine Gestalt perception to proceed schematically as follows in figure 2.

If we apply now the above inferences to the aspectual, i.e., compound spatial/temporal, distinctions foreground vs. background and totality vs. partiality, we are in a position to suggest that there is, here, too, a more general perceptual-sensory distinction between 'totality' and 'partiality' from which both the situation-aspectual foreground-background distinction and event-aspectual totality-partiality distinction apparently are derived (in the latter case by equipollent application of the general distinction; see below). This general distinction is implied by superordinate privative partitioning according to my proposal of hierarchical-successive selection (conditioned by Gestalt perception). From this we may conclude that this general, privative distinction, which we more properly should call PARTITIONING vs. NON-PARTITIONING (or FURTHER PARTITIONING vs. NO FURTHER PARTITIONING) is of such hierarchical dignity that it applies to the basic levels not only of aspect-perspectival organization but also of perceptual organization in general, including Gestalt perception, and, therefore, also causes us to view the latter and the interrelations of its distinctions in a new light.

This conclusion agrees with my assumption that hierarchical-successive chunk-wise selection is primarily a perceptual-sensory strategy (according to principle [a] above). On subsequent levels of perceptual-abductive processing, represented by spatial and compound spatial/temporal analysis of things and situations in terms of the distinctions part-whole/figure-ground and aspectual foreground-background, respectively, as well as the compound spatial/temporal analysis of individual events in terms of the subordinate, aspectual totality-partiality distinction, the superordinate PARTITIONING-NON-PARTITIONING distinction is understood to interact with cognitive-pragmatic elements in perception. This interpretation suggests a more dynamic view also of the figure-ground and foreground-background distinctions than was traditionally the case. A corresponding tendency toward a hierarchical differentiation has been witnessed in aspectology by the proposal to introduce the concept of *close background* as distinguished from *remote background* (today I would prefer these notions to my original *actual background* vs. *proper background*; cf. Thelin 1984a: 266; forthcoming a; see section 11 below) and by the proposal to develop further

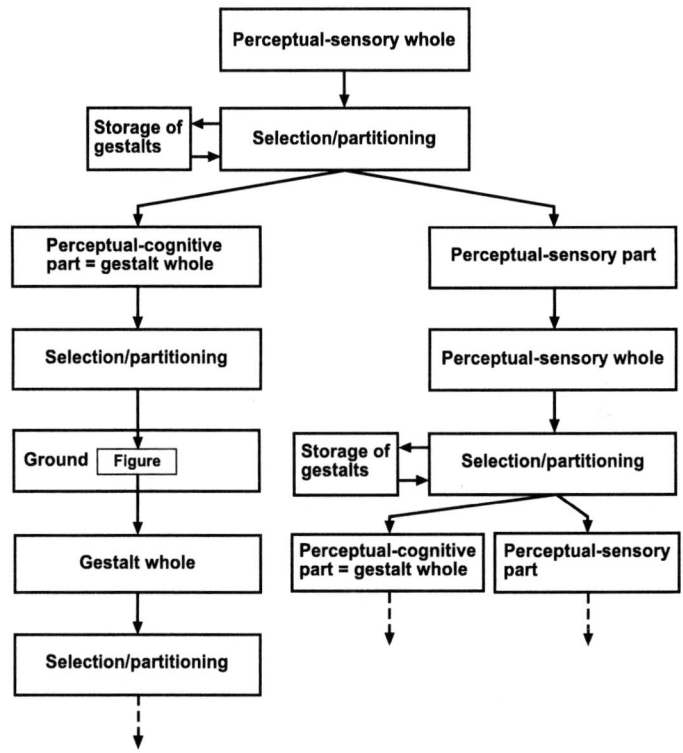

FIGURE 2 Gestalt Perception

the hierarchical differentiation of the concept of background in general, especially in regard to conditions of causation (Thelin 1990a: 64–67).

According to the above interpretation, theories of Gestalt perception may thus profit from a confrontation with linguistic-semiotic theories of aspect. But, as we have seen, aspectology can also learn from Gestalt perception, if understood to be integrated in a coherent hierarchical model of perceptual-abductive processing as suggested by the idea of successive chunk-wise selection. The latter should have consequences, however, for our understanding of the binary aspectual opposition totality vs. partiality, if ascribed (as it is by me) equipollent status. The latter would not, naturally, be reconcilable with the general idea of successive privative partitioning as the governing principle, creating new wholes to be partitioned further. Under these circumstances my proposal to treat the distinction between state-changing (sequential) events in the foreground (plot line), on the one hand, and simultaneously ongoing events in the close background, on the other, as an equipollent opposition between a total and partial aspectual view of events, respectively, would appear doubtful. I think there is a natural solution to this problem, however. Before we proceed to a more incisive discussion of these matters, let me just indicate this solution by the following questions: If the idea of hierarchical-successive chunk-wise selection, i.e., partitioning/discontinuation, is adequate, how far may we assume this procedure to continue? Is it possible to determine its perceptual/cognitive-pragmatic limit? Can it, accordingly, be the case that the aspectual perception of events in terms of the totality-partiality distinction represents such a limit, and its equipollent nature is motivated by the fact that no further partitioning is possible, or, at least, not subject to rule formation?

In his comments on my manuscript, "The conceptual structure of space and time and the organization of narrative texts" (Thelin forthcoming b), Michael Shapiro (personal communication) made the insightful suggestion to examine more closely the role of *metonymy* in connection with my discussion of aspectual totality-partiality and Gestalt perception. My attention had previously been directed primarily toward the central role of *metaphor* in the underlying cognitive derivation of time from space (cf. Thelin 1999; see Appendix below). My frequent references over the years to the Gestalt distinctions figure-ground and part-whole in support of the aspectual distinctions foreground-background and totality-partiality had no doubt lacked a full understanding of their correlations (in part, to be sure, due to the vague interrelations of the two Gestalt distinctions). Shapiro's suggestion, however, appears to indicate a proper way to clarification.

My attempt above to remedy the lacking clarity does not involve metonymy explicitly, but it is evident that the idea of hierarchical-successive chunk-wise selection, as a process selecting parts of wholes (and subordinating the rest of them), can be conceived of as metonymic in essence. If this idea is correct, it implies that metonymy may indeed be involved on levels hierarchically prior even to metaphor (precisely as this was suggested by Michael and Marianne Shapiro; cf. Shapiro and Shapiro 1988: 34), since partaking, apparently, already of perceptual-sensory processing, whereas metaphor, judging by all, even in this fundamental pretropal sense, is introduced in perception only by cognitive, more specifically abductive-analogical processing. By also interpreting figure-ground as resulting from the superordinate metonymic PARTITIONING-NON-PARTITIONING distinction, we infer as well the metonymic nature not only of figure-ground but also of the concept of *gestalt* comprising the latter in a hierarchical fashion as a function of part-whole.

The confrontation of Gestalt perception and aspectual perspective still leaves us with the problem of incongruity indicated already. According to the metonymy interpretation, applying satisfactorily to Gestalt perception, we would expect also the corresponding binary oppositions accounting for aspectual distinctions to exhibit the typical features of metonymy, i.e., inclusion and hierarchical prominence of the marked value (cf. Shapiro and Shapiro 1988: 30–31), demonstrated by 'part' and 'figure'. However, this is apparently not the case. Overtly, this incongruity is evidenced by the fact that, in aspect cognition, totality (the total view of events) is correlated to foreground, whereas Gestalt whole is correlated to ground (corresponding rather to aspectual remote background); further, that aspectual partiality (the partial view of events, i.e., in one of their phases) is correlated to close background, whereas Gestalt partiality is correlated to figure (corresponding to aspectual foreground). Why is this so? Is something wrong with either Gestalt or aspect theory? My hypothesis is—and that is the only reasonable solution I can think of so far—that it is rather a matter of hierarchy.

As indicated already by my preliminary questions above, I would, in regard to the aspectual distinction totality vs. partiality, say that this is apparently an equipollent choice we encounter at the bottom of a hierarchy of preceding successive partitioning (into ever smaller chunks of the observed world) in the shape of privative choices in the process of abduction. In other words, we have arrived at the level of perceptual-perspectival analysis of individual events where there are merely two possibilities left—either the total view or the partial view of them—because no further partitioning beyond phases of motion is conceivable. This equipollent (non-metonymic) totality-partiality distinction may, however, by way of feedback, very well be assumed to partake of basic discontinuation of divisible/diagrammatized continuous chaos hand in hand with privative (metonymic) partitioning (see section 9 below).

In regard to the distinctions between aspectual foreground and close and remote background, already the differentiation of background indicates a cognitive-semantic structure dissolving an unambiguous polarization of inclusive and prominent foreground, on the one hand, and background understood as subordinate whole including the former, on the other. For one thing, the close background takes a mediate position, even closer to the foreground than to the remote background by its temporal relatedness to it. More generally, aspectual background, as distinguished from Gestalt ground, is (in agreement with its differentiation) something that can be paid attention to, even focused upon, in regard not only to its temporal and causal relations to the foreground, but sometimes also in its own right. My preliminary suggestion is to interpret also this incongruity along the previous lines, i.e., as the result of a transition at a determinate stage of hierarchical-privative partitioning (according to perceptual-sensory focus/non-focus, conditioned by figure-ground) to a differentiation in terms of equipollent choices. This dynamic understanding could be coupled to the above model of perceptual-abductive processing (figure 1) in such a way that privative choices correspond to abduction, selecting, in cases of non-matching, a rule for further partitioning of case data, whereas equipollent choices correspond to abduction, selecting, in cases of matching, a rule applicable to the chunk represented by the present case data.

9. From Biological Survival to Temporal Perspective on Situations and Events

Teleology in human behavior can be said to start in the 'final' cause (see discussion below, section 14) represented by the biological motive of the continued existence of the species. This motive is realized in the individual's instinct for survival/self-preservation and his/her corresponding endeavor to control situations of life, i.e., by attending to them, by perceiving, emotionally evaluating, and cognizing them, and by acting in accordance with them. To control changes of situations is vital to self-preservation, and we react to changes in order to retain status quo, or we adapt to them, if this is more adequate, by way of selection. In order to do this, we must discern new states and the events (actions) causing these new states, i.e., we have to perform a perceptual-sensory, an emotional-evaluative, and a perceptual-cognitive analysis, the last of which comprises cause-effect relations.

This entire procedure, according to my suggestion, requires the discontinuation of chaos, enabled by biological rhythmization assigning to it divisibility and, accordingly, continuity. Only under these conditions are we in a position to select, in agreement with the strategy of hierarchical-successive chunk-wise partitioning (conditioned by Gestalt dispositions), parts of this continuity perceived as events causing the change from an old state of affairs to a new one. This is where space and time as means of analysis/discontinuation become involved. Relations between *things* are conceived, by way of discontinuation, as relations 'in' *space*. Changes of these relations are conceived as caused by *motion* of things 'in' space. Motion, in turn, is conceived, by way of discontinuation, as 'taking place in' *time* (for a detailed account, see Appendix). The reason for conceiving a change in the relations of things in space as a change in time is, I suggest, that cause-effect analysis implies a reinterpretation by abstraction of the change in space as a change from one state (the old one) to a subsequent state (the new one), introducing thereby (on the basis of compound spatial/temporal, i.e., aspectual, discrimination of events; see below, sections 10 and 12) the primary temporal distinction between *before* and *after*.

Precisely as perception-cognition of things is assumed to take place by way of superordinate hierarchical-successive partitioning conditioned by *gestalt* dispositions of things, perception-cognition of situations and events may be assumed to take place by way of such partitioning conditioned by *gestalt* dispositions of situations and events. The recognition of *gestalt* wholes of events may further be understood to be closely related to the interpretation of their causal-temporal relations to other events discerned in the process of partitioning. That is the reason for my assumption that temporal-perspectival (i.e., in fact, compound spatial/temporal) analysis, in the form of aspect distinctions, is involved, through *gestalt* wholes, already in primary discontinuation of chaos. Thus, I suggested above that, integrated with primary perceptual-sensory selection according to the superordinate privative PARTITIONING-NON-PARTITIONING (i.e., the promoted-generalized part-whole) distinction, there is, by way of feedback, also a preliminary aspectual analysis in terms of the equipollent totality-partiality distinction.

The latter analysis is obviously required by change-of-state and cause-effect analysis, since the totality-partiality distinction enables a singling out, by totalization, of the immediately causally related events of the state-changing foreground as distinguished from the events of the close and remote background, causally related to the foreground only in mediate ways. (It is an open question as to what extent the direct temporal relations of the close background with the foreground may be said to imply also closer causal relations.) Further, aspectual totalization is necessary for the delimitation of state-changing foreground events from each other as a prerequisite for their being sequenced and causally interconnected (see also section 10 and the end of section 13).

Closely related to abductive-cognitive processes of Gestalt perception, the aspectual totality-partiality distinction thus interacts with perceptual-sensory selection (the superordinate PARTITIONING-NON-PARTITIONING or focus/non-focus distinction) in dividing the perceptual field into the spatial/temporal/causal distinction between foreground and background. In spite of their integration in this process, four hierarchical levels of partitioning may still be distinguished, characterized by the following—in essence, perspectival—distinctions: (1) the perceptual-sensory one between focus and non-focus; (2) the Gestalt ones between part and whole, as well as figure and ground; (3) the aspectual one between foreground and (close and remote) background; and (4) the aspectual one between a total view of events, i.e., totality, and a partial/phasal view of events, i.e., partiality, distinguishing foreground and close background, respectively. To this hierarchical differentiation corresponds the degree of perceptual-abductive progression. In light of my hierarchical-processual understanding, it should be no surprise that the situation-aspectual distinction between foreground and background is intuitively, and correctly so, conceived of as prior to the event-aspectual distinction between totality and partiality, although the latter partakes already of the creation of the former. This is a consequence of constant circuit feedback in abduction allowing for the actualization of hierarchically subordinate distinctions as subsidiary hypothetical questions in the successive search for answers to superordinate hypothetical questions. Whereas the situation-aspectual distinction between foreground-background can be said to be hierarchically subordinate to the general (privative) PARTITIONING-NON-PARTITIONING distinction (represented by perceptual-sensory selection conditioned by Gestalt dispositions), it is thus still hierarchically-processually superordinate to the event-aspectual equipollent totality-partiality distinction.

10. Change-of-State, Cause-Effect, and Aspectual Perspective in the Individuation of Events

My above suggestion that compound spatial/temporal (aspectual) analysis is involved already in the discrimination/individuation of events by discontinuation, and thus partaking of primary change-of-state and cause-effect analysis, implies a revision of prevailing philosophical treatments. This has to do in the first place, I believe, with the shortcomings of the traditional philosophy of time, which restricts its attention to tense by completely neglecting aspect, and usually treats time in terms of intervals and truth-condition. In his discussion of criteria for the identity of events, Donald Davidson (Davidson 1980 [1969]: 175–80), having questioned the criteria of sameness of place and time as not "clearly acceptable," suggests instead another criterion: "[E]vents are identical if and only if they have exactly the same causes and effects" (179). It is true that Davidson discusses *sentences* about identities (of events), but if we assume that there is a hierarchical-processual equivalence in the mode we perceive and cognize events irrespectively of whether they are interpreted on the basis of immediate perception or propositional mediation, we are entitled to understand his suggestion to represent a general standpoint in regard to the cognitive-hierarchical interrelations of causation and space/time. There should be no doubt that causes and effects are crucial to discontinuation also in my model, but what Davidson (ibid.) appears to overlook when he (most pertinently) observes that "they are features guaranteed to individuate [events] in the sense not only of telling them apart but also of telling them together" is that this process of causal individuation and interconnection of events—as demonstrated above—is inconceivable without the simultaneous interaction of spatial and compound spatial/temporal, viz. aspectual, analysis and the corresponding individuation and ordering of things 'in' space, and events 'in' space/time, by way of discontinuation. By concluding that "perhaps sameness of causal relations is the only condition always sufficient to establish sameness of events (sameness of location in space and time may be another)," Davidson (ibid.) obviously admits his irresolution as to an interplay of these conditions.

Furthermore, if there is such a thing as a causally 'natural' direction and order of events (compare Peirce's 'finious actions', CP 7.471), this would not apparently predict temporal order in an absolute and immediate sense but rather as a mediate potentiality, since the former is dependent on individual interpretations in regard to change-of-state and cause-effect. Only events perceived as (potential) changes-of-state can, in turn, be subjected to cause-effect analysis. Generally, we first ask ourselves whether there is a change, then, if there is, what caused it. If temporal (in fact, compound spatial/temporal) perspective in the shape of aspect distinctions is involved already in change-of-state analysis, one would not thus expect temporal analysis to be predicted directly by causal analysis (as maintained by 'causal' theories of time), but rather—as suggested above—to partake of the entire hierarchical process of change-of-state and cause-effect analysis. The statement that "causal order fixes temporal order" (Mellor 1981: 8; see also Reichenbach 1956: 15; Faye 1989: 16ff.), then, apparently neglects the condition that they are in a relation of interdependence (by way of processual feedback) with subjective change-of-state interpretations. If understood to imply that there can be no temporal order without causal order, the latter claim is too strong, however. Events certainly can be temporally ordered without being causally ordered. Causal order cannot, consequently, be objective either (in an absolute sense), as suggested by Faye (op. cit.: 17), since it would depend on subjective interpretations of change-of-state and cause-effect according to individual perspective (intentions, etc.). This understanding of mine was expressed indirectly also by Davidson (op. cit.: 172): "... [I]t is not events that are necessary or sufficient as causes, but events as *described* in one way or another."

The ontogenetic development of perception and cognition obviously takes place along with the development of man's consciousness of his own existence, i.e., the process and conditions of life. Part of this consciousness are the experience of thought as a corresponding, continuous process and the ability to observe to some extent this process. In the latter case we may provisionally speak of 'internal perception'. Observations of conditions beyond the cognitive process, in or outside our bodies, we may then call 'external perception'. In both cases, perception, obviously, is in an abductive relationship of mutual dependence to cognition as a means of rationalization (see above), i.e., in the first case, constituting what we may understand as 'self-reflecting' cognition. The experience of continuous process applies to conditions of 'external perception', as well. The question arises as to whether this is the outcome of an unconscious projection of internal processuality onto conditions of 'external perception'—as assumed by Locke (1961 [1689]: book II, chap. 14) and Peirce (CP 1.489; W 3.68ff., 105ff.) and reflected by the assignment of divisibility/continuity to chaos by the above model—or an inherent property of these conditions. According to the latter alternative, man in nature would experience processuality equivalent to that of his own thought, i.e., as a property of one unitary system of biological and physical processes. The first alternative is favored by the thesis of biological rhythmization, originating in man and, according to my suggestion, applied by man as a constitutive part of attention and perception to chaos as a precondition for its discontinuation and ordering. This does not exclude, however, the possibility of a combination, i.e., man's superimposing endogenous rhythms onto processuality (phasality) in nature (see section 13 below).

At this point we have to ask whether perceived processes—besides a nature-inherent direction as potentiality—can be said a priori to imply a causal and temporal order between their elements. This was in effect maintained by Mellor as a consequence of his rather absolute understanding of time: "[A]ny possible world ... must have at least one dimension, that of time" (1995: 235); "time is the causal dimension of spacetime" (op. cit.: 243); "causation is what gives time its direction and makes it linear" (op. cit.: xi). This would not be the case according to a perspectival-relational theory of time. The primary "linear" process here is void of elements that are discerned and ordered causally and temporally, i.e., we have merely the divisible continuity superimposed on the chaos of immediate perception. Only when the observer discerns phases of this continuum as (potential) changes-of-state would an analysis, as part of overall partitioning, be initiated, which leads to discontinuity. This analysis presupposes from the very beginning an intimate cooperation of cause-effect and temporal (primarily aspectual, i.e., compound spatial/temporal) interpretation, but change-of-state distinctions may be understood to trigger this complex procedure of situation analysis. Causation and time (temporal order) presuppose each other. Neither of the two is a priori in the sense both were regarded by Kant, and causation was by Mellor (1995: 243): "[T]he form of inner sense is causation." The significance of subjective interpretations according to a perspectival-relational theory of time otherwise harmonizes with the "explanatory and means-end connotations of causation" pertinently pointed out by Mellor (op. cit.: 58ff., 79ff., 220).

The complex analysis in terms of cooperative change-of-state, cause-effect and temporal (aspectual) perspective may be assumed, thus, to hold for 'external' as well as 'internal perception'. In sum, if there can be any talk of causally-temporally ordered continuity, this would be the derived continuity resulting from the *synthesis* taking place after the causal-temporal analysis (see Appendix below).

Causal or 'natural' order of events, to the extent that it exists, is obviously accessible to man only by means of (provisory) temporalization in complex interpretations-by-construction (including Gestalt/pattern-matching analysis) triggered by change-of-state or, rather, hypotheses of change-of-state, since the latter, too, can be tested only by means of aspectual temporalization. Although there should indeed be a cognitive hierarchy insofar as cause-effect analysis generally presupposes the establishment of change-of-state, the prominent mechanism of processual feedback, in effect, would enable also the influence of cause-effect experience upon the successive establishment of change-of-state.

11. Space/Time Cognition, Grammar, and Biological Rhythmization

When I some 25 years ago—inspired by discussions with, among others, Rudolf Růžička and Hansjacob Seiler—began to study the temporal categories, in particular, the aspect category, in Slavic languages, I could not foresee that these studies would take me to the very heart of human behavior. Today I realize that it was consistent that the path I followed then should lead me eventually not only to the cornerstones of human perception, thought, and action, i.e., the concepts of space and time, but also to questions about their neurobiological substrata.

One of the early discoveries I made was that traditional philosophy of time thoroughly treated the category of tense, but completely lacked knowledge of aspectual distinctions. Accordingly, it became my privilege to suggest the relevance of aspect for the general concept of time and thus for a solution of the 'eternal' philosophical problem of time, as well (cf. Thelin 1990a, b; 1999; see section 12 below).

Semantic studies of aspect in Slavic and other languages led me to fairly qualified hypotheses about time as a hierarchical-processual complex of conceptual distinctions, basically universal by nature. The most prominent feature of these distinctions turned out to be their *perspectival function*. It is precisely the lack of this function in traditional philosophical as well as physical theories of time that I consider to be one fundamental reason for their insufficiency. The established dependence of temporal perspective on spatial perspective further made it evident that the cognition of time can be studied exhaustively only in connection with the cognition of space.

We are entitled to ask now: Are these conditions indeed relevant to our grammar models? If we consider this to be the case, we ought to ask, as well: Which type of grammar is best suited for incorporating this knowledge? The recent development toward cognitive grammar, in my opinion, is a positive answer to the first question, but not necessarily an exhaustive answer to the second question. The universal role of space and time in language, action, and thought demonstrates convincingly that the study of corresponding grammatical structures can no more take place in a closed language-specific or typological system.

Expressions of space and time in language and their role for the organization of communication are thus the manifestations of basic human behavior, including situation analysis in terms of change-of-state and cause-effect. We cannot imagine that man, without an analysis of things and events in space and time, would be able to react properly to changes of current states of affairs. Ultimately, this capability is indeed a precondition for man's survival as well as the continued existence of the human species. These considerations give preference to a grammar capable of founding its hypotheses on knowledge of man not only as a social being but also as a part of biological evolution. They also give preference to a grammar based on a general theory of action of the kind suggested by Peirce, and, subsequently, for example, by psycholinguists of the Vygotskij School (cf. also Thelin 1985: 158).

The answer to the second question, therefore, ought to be that we need a grammar which—in the spirit of Peirce and other pragmatists—recognizes as a relevant basis the study of human cognition as part of a superordinate theory of action. It is not important whether we call such a grammar cognitive-pragmatic or simply pragmatic. From the standpoint of biopragmatism, it is important, however, that its explanatory and predictive adequacy should be viewed as dependent on the degree to which it is supported by a biological theory of human behavior. Such a theory, as we know, was suggested by Konrad Lorenz (1978), the founder of modern ethology. Related to language, it received its hitherto most perfect expression in Eric Lenneberg's *Biological Foundations of Language* (1967). In a century starting with the complete mapping of the human genome and promising to become the very century of biology, the time has hopefully come for Lenneberg's pioneering work to receive its full recognition.

Even against this background, I was surprised when I recently found out that my cognitive-linguistic models of aspect and time are supported, as a matter of fact, by *the behavior of earthworms*. That I realized this, at first glance improbable, connection I owe to Konrad Lorenz (1996: xxxvii), who was the first to recognize the enormous importance of Erich von Holst's (1969–70 [1936]) discovery of *the endogenous production of rhythmic stimuli*. Lorenz understood that the latter is the foundation not only of motion in earthworms and fishes but of behavior in general, also in higher animals, including man. The connection with man's cognition of space and time, however, Lorenz did not see. Conceived as an empirical base for hypotheses about man's perception and cognition, biological rhythmization, however, offers a new understanding also in this respect. This condition was evident, in general terms, to Colwyn Trevarthen (1990a: 339ff.), who understood endogenous rhythmization (biological 'clocks') to constitute "the anatomical space/time frame of behaviour [formed by] regulator neurones of the reticular core" (cf. also Trevarthen 1999). But how are we to understand more specifically the connection between biological rhythms and man's analysis of the world in terms of space and time?

Let us begin with the following question: What is the reason for our conceiving space and time as continuous? My suggestion is that it is our unconscious strategy of 'preparing', as it were, the immediately perceived chaos by applying to it what we may compare to a homogeneous screen. In this way, chaos becomes *divisible* and *continuous*, and thus manageable to perception and cognition. Now we are in a position to apply space and time as the perspectival-relational instruments with which we perform the analysis—i.e., discrimination-by-discontinuation—of things and events. In divisible continuity I want to see the fundamental medium of which temporal research until now had only a faint idea. Peirce (CP 1.383, 2.778) was close to a solution in this sense when he suggested his hypothesis of 'diagrammatic patterning' as a prerequisite for human perception (see above), but—like William James (1890: 224–90, 605–42) and Henri Bergson (1889, 1911: 32, 1923: 54ff.)—he erroneously understood the resulting continuity as identical with time itself. For an extensive discussion of the concept of continuity with Peirce, see Thelin (1999: 289–97).

It should be evident by now that it is precisely in the biological rhythms, discovered by von Holst, that we, according to my suggestion, shall see the origin of divisibility and continuity, concepts that are so essential for the construction of space and time. Without the homogeneous divisibility of extension in things, their distances, motion, and trajectories, the analysis in terms of discontinuous spatial and temporal definitions—such as, for example, the aspectual distinction totality vs. partiality, but certainly also procedures of measure—would be literally unthinkable. *The divisibility and continuity of (potential) perceptual objects may thus be assumed to originate in a neurobiological reality, viz. the production of rhythmic stimuli, 'directed', so to say, by perception and cognition toward these objects.*

The fundamental role assigned to rhythmic stimuli in this theory of space and time cognition finds independent support in other observations. Lenneberg (1967: 98, 107–20), accordingly, demonstrated the significance of rhythmization for human behavior in general and for the *seriality of speech* in particular. Wilhelm Wundt's (1874) 'pulses of attention' is a further indication of rhythmization as constitutive of perception. In agreement with my above interpretation is also the early discovery by Trevarthen (1974, 1990a: 339ff.; see also Lenneberg 1974: 571ff.) that the perception of visual space in newborn children is characterized by a *regular scanning rhythm*.

Against this background, it appears legitimate for cognitive-pragmatic grammar, as distinguished from autonomous grammar, to ask questions also about the specific neurobiological (processual-physiological and anatomical) correlates of space and time. For example, is there a connection between the growth of the brain, in particular, the frontal lobe, in hominids and their developing instruments for spatial and, especially, temporal analysis (as a constitutive part of a general ability of rationalization by symbolization)? Further, isn't it reasonable to assume that cognitive-linguistic knowledge of space and time, incorporated in the praxis of neurosciences, might contribute to a proper formulation of neurological problems connected with disorders in spatial and temporal orientation due not only to brain injuries, lesions such as tumors and stroke, and neural dysfunction such as schizophrenia, but also to age-related impairment of memory? The acquirement of concepts of things and their spatial and temporal relations in early childhood, but, equally, their successive loss due to aging and disease, was the thought-provoking theme in Jurij Olesha's story *Liompa* (cf. Björling 1981; Thelin 1984b).

12. Time in Philosophy and Physics, and the Aspectual Renewal of Temporal Studies

Ever since man began to reflect on matters of existence, the essence of time to thinkers has been a permanent cause for worry. Of course, we know how to use calendars and clocks, how to divide, measure, and indicate time according to the conventions historically founded primarily in the apparent motion of the sun and the cycle of day and night. But how essential is this so-called *chronological time* to the overall concept of time?

On closer reflection, is it indeed time that is being determined? Is it not, conversely, motion and events that are being determined with the aid of time? We may, against the background of what has been said above, assume that what gave birth to time was probably regular, cyclic motion (cf. also Thelin 1990b: 104–7), viz. when man turned such rhythms of nature (conditioning, apparently, in turn, phylogenetically certain macro-types of endogenous rhythms; see section 13 below) into standards for the analysis of specific *gestalts* and on this basis developed (as the hierarchical-processual continuation of superordinate partitioning conditioned by Gestalt perception; see above) *time proper* as an instrument primarily for the aspect-perspectival discrimination and ordering of events in terms of *before-after*, and secondarily for their measurement and tense-perspectival correlation to moment of speech. The common ideas of continuous time (see above) and, specifically, of 'moving time', accordingly, would not under these circumstances reflect essential features of time. We have suggested (see Appendix below) that the latter idea should rather be understood as a metaphor of secondary nature—not without influence, though, on our conception of reality. If this assumption is correct, we will have to regard time in a more proper sense as an *immobile* instrument for the perspectival analysis of motion, i.e., of what we perceive as events. The notion of 'immobility' is understood to allow merely for *operational mobility*, i.e., the focus of temporal distinctions is directed by the observer toward events wherever they are located in the perceptual field.

Already at this point we realize that our spontaneous understanding of time is insufficient to give us an idea of its essence. Wittgenstein's (1958: 42e, 89) response to St. Augustine's (*Confessions* XI: 14, 17) famous words of resignation in this respect ("If nobody asks me I know; if someone puts the question and I have to explain, I do not know any more") was his advice to "remind ourselves" of this knowledge, i.e., to make available to our consciousness the concept of time underlying language. As distinguished from the outspokenly skeptical view that time is indefinable (cf. Gale 1968a: vii, 1968b: 4ff.), our present reflections are governed rather by the constructive spirit of Wittgenstein's viewpoint (although in more outspokenly cognitive-processual ways than he would have agreed to).

A discussion of time still cannot get round the idea of its motion ('passage of time'). We observe, in the now, how events take place and disappear, as it were, into the past, thereby experiencing that time goes by as well, i.e., when we look back or remember. When we look forward in expectation, we experience, conversely, that events, and with them time, move toward the now, before they, in turn, also become past. In this image of time's motion, our point of observation—the now—is fixed. We appear to stand on the shore of the 'stream of time' and see it passing, moving backwards. According to an alternative image, we move forwards ourselves, together with the now, along a fixed succession of events that change from future to present and finally past ones. In reality, in both cases we idealize observations of concrete events made in a given now. No observer can ascribe to an actual event all three temporal meanings. By abstracting unconsciously from concrete observations, we free ourselves from the now as the point of departure and have the feeling that we can move freely both forwards and backwards in time. Time itself receives the character of a medium in permanent and uniform motion independently of the events it orders and measures. This idealized image ever since Newton (1962 [1687]: 6–8) was the basis for the *absolute* concept of time in classical physics.

The essentially *relational* nature of time, maintained by Leibniz (1981 [1765]: 152, §16), was evident already to Aristotle (*Physics*: §§ 217–23). He defined time as measure ('number') of motion in regard to 'before' and 'after'. As pointed out by von Wright (1969: 17), we may assume that time as duration, i.e., measure of the distance between 'before' and 'after', is preceded by temporal order, i.e., this very distinction between 'before' (old state) and 'after' (new state) as the origin of temporal meaning (together, according to my analysis, with its underlying compound spatial/temporal, i.e., aspectual, analysis; see below, this section, and section 13). This understanding harmonizes with intuitive cause-effect analysis and a corresponding primitive stimulus-response behavior. It has also found support in the inherent direction of events that according to thermodynamics has been assumed to follow from increasing disorder (entropy). The opposite view is maintained by Prigogine (1997: 3, 26), who holds that this direction is rather a result of increasing order established by natural processes of evolution through 'self-organization' ('order from chaos'). In favor of this view is the striking parallel of situational analysis by human observers in assigning order to chaotic happenings, prominently by the instrument of aspectual time.

A relational theory of time rejects, however, Prigogine's fusion of events and time on one cognitive level, which ascribes, metaphorically, to time itself motion and direction (cf. the notion 'arrow of time' inherited from Eddington, 1932) as essential properties and, in effect, absolute existence in a reality without observers (even before the Big Bang). This assumption leads to a circular argument as demonstrated by the view (Prigogine and Stengers 1993: 310) that "time cannot come from timelessness." A perspectival-relational theory shows that it can. Time, accordingly, is primarily an immobile instrument used by man to create order in chaos by assigning perspective and coherence to events (rather than an observer-independent dimension resulting, in inanimate matter, from "spontaneous transformation of disorder to order," Swenson 1999: 577). A 'natural' direction of events is not necessarily considered in our interpretations of their causal and temporal relations but rather depends on whether we perceive them as changes-of-state and, indeed, *actualize* their inherent (potential) direction as order—i.e., by a chain of events in the foreground of a situation—or *neutralize* it in its background.

As soon as one has realized that the distinction *before-after* implies not only points of reference delimiting an event or the distance between two events, but also the very procedure of ordering events—in respect to each other and to the moment of speech—the relational nature of time becomes more evident. Ordering events, precisely like ordering things 'in' space, proceeds from and is dependent on an individual point of observation. Time, as well as space, therefore is a matter of perspective. One type of observational point is, as we have seen, the now, i.e., the moment of the speech event. From the latter, observed events are determined in regard to *tense*, i.e., as belonging either in the past, present, or future. The category of tense was the almost exclusive object of exploration in classical philosophy of time.

As indicated already above, linguistics discovered, however, another temporal (by nature rather compound spatial/temporal) category preceding hierarchically not only tense but also the primary temporal distinction *before-after*: the *aspect* category. Although this category had been a central object of research, especially in Slavic grammar, for almost a century, it only recently was freed from its traditional confusion with either tense (and taxis; cf. Thelin 1991, 1999: 247) or the semantico-syntax of the verb (cf. Thelin 1990a). We know this category through its specific modes of formalization, for example, in Slavic languages, English, and French, but (as distinguished from tense) its cognitive-pragmatic content appears to be universal in essence. One well-known expression of aspect is the distinction between the so-called simple and continuous forms of the verb in English: *to read* vs. *to be reading* (see below).

The aspect category is based on a complex point of observation abstracted from (but still including as a hierarchically subordinate component) the moment of observation/speech and possible tense distinctions. From this point of observation, actual perception and accumulated experience cooperate in determining the role of events in the observed situation in regard to change-of-state and cause-effect. We can imagine the situation as a theatrical scene. If events in it are understood by the spectator to represent essential changes, then he regards them as part of the scene's *foreground*, if not, of its *background*. In the latter case, events can be related directly to the foreground; in this instance, it is a matter of the *close background*. Or they are related merely indirectly to the foreground events, in which case it is a matter of the *remote background*, beyond the actual scene.

Consider, for example, the dramatic climax of Shakespeare's *Hamlet*. Obsessed by the suspicion that Claudius had murdered his father (remote background), Hamlet, during the theatrical performance, was watching (close background) how his uncle, at the poisoning of the theatrical king (foreground), reacted by suddenly rising and thus betrayed himself (foreground).

In order to understand foreground events that advance the plot, we have to know as a rule their causal connections with both kinds of background. Parts of the close background may be not only simultaneously ongoing events but also new states, resulting from preceding changes. Parts of the remote background are previous scenes or scenes expected by the spectator to succeed. The tense dimension thus is normally involved as a component subordinate to aspectual analysis.

Like scenes, we interpret—and act in—situations of life on the basis of actual perception and accumulated experience. The latter two are individualistic as are the factors by which they are conditioned: personal needs, desires, interests, emotions, convictions, expectations, apprehensions, and so forth. Causal-temporal analysis is decisive for our ability to adapt to changing situations.

According to different interpretations of situational changes, there may, for example, be different opinions as to whether an event at the moment of speech, such as a rise on the Stock Exchange, has ceased or continues. This shows that *tense perspective* (in temporal logic, as such first paid serious attention to by Paul Needham, 1975) is dependent on *aspect perspective*. This dependence is evident also from the fact that in certain ('generic') cases of remote background events, one cannot use any other tense than the present; cf.:

Mammals give birth to living babies

Now, ordering events in the foreground and background, respectively, according to the distinction between change-of-state and non-change-of-state, i.e., applying a *perspective on situations*, requires a simultaneous aspectual analysis of these events themselves, i.e., a *perspective on events*. More than 20 years ago, aspectologists (cf. Thelin 1978: 31ff., 1990a: 30ff.) discovered that events (except those belonging in the remote background) can be subjected to either a total (+TOT) or partial (-TOT) perspective. The total perspective on an event, i.e., its delimitation with a beginning and an end, has been shown to be a prerequisite for its being included in a chain of foreground events; cf.:

Mary LOCKED herself in her room, READ the letter, and BURST into tears

The aspectual total perspective, accordingly, is also a prerequisite for the primary temporal distinction *before-after*. The partial perspective, i.e., a reference to a part (phase) of an event, has been shown to be a prerequisite for its presentation as going on simultaneously with a foreground event; cf.:

Mary WAS READING a letter when I came into her room

or with the moment of speech; cf.:

Mary IS READING the letter now

i.e., as taking place in the close background.

There is some evidence that aspectologists, precisely in this event-related distinction of totality vs. partiality, have found the key to understanding the essence of time. For more than two thousand years philosophers and natural scientists have thought of time as a riddle, apparently, because they did not manage to penetrate language and its temporal categories. Today, a linguistically based philosophy of time in the aspect category has at its disposal an instrument that among other things would explain why some of our greatest thinkers, such as Aristotle, St. Augustine, and Einstein, have been at a loss for a reply to one and the same problem, viz. that the present, as distinguished from the past and the future, does not allow for measurement of time (cf. Thelin 1999: 246, 280ff., 299ff.). One can say that someone read for an hour but not that someone in this very moment is reading for an hour. The explanation is conditioned not by tense but by aspect.

Measurement of time, or more properly, of the extension of events, thus requires the delimiting, total (+TOT) temporal perspective that conveys either foreground changes or, as here, embedding into these; cf.:

Mary came home, READ for an hour, and then went for a walk

This perspective is irreconcilable with the *actual* present meaning, which—as we saw above—is based contrarily on the partial temporal perspective (-TOT), i.e., a reference to events in that part (phase) of them that coincides with the moment of speech. This also explains why as a rule English simple forms in the present can be used only in their second meaning, i.e., of remote background, as, for example, in cases of habituality; cf.:

Mary READS a lot

but not in the meaning of foreground (for well-defined exceptions, e.g., the 'historical present', see Thelin 1990a: 34, 57ff., 1990b: 99).

Having become aware of the significance especially of aspectual analysis for the concept of time, we understand that the problem with which philosophers and physicists have been confronted until this day is their inability to reconcile the idea that time is continuous with the discontinuous nature of observation and temporal perspective. THIS IS THE ROOT OF THE CLASSICAL TIME PROBLEM.

Closest to achieving this insight was Henri Bergson (1911: 32), who actually spoke of "partial views on the whole," although by this he meant general fragmentation (without a clear distinction between courses of events and temporal categories), deforming, according to him, an original continuity ("durée-qualité"). Peirce

(NEM 4.332) had, to be sure, in a corresponding way considered Firstness or 'quality' to be 'without parts' (cf. Dewey 1935; Thelin 1994; Innis 1998). Of importance in this connection is also the observation made by von Wright (1969: 7ff., 31) of the purport that the logical analysis of change-of-state leads to contradictions, unless one postulates two temporal levels: one linear time and one time "divided into bits." He understands the former as a "macro-aspect," the latter as a "micro-aspect." In these notions von Wright is close to an instrumental, perspectival conception of time in spite of the fact that he summarizes his analysis as a logic for "division of time" (rather than of events).

The time problem was not solved by the theories of relativity, and it became the outspoken dilemma of quantum theory. According to Bohr (1934: 98), a causal, i.e., continuous, study of atomic processes is impossible: "[A]ny attempt at an ordering in space-time leads to a break in the causal chain." This discontinuity is no surprise to a perspectival-relational theory of time. It is interesting that Bohr actually took the first steps precisely in this direction and, apparently, did so under the influence of his mentor, the Danish philosopher and psychologist Höffding (for an excellent account of this background, see Faye 1991). Inspired by Einstein's special theory of relativity, Höffding had indeed already in 1921 suggested a subjective-perspectival interpretation of time (irrespectively, though, of relative motion). Bohr was convinced that the meaning of physical discoveries must be viewed as part of a philosophy related to human cognition. The observational problems of quantum theory led him thus to a dynamic-perspectival understanding of the *subject-object relations* that he, in the spirit of Höffding, considered to be "the very root of the problem of knowledge." He suspected that the answer to these problems had to be looked for in language and our mode of thinking: "[A]ll account of physical experience is, of course, ultimately based on common language, adapted to orientation in our surroundings and to tracing relationships between cause and effect" (Bohr 1963: 1; cf. also Chevalley 1994: 49).

The idea that the dilemma of quantum theory (represented also by the wave-particle complementarity) might be explained by a hierarchical reconstruction of cognitive-pragmatic processes based on language appears to have been in Bohr's mind when he (1958: 52, 68) referred to the *analysis-synthesis strategy* as one possible expedient (and, apparently, did so under the influence of Höffding; cf. Faye 1991: 148). Since this, as we have indicated (see also below, Appendix), is indeed one of the instruments necessary for a reconciliation of discontinuity with continuity in one unitary system, Bohr may thus be considered to have anticipated, at least in part, the foundation for a cognitive-hierarchical model of time derivation of the kind suggested here. That discontinuation represents analysis, like the temporal one, is obvious. Continuity, however, is more than synthesis if we assume that temporal perspective fragmentizes precisely the continuity of unanalyzed courses of events. The traditional concept of synthesis in the primary function intended by Kant (cf. discussion in Peirce CP 1.384) can therefore be replaced by the hypothesis of a homogeneously divisible continuity (A). The latter functions, in the spirit of Peirce's (CP 1.383, 2.778), as a screen we superimpose on the chaos of immediate perception in order to enable (temporal-perspectival) analysis (B). The latter implies discontinuity, which is subsequently subjected to synthesis proper (C). The outcome is heterogeneous continuity of causally-temporally related events. It is most remarkable that Peirce (CP 4.642) in 1908 with the following words announced a paper on continuity that was never to be written: "I have, in the interval, taken a considerable stride toward the solution of continuity, having at length clearly and minutely analyzed my own conception of a *perfect continuity* as well as that of an *imperfect continuity*, that is, a continuum having topical singularities, or places of lower dimensionality where it is interrupted or divides."

Against this background, we understand that the problem in physics arose when the continuous screen, which had worked satisfactorily for the macro-objects of classical physics and everyday life, turned out not to be fine-meshed enough to give us a simultaneous grip on the chaos represented by atomic micro-objects and their extreme velocities. Quantum theory, in effect, revealed the present limits of the human faculty of observation. Since micro-objects do not allow for a coherent interpretation of space/time and change/cause-effect at the level of analysis, subsequent synthesis is not possible either. Classical physics, conversely, overlooked a possible analysis and generalized synthesis, instead, as the isolated object of exploration—without giving up, though, the continuous screen. This gave birth to the idea of time's homogeneity, mobility, and symmetric directionality as fundamental, absolute properties.

From the point of view of cognitive reality, there is no sense in denying absolute time, but it should be understood as derived secondarily from relational time. The theory of special relativity did not really remove temporal absolutism by making time dependent on the position and relative motion of observers. Relativistic time (the observer's 'Eigenzeit') in the shape of space-time fulfills an a priori coordinate function without the necessary prerequisites for relating space and time in a hierarchical process. Time as general 'container' was just changed into a "personal container" (as Mellor coined it in a discussion) in which there is no place for the subject's *choice* of perspective on events. Only quantum mechanics allowed for a basic discontinuous understanding of time as a relational and perspectival instrument within a unitary cognitive-pragmatic model. The asymmetry of thermodynamic entropy (or negentropy) refers to processes preceding their temporalization.

The possibility of so-called time travel, founded in the general theory of relativity, is by definition excluded by a perspectival-relational theory of time. According to the latter, it is also unreal that time would go more slowly because clocks (and biological processes such as aging) do, owing to increasing gravity and/or relative motion.

On the other hand, a perspectival-relational theory of time allows for a new understanding of Zeno's paradoxes. The illusion of Achilles never catching up with the tortoise or of the ever resting arrow is due to *the infinite division of space and time* that follows from the confusion of two distinct cognitive levels: the level of homogeneously divisible continuity of non-perspectivized motion, on the one hand, and the level of motion made discontinuous by temporal-perspectival analysis, on the other.

Another classical riddle, viz. Heraclitus's river into which we (according to the original Greek wording) both can and cannot step twice, now becomes explainable as an expression of two different temporal perspectives on the action, with focus on its object: in the former case, the river and our stepping into it as part of the remote background, with permanent identity; in the latter, the river as part of the close background, in permanent change related directly to the foreground event of our stepping into it. This very distinction may at first glance be blurred by the condition that both propositions are embedded hierarchically in a superordinate remote background perspective due to their proverbial function.

13. Abductive Hypotheses in the Perception of Events, and the Assignment of Aspectual Perspective

We are now in a position to apply the above model of abduction (figure 1) to the perception of events and formulate tentatively the hypotheses (hypothetical questions) emerging from the rules implicit in the proposed treatment of aspectual perspectivization. According to these rules, the latter takes place in cooperation not only with change-of-state analysis, as explicated below, but also with cause-effect analysis. The explication of the last (and its interrelations with the two former) would demand an immensely more complex picture (still understood only in rough outlines) due to the necessary simultaneous inclusion of at least two events (instead of one at a time, as is the case below) and their multitude of possible interconnections, depending on whether causes and effects are activities or states (see below), and whether they belong in the foreground, close background, or remote background, respectively. These conditions give us an idea of the complexity involved in perception and cognition of events and the corresponding scope of future research (and thus justify my simplification).

Another important preliminary concerns the relation of human endogenous rhythms in perception to processuality (phasality) inherent in external nature (see section 10 above). According to my understanding, subordinate to human perception and rhythmization, there are two forms of existence in nature: *motion* and *rest*. Motion and rest—to which we may refer also as *activities* and *states*, respectively—differ by one essential feature: activities have *phases*, states do not. The presence or absence of phasality is one decisive feature made discernible in the chaos of nature by human endogenous rhythmization and the corresponding assignment to chaos of divisibility/continuity. In cases of phasality, endogenous rhythms are apparently superimposed on external rhythms of nature. Both kinds of rhythms may be assumed to appear in various kinds and to differ, accordingly, as to the length of their phases. By way of processual feedback, endogenous rhythms may in the latter respect adapt to external rhythms (cf. the day and night rhythm). They would, apparently, in a similar way coincide with the latter also in cases of performance and perception of identical activities. However, there is no reason to consider endogenous rhythms to be dependent on external rhythms in any absolute sense. They are, of course, by origin 'natural', too, but it is important to understand that they are *applied* by man for the purpose of partitioning as a composite perceptual-sensory and cognitive-pragmatic procedure, and are thus, by processual feedback, dependent on conditions of change-of-state and cause-effect analysis in cooperation with spatial/temporal (aspectual) perspectivization (subsumed in Gestalt dispositions/patterns).

According to this understanding, endogenous rhythms may, as well, not adapt to external rhythms, but still use the latter's individual phases as a basis for partitioning, i.e., for the discrimination of events, according to their own requirements. It is an open question as to whether such a differentiation takes place as conditioned selection of primary rhythms or at an intermediate level for the assignment of specific types of divisibility sensitive to cognitive-pragmatic conditions.

As distinguished from activities, states cannot be discerned directly by endogenous rhythmization and partitioning because they lack phases to be operated upon. States can be delimited thus exclusively by surrounding activities (changes) and partitioned merely by conventional means. Only to the extent that the selection of endogenous rhythms, by way of processual feedback, is restricted by perceptual-sensory partitioning, the former may be assumed to be dependent on external rhythms, since perceptual-sensory partitioning, as we have seen (see section 8 above), cannot proceed beyond phases of the latter, unless such a procedure is made conceivable conventionally (theoretically, experimentally, etc.). In the absence of tangible evidence, these reflections on the relationship between endogenous and external rhythms must by necessity remain rather speculative. For the purpose of further exploration, I will still, on the basis of these reflections, assume provisionally that external rhythms—more specifically, *phasality* in the nature observed—are subordinate to the endogenous rhythms applied in observation.

After these preliminary remarks, we may, by way of simplification, imagine aspectual (i.e., compound spatial/temporal) perspectivization in cooperation with change-of-state (and, implicitly, cause-effect) analysis to partake of perception/abduction of events according to the hierarchically ordered, hypothetical questions suggested in figure 3.

In the process schematized in figure 3, the distinction between aspectual totality and partiality can (as indicated previously) be realized only as part of change-of-state analysis. Events that are interpreted as bringing about a situational change (and thus are referred to the foreground) can be so only by their delimitation or totalization

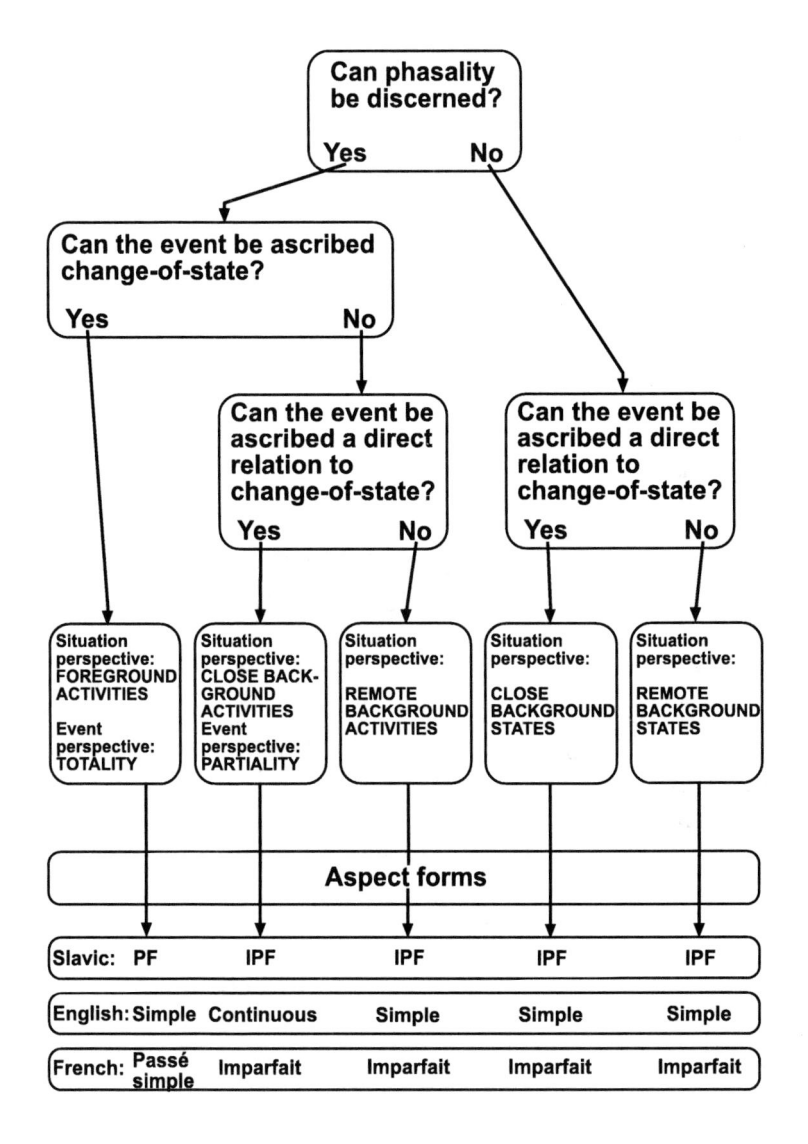

FIGURE 3 Aspectual Perspectivization

in divisible/diagrammatized chaos. This does not mean that totalization can be said to be predicted by change-of-state, or partialization by change-of-state-relatedness, but rather that the distinction totality-partiality as perspectival instrument is itself (by processual feedback) involved in the analysis of events before their change-of-state properties can be determined. This very distinction may thus be assumed to be a crucial tool for man's analysis of situations (see section 12 above), that is to test hypotheses about what is going on, viz. as part of attempts to discern (by totalization) and order events to see if they make sense as change-of-state (supported, in turn, by cause-effect experiences), or if they do not; or to discern (by partialization) merely phases of events that might be temporally (and possibly causally) related to but not part of change-of-state.

The above scheme represents linguistic *encoding*. *Decoding* would, in principle, take the opposite direction, but is complicated, among other things, by the extensive polysemy of aspect expressions. This, obviously, causes decoding to rely heavily on coherence in situation/discourse to establish compound spatial/temporal (aspectual) perspectives consistent with the actual interpretations of change-of-state and cause-effect. For a discussion of these still poorly known conditions, see Thelin (1990a: 29).

14. The Distinction between 'Final' and 'Efficient' Causation: Toward a Hierarchical-Processual Alternative

Against the background of the above account of space/time cognition in event perception and, in particular, the proposed procedure of aspect-perspectival selection involved in partitioning/discontinuation of chaos (assigned divisibility and continuity by biological rhythmization), would it be possible to make any qualified inferences in regard to the conditions of teleology involved, more specifically, to the distinction between 'final' and 'efficient' causes? According to Peirce's (CP 1.211–12) definition, based on Aristotle's proposals, the former are 'ideal', the latter, 'forceful': "[W]e must understand by final causation that mode of bringing facts about according to which a general description of result is made to come about, quite irrespective of any compulsion for it to come about in this or that particular way.... Efficient causation, on the other hand, is a compulsion determined by the particular condition of things, and is a compulsion acting to make that situation begin to change in a perfectly determinate way."

What if we apply this distinction made by Peirce to the proposed abductively governed process of perception and mental/physical action (figure 1), more specifically, to rules ('laws') and action, respectively? This is actually what Peirce (CP 1.212) himself does when he says that "[a law] is something general ... not a force. For force is compulsion; and compulsion is *hic et nunc*." Whereas 'laws', accordingly, may be considered to be 'final' causes, action cannot simply be identified with force/compulsion and 'efficient' causes. The reason for this is that Peirce (CP 1.265), by characterizing 'final' causation as 'mental' and 'efficient' causation as 'material', in effect makes a further distinction between mental and physical action: "There can be no objection to a man's engaging at one time in tracing out final, or mental, causation, and at another time in tracing out material, or efficient, causation." Strictly applied to the above account of perception and cognition of events, including aspectual perspectivization, this interpretation of Peirce would consequently treat not only primordial biopragmatic motives (see above, sections 2 and 9, and below) but the entire system of subsequent cognitive rules and procedures as 'final' causation, leaving for 'efficient' causation, actually, merely the physical/linguistic (phonetic-graphic) implementation of aspect expressions.

Are these consequences indeed reconcilable with Peirce's intentions? Yes, they appear to be confirmed by his further explication (CP 1. 212) of the relation between 'laws' and (physical) action: "[T]he relation of law, as a cause, to the action of force, as its effect, is final, or ideal, causation, not efficient causation." If my interpretation is correct, this would mean that the distinction between 'final' and 'efficient' causes may be questioned as to its usefulness in semiotic analysis, and should, perhaps, instead be replaced by an exploration of hierarchical distinctions in causation (understood, so far, mainly as 'final').

A corresponding differentiation of causation should, I suggest, proceed from the processual hierarchy of cognitive rules and procedures according to the logical order of perceptual-abductive processing, i.e., the proper order to ask hypothetical questions. This order implies (in accord with Peirce) causal order merely in a *mediate* sense. For example, the reason for asking for the cause of change only after we have asked whether there *is* a change (and know that this is the case) is primarily a matter of perceptual-cognitive and pragmatic logic, and only secondarily a matter of causation, viz. mediate causation. When we say that *a change 'causes'* us to ask for its cause, this is not a matter of immediate causation (i.e., an effect caused immediately by change itself) but of mediate causation, because the immediate cause is that we, in order to react properly on the change, normally must know its cause.

Like, in turn, asking the question whether there is a change can be said to be ordered causally as a mediate effect of the need for situation control and, ultimately, biological survival, the need to react on change (through its causes) can be included in this very hierarchy primarily as mediate effect of change. Immediate causation takes place only at a level where reaction to change causes determinate action (see below). One central, biologically founded hierarchy of mediate causation (leading eventually to adequate action) might hypothetically contain elements such as the following: CONTINUED EXISTENCE OF THE SPECIES > SELF-PRESERVATION > SITUATION CONTROL > CHANGE-OF-STATE/CAUSE-EFFECT/SPACE/TIME ANALYSIS. Hierarchies such as this should, from a biopragmatic standpoint, be understood to be superordinate to and determine generally the order of perceptual-abductive processing (and subordinate cause-effect relations). Why should we, in the first place, ask whether there is a change, if change would not (under circumstances) be a threat in a biologically motivated sense?

This standpoint does not prevent us, as I suggest, from replacing the distinction between 'final' and 'efficient' causation by one unitary hierarchy of causation, including superordinate biological causes. This presupposes, to be sure, a dissolution of Peirce's strict distinction between 'mental' and 'material' causation, and, as a consequence, between mental and physical action. Causation will now be differentiated only by hierarchical order and the distance between cause and effect. In this overall hierarchy we thus order causes with mediate effects (including superordinate biopragmatic causes) as well as causes calling for immediate effects, irrespectively of the latter causes being mental or physical by nature (i.e., representing logical or physical 'force', respectively). That is, mental, or cognitive, causation and physical causation may, according to this view, both have immediate effects. This new understanding appears natural in the light of growing neurobiological knowledge of processual coherence in perception, cognition, and action; and it finds, as we shall see, some support also in observations made by Peirce himself.

In his discussion of the classification of the sciences (CP 1.220), Peirce relates the distinction of 'final' and 'efficient' causation to the part-whole distinction as follows: "Efficient causation is that kind of causation whereby the parts compose the whole; final causation is that kind of causation whereby the whole calls out its parts. Final causation without efficient causation is helpless; mere calling for parts is what Hotspur, or any man, may do; but they will not come without efficient causation. Efficient causation without final causation, however, is worse than helpless, by far; it is mere chaos; and chaos is not even so much as chaos, without final causation; it is blank nothing."

This statement is remarkable in at least two ways: first, it appears to demonstrate the applicability of the distinction between 'final' and 'efficient' causation to a cognitive procedure such as classification; second, it could, indeed, have been written to capture my idea of divisibility assigned to chaos by biological rhythmization as a precondition for partitioning. If we, as I suggest, regard the distinction between 'final' and 'efficient' causation rather as one of processual hierarchy and of mediateness/immediateness of effects, it becomes evident that superordinate ('final') causation ("whereby the whole calls out its parts") corresponds neatly to the mediate assignment of divisibility/continuity to chaos, whereas subordinate ('efficient') causation ("whereby the parts compose the whole") corresponds equally neatly to immediate partitioning/discontinuation of chaos on this basis. To paraphrase Peirce, the former without the latter, i.e., assignment of divisibility without subsequent division=partitioning, would indeed be senseless ("helpless"), but the latter without the former, i.e., division=partitioning without divisibility (assigned to chaos), would simply be impossible ("worse than helpless") because "it is mere chaos; and chaos is not even so much as chaos, without final causation; it is blank nothing." This interpretation appears to be supported further by Peirce's (CP 1.227) observation of the hierarchical relationship involved in "the genesis of objects classified": "[B]y genesis must be understood, not the efficient action which produces the whole by producing the parts, but the final action which produces the parts because they are needed to make the whole" (i.e., according to my interpretation, the whole of synthesis following upon analysis; see Appendix below).

The proposed reinterpretation of 'final' and 'efficient' causation into *one unitary hierarchy of mediate and immediate causation*, coherently running through the entire system of semiotic processing (allowing for superordinate biopragmatic causes to determine the order of other causes), appears to be called for by further considerations. One of these is the need to integrate on various levels of semiosis the central function of perspective (see section 2 above). Another concerns the obvious problems we encounter when attempting to reconcile the distinction between 'final' and 'efficient' causation (as defined by Peirce) with the requirements of *decoding*, for example, linguistic decoding. Here we would face a situation in which effects of 'efficient' causes, such as, for example, spoken or written aspect expressions, rather trigger 'final' causation. That is, we must conclude that effects of 'efficient' causes here are not 'efficient' causes (because such are supposed to be "a compulsion acting to make [the] situation begin to change in a perfectly determinate way," CP 1.212), so they must be 'final', but, accordingly, of the lowest possible hierarchy. Doesn't this demonstrate that, primarily, it is not the kind of effect as such of a cause that (according to Peirce's definition) determines the latter's semiotic function, but rather its hierarchical relation to other causes together with the (specified) mediacy/immediacy of its effect, irrespective of the direction of semiosis (according to encoding or decoding, respectively)?

15. Trevarthen's Theory of Motives, and the Biopragmatic Sense of Language

In harmony with my above hierarchical-processual understanding of biologically founded causation is the theory of motives suggested by Colwyn Trevarthen (1990a, 1997). In a logically persuasive way, Trevarthen ascribes to *endogenous motives*—among which he gives precisely the production of rhythmic stimuli in the reticular core (1990a: 339ff.; see section 11 above) a central position—a decisive role in cognition by setting the intrinsic conditions for brain growth and cultural learning and thus realizing the fundamental idea of *genetic regulation*.

Trevarthen refers clearly enough to the role of emotions and emotional evaluations for these processes. Indeed, his notion of motives is embedded, I understand, in a cognitive theory based on communication of emotions as an innate human property (1990a: 324) and itself a primary motive for ontogeny (cf. also Trevarthen 1994). This communicative understanding is very appealing to a cognitive-pragmatic linguist and semioticist. It enables the early foundation of cognition as an integrated part of social interaction and a dynamic view of language development as a successive process of *motivated* communicative refinement and adaptation to the dominating system of signs, anatomically prepared for—spoken language.

One decisive advantage of Trevarthen's model, in comparison to Jean Piaget's framework, is that we, on its basis, may assume that symbolism begins early, and before language, by the primary coupling of distinct percepts with distinct emotions, viz. as the realization of fundamental biological motives or needs (dictated ultimately by the instinct for survival). Inspired by Trevarthen's proposals, I allow myself the following reflections on the biopragmatic foundations of language.

The primary set of emotions is, obviously, represented by a simple opposition: 'good' or 'bad' *for me*. Accordingly, we have to presuppose for an early phase of cognitive development also the parallel, successive differentiation between the self and the other (what we may understand as the motive of *socialization*, in a primordial sense). This would, indeed, be a precondition for, or rather integrated part of, the activation of the motive of *communication*. Cognitive development, roughly, would then begin as the successive rationalization of relations between percepts (sensations, 'senses') and their emotional values, and, by integration, between subjects, communicating emotions and their underlying biological causes. Although differentiated further by abstraction, the underlying primary set of emotions obviously remains in force throughout ontogeny. The number of percepts (with their corresponding relational content), however, increases continuously. This could not be otherwise in an ever changing world. This brings us to another central, assumedly innate, motive: the child's *attention to change-of-state*.

From primarily reflexive reactions on changes of states (felt as 'good' or 'bad'), the child is motivated to develop logical connections between these reactions and their consequences, realizing thus the motive of *rationalization*. That is, coupled with the motive of attention to change-of-state, it activates by necessity also the rational motive of *discerning cause-effect* relations, viz. as instrument for predicting the consequences of actions, assuming thereby the role of causes, and thus for acting adequately itself. Motivated action may, consequently, be thought to start in the shape of primarily 'emotional communication'. That is, the motives of change-of-state and cause-effect analysis, as distinguished from Piaget's 'mental schemata' (and rather in harmony with Vygotskij's conception), are realized as cognitive tools already in *the primordial system of emotional symbolization*. Within this framework, trial and error and conditioned reinforcement of new sensorimotor connections may, in my view, probably still be ascribed a definite role, albeit as a learning strategy subordinate to (directed by) the realization of motivational structure.

My interpretation of the primordial system of emotional symbolization implies a hierarchical distinction between emotions and 'senses'. More specifically, I assume that emotionality constitutes an 'archisense', succeeding 'senses', i.e., sensory percepts, hierarchically-processually, but fulfilling by way of feedback *the superordinate function of evaluative coordination*. Emotion expresses value, and value presupposes symbolization on various levels, ranging from primordial emotional evaluation of 'senses' to increasing degrees of rational evaluation.

According to my interpretation of Trevarthen's theory of motives, the latter takes a stand that differs not only from Piaget's, but also from Chomsky's proposals. It may appear, perhaps, to be closer to Chomsky's thesis of innate cognitive (i.e., linguistic) capacities, but it does not, to be sure, agree to give absolute preference to the semiotic system of spoken language. This is also my understanding. The crucial question now is how specific we understand the motivational program to be (op. cit.: 335). There is no compelling evidence, as far as I can see, for postulating universal, specifically grammatical motives, as suggested by Chomsky.

There are other candidates, however, for innate motives for emotional-cognitive development, viz. of a general regulative kind, from which linguistic behavior as part of general human behavior—i.e., specifically, language structure on a par with other semiotic systems—can be derived. Besides the fundamental system of logical procedures governed by abduction, we have already observed *rhythmization* (with resulting divisible continuity) and the corresponding strategy of *partitioning/discontinuation* by way of primordial metonymy (see section 8 above). There is, further, as a complement to this primarily horizontal motive, the vertical strategic motive of *hierarchization* and corresponding decomposition in terms of hierarchically ordered binary oppositions (Roman Jakobson's binarism was understood by him to be an innate cognitive feature). A precondition for the role of change-of-state and cause-effect analysis in increasing *rationalization* (itself a superordinate motive), as well as for the motives of *socialization/communication*, is the fundamental motive of *memorization*. Knowledge of the growth of short-term memory and long-term memory and their cooperation in emotional-cognitive development is crucial to our understanding of human behavior in most aspects. Rationalization is carried out further by the motive of *symbolization* and strategies of abstraction by analogy subordinate to it, such as the motives of *imagization* (I cannot think of any better word; see below) and *metaphorization*. The latter is demonstrated to be active in deep cognitive processes of ontogenetic development, such as, for example, the construction of space and time on the basis of rhythmization (see Appendix below). Understood as innate regulative predispositions for emotional-cognitive development, motives, as we can see already from this spontaneous outline, appear to form a complex logical hierarchy open to further exploration within Trevarthen's framework.

Against the above background, the cognitive strategy of analyzing the world by modeling it in the form of *images* (referred to sometimes as 'internal space' by omission of the temporal component) may be understood as an ability of symbolization, activated before, and thus, conditioning, linguistic symbolization. It appears reasonable to assume that the growth of the latter, accordingly, is an outcome of the general, primary growth of rationalization from primordial bio-emotional structure. This development leads successively to a relationship between *emotional* and *rational* symbolic content, characterized by the latter's continuous accumulation and differentiation, but equally by the former's unchanging status as superordinate regulative factor. Linguistic symbolization develops rationalization further through original image-based modeling to an extent vastly exceeding basically bio-emotional symbolization. That is apparently why (images of) predominantly rational (factual) states are more readily described in explicit and logically coherent ways by language than are emotional states. In other words, with the growth of linguistic symbolization, there is a successive increase in rational thought accompanied by a corresponding differentiation and refinement of its crucial tool of image-based manipulation.

* * * *

This might, roughly, be how language and thought, emotionally motivated, are successively and inseparably entwined in ontogeny, and, thus, inveigle us into believing that this was so from the beginning. The complexity of linguistic structure already in early-preschool-age children reflects, according to this view, the complexity of their symbolic thought as a universal feature of ontogenetic development, predicted, independently of language, by bio-emotionally motivated cognitive strategies of the human species. Universal semantic and syntactic features are expressions of properties and relations of things and events in situations perceived and cognized according to such innate motivational structure. That is, there are no innate linguistic universals, but there are innate cognitive motives predicting the universal basis for the ontogeny of spoken language, or any other semiotic system fulfilling the role of basic instrument for human communication, and thus activating these motives. This biopragmatic interpretation of language, which I understand to be in harmony with Trevarthen's emotionally based theory of motives, does not contradict the condition that, in the course of human evolution, linguistic communication has had a definite impact not only on the anatomical adaptation of the speech organs and the central nervous system, but probably also on the development especially of those genetic dispositions for cognition, the activation of which is enhanced by linguistic communication, in particular, the motive of symbolization. Equivalent conclusions were arrived at independently by Deacon (1997: 122, 141ff.) and Hoffmeyer (1999: 341).

16. Conclusions

It is difficult to think of any other categories as suitable as space and time to trust the guidance through the complex hierarchy of semiotic processes manifested by language. Only through language can we proceed to the semiosis of perception, emotion, rational thought, and action, and approach the biological foundations of all these forms of human behavior. It would thus be encouraging if my attempt to correlate the categories of space and time—in particular, regarding their role in the linguistic category of aspect—with the biological-regulative motive of reticular rhythmization (Trevarthen 1990a) would not only indicate a feasible way toward an adequate model of space and time as pivotal human, i.e., universal, cognitive instruments, but also give us a general idea of the nature of semiosis involved.

In the latter respect, more light appears to be shed on the conditions of teleology/causation implied by processes of selection throughout the various levels of the overall hierarchy of semiosis. Based on the distinction between mediate and immediate causation, a processual-hierarchical treatment is proposed as an alternative to the distinction between 'final' and 'efficient' causation.

Fundamental, biologically founded hierarchies of causation are understood to be superordinate to and determine generally the order of perceptual-abductive processing. Abduction, accordingly, is related processually to induction and deduction in a circuit feedback model, and, most importantly, ascribed the regulative-coordinating role in the semiosis of perception and mental/physical action (based on emotional primacy).

With the evolutionary support of the human organs of speech and hearing and a powerful central nervous system, language, as the result of goal-directed selection, develops ontogenetically by the activation of genetically inherited dispositions of general nature, i.e., for perception and mental/physical action, conditioned by emotional evaluation and, linked to it, the growth of self and of socialization. Rational thought and symbolization have their origin in the logic of primordial emotional evaluation. Emotional-social conditions should be understood as an essential constituent of biopragmatist philosophy.

Processual feedback, the crucial role of which has been demonstrated above for semiosis, applies, apparently, also to the evolution of the human central nervous system. It appears reasonable to assume that there was not and could not be any simple, unidirectional evolution of symbolic thought and language from an initially developed human neocortex. This would have contradicted the principles of successive adaptation through selection, conditioned by evolutionary feedback. Therefore, if we, conversely, maintained that the growth of the neocortex is the result primarily of the human language capacity, this would appear reasonable only if this capacity were subject to the same condition of successive evolution. But are we then at all entitled to speak of 'language capacity' at that point of evolution when, by the chance of mutation, human adaptation was confronted with the possible choice of developing language capacity and corresponding anatomical and neurobiological means? No, it appears necessary rather to view this very act of selection as the evolutionary trigger, viz. of the successive, parallel growth of symbolic thought and further cognitive dispositions for linguistic semiosis, on the one hand, and of the organs of speech and hearing and the neocortex, on the other.

This is a simplification, naturally. We have to assume an increasing complexity of social behavior—developing initially on the basis of prelinguistic, primarily emotional (emotional-iconic), iconic, and indexical semiosis—to have played an important role in this process, as well. More specifically, we may understand dispositions for spatial and temporal analysis to have evolved as a cognitive capacity by way of symbolization starting from primitive indexical semiosis of things and events.

Against this background we may assume that language as such has no phylogeny, i.e., linguistic structure is not inherited genetically. Accordingly (however trivial this statement may sound), language change cannot be a matter of phylogeny, either. It takes place only by way of social-conventional activation ('cultural learning') and development in ontogeny, i.e., as a result primarily of abductive selection (and implied teleology) determined by non-linguistic (or pre-linguistic) hereditary dispositions of biopragmatic nature. Language change can, consequently, be explained adequately only on the basis of these general genetic regulative motives and cognitive capacities, which rule the ontogeny of language and carry in them the universal direction of language diachrony subsumed in the notion of teleology. Accordingly, teleology cannot be applied directly to historical change, because our explanations of the latter must by necessity start in the ontogeny of language. In other words, language change is the empirical evidence of selection processes in ontogeny and their implicit, genetically preprogrammed teleology. The crucial role for language change ascribed to abduction is derived, according to the proposed model, from its responsibility for selection. All change thus starts with and is monitored by abduction, primarily through selection.

Selection in the form of partitioning/discontinuation is interpreted as the fundamental composite perceptual-sensory and cognitive strategy for the individuation (objectivation) of things and events in chaos, assigned divisibility/continuity by biological (reticular) rhythmization. Subordinate to (but, by processual feedback, conditioning) perceptual-sensory part-whole relations are the cognitive part-whole relations represented by Gestalt/pattern matching perception, on the one hand, and the subordinate aspectual-temporal perspective of events in terms of totality vs. partiality, on the other. The latter distinction, in which we may have found the key to a solution of the classical philosophical problem of time, cooperates by way of processual feedback with change-of-state and cause-effect analysis in perception and cognition of events, including action performed by the observer.

If it should turn out that my above suggestions have brought us somewhat closer to revealing the 'secret' Peirce (CP 6.418) felt still to remain after his valiant attempt to bridge the gap between space and time—understood by him as constituents of 'fundamental', i.e., physical, 'laws'—on the one hand, and their corresponding human concepts, on the other, the credit for this goes alone to him, for his incessantly inspiring, and challenging, guidance in the search for sense in human behavior, including language:

> ... as that animal would have an immense advantage in the struggle for life whose mechanical conceptions did not break down in a novel situation ..., there would be a constant selection in favor of more and more correct ideas of these matters. Thus would be attained the knowledge of that fundamental law upon which all science rolls; namely, that forces depend upon relations of time, space, and mass. When this idea was once sufficiently clear, it would require no more than a comprehensible degree of genius to discover the exact nature of these relations. Such an hypothesis naturally suggests itself, but it must be admitted that it does not seem sufficient to account for the extraordinary accuracy with which these conceptions apply to the phenomena of Nature, and it is probable that there is some secret here which remains to be discovered.

My present reflections are carried out in a philosophical framework that I conceive of as biologically founded cognitive-pragmatic realism, or, simply, biopragmatism. Essential components of this project (besides the methodological/metacognitive tools of hierarchy, process, feedback, decomposition, and binarism) are: fundamental biological motives; teleology implied by processes of selection throughout the entire hierarchy of semiosis; emotional evaluation as the origin of rational thought and symbolization; perceptual-abductive regulation of semiosis in mental/physical action; the growth of self and socialization; perspectival variation realized permanently by abductive selection; the interface between phylogenetic dispositions for perception and mental/physical action, on the one hand, and their activation through 'cultural learning' in ontogeny, on the other.

The proposals brought forward here represent a further development and, in part, revision of ideas suggested in previous work (see, especially, Thelin 1978, 1985, 1990a, 1990b, 1994, 1999).

APPENDIX

Space/Time Cognition: Hypotheses in Summary
(cf. also Thelin 1999, forthcoming a, forthcoming b)

1. Spatial and temporal analysis of the world as immediately perceived chaos is enabled by *biological rhythmization* and the corresponding assignment to it of divisibility and continuity. This procedure—and prerequisite for *analysis* by way of perceptual-sensory and cognitive partitioning/discontinuation—is thus the manifestation of an endogenous regulative motive (Trevarthen 1990a) underlying perceptual and mental/physical action. Rhythmization can, accordingly, be understood to be directed by attention and perception-cognition toward (potential) objects in the perceptual field.
2. *Space* is not a physical reality but rather a perceptual-cognitive construction based on the *analysis* (discontinuation) of divisible continuity applied first to the *extension of things* (assumed to be a priori), and then—by way of METAPHOR I—to their *distances*: either constant distances or changing distances, traversed by moving things, i.e., their *trajectories*. By means of space, man thus establishes relations between things at rest and in motion.
3a. *Time* is not a physical reality but a perceptual-cognitive construction based on the *analysis* (discontinuation) of divisible continuity applied to *motion*. By the reinterpretation of changing spatial distance as changing distance between old and new states (the prototypical temporal distinction before-after), divisible continuity—by way of METAPHOR II—is transferred from trajectories to motion itself. This may be assumed to come about in such a way that motion emerges, as a concept of divisible (phasal) and continuous *object*, from the conceptual amalgamation of a moving thing and its trajectory.
3b. *Time proper* is represented by the *analysis* (discontinuation) of motion by means of temporal-perspectival distinctions (aspect, tense, taxis).
3c. By subsequent *synthesis*, discontinuity is replaced by a new continuity of temporally related instances of motion, i.e., events.

3d. By non-penetration of the analysis underlying secondary, synthesized continuity—i.e., by amalgamating the steps represented by 3a and 3b, under the influence of 3c—motion with its features of divisibility and continuity ('linearity') is ascribed by the superficial METAPHOR III to time itself.
4. *Space* and *time*, accordingly, are analytic instruments by means of which man, from a given perspective, operates when perceiving and cognizing the world. Spatial and temporal (spatial/temporal) analysis is integrated in a complex process of perceptual and mental/physical action based on *change-of-state and cause-effect analysis*. The goal of this process is to keep control of life situations and, ultimately, ensure survival.
5. The derivation of time from space, illustrated by the emergence of the before-after distinction (see 3a), is evidenced still more clearly by the compound spatial/temporal nature of the situation-perspectival *foreground-background* distinction and the event-perspectival *totality-partiality* distinction. The latter distinctions may, accordingly, be assumed to precede hierarchically the before-after distinction, which appears reasonable since events can be ordered only when ascribed to the foreground and, correspondingly, individuated by way of totalization. The situation-perspectival distinction between *foreground* and *close background* is realized by the event-perspectival distinction between *totality* and *partiality*, respectively. Operating on divisible continuity (subordinate phasality), totalization and partialization function as topographic definitions of events and their relations to other events, prominently in terms of sequential order within the foreground (totality) or simultaneity of events of the close background (partiality) with events of the foreground.

Works Cited

CP = *Collected Papers of Charles Sanders Peirce*. 1931–58. Ed. Charles Hartsborne and Paul Weiss (volumes 1–6) and Arthur Burks (volumes 7–8). Cambridge, Mass.: Harvard University Press.
NEM = *The New Elements of Mathematics by Charles S. Peirce*. 1976. Ed. Carolyn Eisele. The Hague: Mouton.
W = *Writings of Charles S. Peirce: A Chronological Edition*. 1982– . Ed. Max H. Fisch et al. Bloomington: Indiana University Press.

Andersen, Henning. 1973. "Abductive and deductive change." *Language* 49:765–93.
Anttila, Raimo. 1972. *An Introduction to Historical and Comparative Linguistics*. New York: MacMillan.
Aristotle. 1936. *Aristotle's Physics*. Rev. W.D. Ross. Oxford: The Clarendon Press.
Bergson, Henri. 1889. *Essai sur les données immediates de la conscience*. Paris: Félix Alcan.
_____. 1911. *Creative Evolution*. New York: Holt.
_____. 1923. *Durée et simultaneité*. Paris: Félix Alcan.
Björling, Fiona. 1981. "Verbal aspect and narrative perspective in Olesha's 'Liompa.'" *Russian Literature* 11:7–23.
Bohr, Niels. 1934. "The quantum of action and the description of nature." *Atomic Theory and the Description of Nature*, 92–101. Cambridge: At the University Press.
_____. 1958. *Atom Physics and Human Knowledge*. New York: John Wiley and Sons.
_____. 1963. "Quantum physics and philosophy: Causality and complementarity." *Essays 1958–1962 on Atomic Physics and Human Knowledge*, 1–7. New York: Interscience Publishers.
Chevalley, Catherine. 1994. "Niels Bohr's words and the Atlantis of Kantianism." In *Niels Bohr and Contemporary Philosophy*, ed. Jan Faye and Henry J. Folse, 33–53. Dordrecht: Kluwer Academic Publishers.
Chvany, Catherine W. 1985. "Backgrounded perfectives and plot line imperfectives (Toward a theory of grounding)." In *Issues in Russian Morphosyntax* (= *UCLA Slavic Studies*, vol. 10), ed. Michael S. Flier and Richard D. Brecht, 247–73. Columbus, Ohio: Slavica Publishers, Inc.
_____. 1990. "Verbal aspect, discourse saliency, and the so-called 'perfect of result' in Modern Russian." In *Verbal Aspect in Discourse*, ed. Nils B. Thelin, 213–35. Amsterdam: John Benjamins Publishing Company.
Coseriu, Eugenio. 1974. *Synchronie, Diachronie und Geschichte: Das Problem des Sprachwandels*. Trans. Helga Sohre. Munich: Fink.
Damasio, Antonio R. 1994. *Descartes' Error: Emotion, Reason, and the Human Brain*. New York: Avon Books.
Davidson, Donald. 1980. "The individuation of events." In *Essays on Actions and Events*, 163–80. Oxford: Clarendon Press. [Originally published in *Essays in Honor of Carl G. Hempel*, ed. Nicholas Rescher, 216–34. Dordrecht: D. Reidel. 1969.]
Deacon, Terrence. 1997. *The Symbolic Species*. New York: Norton.
Deely, John. 1990. *Basics of Semiotics*. Bloomington: Indiana University Press.
Dewey, John. 1935. "Peirce's theory of quality." *Journal of Philosophy* 32: 701–8.
Eddington, Arthur S. 1932. *The Nature of the Physical World*. Cambridge: At the University Press.

Edelman, Gerald M. 1989. *The Remembered Present: A Biological Theory of Consciousness*. New York: Basic Books.
Faye, Jan. 1989. *The Reality of the Future*. Odense: Odense University Press.
———. 1991. *Niels Bohr: His Heritage and Legacy*. Dordrecht: Kluwer Academic Publishers.
Gale, Richard M. 1968a. *The Philosophy of Time: A Collection of Essays*. London: MacMillan.
———. 1968b. *The Language of Time*. London: Routledge and Kegan Paul.
Grimes, Joseph E. 1975. *The Thread of Discourse*. The Hague: Mouton.
Hoffmeyer, Jesper. 1996. *Signs of Meaning in the Universe*. Trans. B.J. Haveland. Bloomington: Indiana University Press.
———. 1999. "Order out of indeterminacy." *Semiotica* 127 (1/4): 321–43.
Holst, Erich von. 1969–70 [1936]. *Zur Verhaltensphysiologie bei Tieren und Menschen*, Bd. I–II. Munich: Pieper.
Hookway, Christopher. 1985. *Peirce*. London: Routledge and Kegan Paul.
Innis, Robert. 1998. "John Dewey et sa glose approfondie de la théorie peircienne de la qualité." *Protée* 26 (3): 89–98.
Itkonen, Esa. 1999. "Grammaticalization: Abduction, analogy, and rational explanation." Proceedings of the International Colloquium on Language and Peircean Sign Theory, Duke University, June 19–21, 1997 (= *The Peirce Seminar Papers: Essays in Semiotic Analysis*, vol. 4), ed. Michael Shapiro, 159–75. New York: Berghahn Books.
James, William. 1890. *The Principles of Psychology*. Vol. 1. New York: Henry Holt and Company.
Koffka, Kurt. 1935. *Principles of Gestalt Psychology*. New York: Harcourt, Brace and Company.
Köhler, Wolfgang. 1929. *Gestalt Psychology*. New York: H. Liveright.
Kull, Kalevi. 1999. "Biosemiotics in the twentieth century: A view from biology." *Semiotica* 127 (1/4): 385–414.
Leibniz, Gottfried W. 1981 [1765]. *New Essays on Human Understanding*. Trans. and ed. Peter Remnant and Jonathan Bennett. Cambridge: Cambridge University Press.
Lenneberg, Eric. 1967. *Biological Foundations of Language*. New York: John Wiley and Sons.
———. 1974. *Language and Brain: Developmental Aspects* (= Neurosciences Research Program Bulletin, vol. 12, no. 4). Boston: n.p.
Locke, John. 1961 [1689]. *An Essay Concerning Human Understanding*. Ed. J.W. Yolton. London: J.M. Dent and Sons.
Lorenz, Konrad. 1978. *Vergleichende Verhaltensforschung: Grundlagen der Ethologie*. Vienna: Springer Verlag.
———. 1996. *The Natural Science of the Human Species*. Cambridge, Mass.: The MIT Press.
Mellor, D. Hugh. 1981. *Real Time*. Cambridge: Cambridge University Press.
———. 1995. *The Facts of Causation*. London: Routledge.
Miller, George A., et al. 1960. *Plans and the Structure of Behavior*. New York: Holt, Rinehart and Winston.
Needham, Paul. 1975. *Temporal Perspective: A Logical Analysis of Temporal Reference in English* (= University of Uppsala Philosophical Studies 25). Uppsala: Liber Tryck.

Nesher, Dan. 2001a. "Peircean epistemology of learning and the function of abduction as the logic of discovery." *Transactions of the Charles S. Peirce Society* 37 (1): 23–57.

———. 2001b. "'Our senses as reasoning machines' prove that our perceptual judgements are true representations of external reality." Paper read at the International Colloquium Peircean Semiotics: The State of the Art, Canet-Plage, June 27–30, 2001.

Newton, Isaac. 1962 [1765]. *The Mathematical Principles of Natural Philosophy.* Trans. A. Motte, rev. Florian Cajori. Berkeley: University of California Press.

Parret, Herman. 1983. *Semiotics and Pragmatics: An Evaluative Comparison of Conceptual Frameworks.* Amsterdam: John Benjamins Publishing Company.

Popper, Karl R. 1959. *The Logic of Scientific Discovery.* London: Hutchinson.

———. 1975. *Problems of Scientific Revolution.* Oxford University Press.

Prigogine, Ilya. 1997. *The End of Certainty.* New York: The Free Press.

Prigogine, Ilya, and Isabelle Stengers. 1993. *Das Paradox der Zeit.* Munich: Pieper.

Reichenbach, Hans. 1956. *The Direction of Time.* Berkeley: University of California Press.

Reinhart, Tanya. 1984. "Principles of Gestalt perception in the temporal organization of narrative texts." *Linguistics* 22: 779–809.

Saint Augustine. 1948 [401 C.E.]. *Confessions.* Trans. E.B. Pusey. Chicago: Henry Regnery Co.

Santaella Braga, Lucia. 1999. "Peirce and biology." *Semiotica* 127 (1/4): 5–21.

Sapir, Edward. 1921. *Language: An Introduction to the Study of Speech.* New York: Harcourt, Brace and World.

Sebeok, Thomas A. 1973. "Between animal and animal." *Times Literary Supplement* No. 3, 734, October 5 (London).

———. 1979. *The Sign and Its Masters.* Austin: University of Texas Press.

———. 1991. *A Sign Is Just a Sign.* Bloomington: Indiana University Press.

———. 2001. "Biosemiotics: Its roots, proliferation, and prospects." *Semiotica* 134 (1/4): 61–78.

Sebeok, Thomas A., and Jean Umiker-Sebeok, eds. 1992. *Biosemiotics.* Berlin: Mouton de Gruyter.

Shapiro, Michael. 1983. *The Sense of Grammar: Language as Semeiotic.* Bloomington: Indiana University Press.

———. 1987. "Sapir's concept of drift in semiotic perspective." *Semiotica* 67 (3/4): 159–71.

———. 1991. *The Sense of Change: Language as History.* Bloomington: Indiana University Press.

Shapiro, Michael, and Marianne Shapiro. 1988. *Figuration in Verbal Art.* Princeton, N.J.: Princeton University Press.

Short, Thomas L. 1981. "Peirce's concept of final causation." *Transactions of the Charles S. Peirce Society* 17: 369–82.

———. 1999. "Teleology and linguistic change." Proceedings of the International Colloquium on Language and Peircean Sign Theory, Duke University, June 19–21, 1997 (= *The Peirce Seminar Papers: Essays in Semiotic Analysis*, vol. 4), ed. Michael Shapiro, 111–58. New York: Berghahn Books.

Swenson, Rod. 1999. "Epistemic ordering and the development of space-time: Intentionality as a universal entailment." *Semiotica* 127 (1/4): 567–97.

Thelin, Nils B. 1978. *Towards a Theory of Aspect, Tense and Actionality in Slavic.* Uppsala: Almquist and Wiksell.

———. 1984a. "Komposition, Perspektive und Verbalaspekt in Puschkins Prosa: Entwurf einer poetisch-linguistischen Methode." In *Signs of Friendship: To Honour A.G.F. van Holk*, ed. Joost J. Van Baak, 275–93. Amsterdam: Rodopi.

———. 1984b. "Coherence, perspective and aspectual specification in Slavonic narrative discourse." In *Aspect Bound*, ed. Casper de Groot and Hannu Tommola, 225–38. Dordrecht: Foris Publications.

———. 1985. "Kognitiv-pragmatische Korrelate semantischer Strukturen in einem Zirkelmodell für prozessuelle Sprachanalyse: der Aspektspezifizierung im Slawischen zugrunde liegende Hierarchien und Komponenten." *Zeitschrift für Slawistik* 30: 153–99.

———. 1990a. "Verbal aspect in discourse: On the state of the art." Introduction, *Verbal Aspect in Discourse*, ed. Nils B. Thelin, 1–88. Amsterdam: John Benjamins Publishing Company.

———. 1990b. "On the concept of time." In *Verbal Aspect in Discourse*, ed. Nils B. Thelin, 91–129. Amsterdam: John Benjamins Publishing Company.

———. 1991. "Aspect, tense or taxis?—The perfect meaning reconsidered." In *Words Are Physicians for an Ailing Mind*, ed. Maciej Grochowski and Daniel Weiss, 421–31. Munich: Otto Sagner.

———. 1994. "Perception, conception and linguistic reproduction of events and time: The category of verbal aspect in the light of C.S. Peirce's theory of signs." In *Living Doubt*, ed. Guy Debrock and Menno Hulswit, 257–73. Dordrecht: Kluwer.

———. 1999. "Knowledge, perspective, and the metaphor of time." Proceedings of the International Colloquium on Language and Peircean Sign Theory, Duke University, June 19–21, 1997 (= *The Peirce Seminar Papers: Essays in Semiotic Analysis*, vol. 4), ed. Michael Shapiro, 243–309. New York: Berghahn Books.

———. forthcoming a. *Time in Language and Thought*.

———. forthcoming b. "The conceptual structure of space and time, and the organization of narrative texts."

Trevarthen, Colwyn. 1974. "L'action dans l'espace et la perception de l'espace. Méchanismes cérébraux de base." In *De l'espace corporel à l'espace écologique*, ed. F. Bresson et al., 65–80. Paris: Presses Universitaires de France.

———. 1990a. "Growth and education of the hemispheres." In *Brain Circuits and Functions of the Mind: Essays in Honor of Roger W. Sperry*, ed. Colwyn Trevarthen, 334–63. Cambridge: Cambridge University Press.

———. 1990b. "Signs before speech." In *The Semiotic Web*, ed. T.A. Sebeok and J. Umiker-Sebeok, 689–755. Berlin: Mouton de Gruyter.

———. 1994. "Infant semiosis." In *Origins of Semiosis: Sign Evolution in Nature and Culture*, ed. Winfried Nöth, 219–52. Berlin: Mouton de Gruyter.

———. 1997. "The nature of motives for human consciousness." *Psychology: The Journal of the Hellenic Psychological Society* 4 (3): 187–221.

———. 1999. "Musicality and the intrinsic motive pulse: Evidence from human psychology and infant communication." *Musicae Scientiae*, Special Issue 1999–2000: 155–215.

von Uexküll, Jakob. 1920. *Theoretische Biologie*. Berlin: Gebrüder Paetel.

———. 1940. *Bedeutungslehre* (= BIOS 10). Leipzig: J.A. Barth.

von Uexküll, Thure. 1992. "Varieties of Semiosis." In Sebeok and Umiker-Sebeok, eds., 455–70.

Wheeler, Benjamin Ide. 1887. *Analogy and the Scope of Its Application in Language*. Ithaca, N.Y.: Cornell University Press.

Wimsatt, William C. 1972. "Teleology and the logical structure of function statements." *Studies in History and Philosophy of Science* 3: 1–80.
Wittgenstein, Ludwig. 1958. *Philosophical Investigations*. Trans. G.E.M. Anscombe. Oxford: Blackwell.
Wright, Georg Henrik von. 1969. *Time, Change and Contradiction*. Cambridge: Cambridge University Press.
Wundt, Wilhelm. 1874. *Grundzüge der physiologischen Psychologie*. Leipzig: W. Engelmann.

João Queiroz and Sidarta Ribeiro

The Biological Substrate of Icons, Indexes, and Symbols in Animal Communication: A Neurosemiotic Analysis of Vervet Monkey Alarm Calls

Introduction

According to C.S. Peirce, there are three fundamental kinds of signs underlying meaning processes—icons, indexes, symbols. The Peircean list of categories (Firstness, Secondness, Thirdness) constitutes an exhaustive system of exclusive and hierarchically organized classes of relations (monadic, dyadic, triadic) (Houser 1997: 14; Burch 1997; Brunning 1997). This system is the formal foundation of his architectonic philosophy (Parker 1998: 60) and of his classifications of signs (Kent 1997: 448). In this context, and relatively to the "most fundamental division of signs" (Peirce CP 2.275), these classes correspond to icons, indexes, and symbols that correspond to relations of similarity, contiguity, and law between S-O (sign-object) of the triad S-O-I (sign-object-interpretant). The properties associated with these modalities are: (1) S-O dependent of intrinsic properties of S (monadic), (2) S-O in spatio-temporal physical correlation (dyadic), and (3) S-O dependent of I mediation (triadic).

Icons are signs that stand for their objects through similarity or resemblance (Peirce CP 2.276), irrespective of any spatio-temporal physical correlation that S has with existent O: "An Icon is a sign which refers to the Object that it denotes merely by virtue of characters of its own, and which it possesses, just the same, whether any such Object actually exists or not" (Peirce CP 2.247; see 8.335, 5.73). In contrast, if S is a sign of O by reason of a dyadic relation with O, then it is said to be an index of O. In that case, S is really determined by O in such a way that both must exist as events, S and O: "An Index is a sign which refers to the Object that it denotes by virtue of being really affected by that Object.... [Insofar] as the Index is affected by the Object, it necessarily has some Quality in common with the Object, and it is in respect to these that it refers to the Object. It does, therefore, involve a sort of Icon" (Peirce CP 2.248; see 2.304). Finally, if S is in a triadic relation with O, a third term, I, is required so that I stands for "O through S." In this case, S is a symbol of O, and the determinative relation of S by O, a relation of law: "A Symbol is a law, or regularity of the indefinite future.... But a law necessarily governs, or 'is embodied in' individuals, and prescribes some of their qualities. Consequently, a constituent of a Symbol may be an Index, and a constituent may be an Icon" (Peirce CP 2. 293; see 2.299, 2.304, 2.249).[1]

The Problem

What is the origin of the symbolic processes that underlie human vocal communication? Since animal communication is ultimately a product of neurobiological processes (see Lieberman 1984, 1998; Pinker and Bloom 1990; Bloom 1999), and all biological phenomena are presumed to be the product of gradual evolution (Darwin 1859), the solution to this problem cannot avoid a comparative study of meaning processes and their underlying neurobiological basis in non-human primates (Hauser 1996; Deacon 1997; Tomaselo and Call 1997; Lieberman 1998). Whether these categories (icons, indexes, and symbols) apply to non-human animal communication is a matter of theoretical debate and controversy (Janik and Slater 2000), and no experimental evidence exists either against or in favor of such a scheme. There is, however, a great deal of descriptive knowledge about vocal communication in non-human primate species, the case of vervet monkeys being perhaps the best studied.

The Meaning of Alarm Calls in Vervet Monkeys

Vervet monkeys inhabit the African sub-Saharan plains and live in groups of up to 30 members. These primates possess a sophisticated repertoire of vocal signs that are used for intraspecific social interactions (confrontation, reconciliation, and alliance formation of different sorts) (Cheney and Seyfarth 1990; Hauser 1996), as well as for general alarm purposes regarding imminent predation on the group (Seyfarth et al. 1980). Field studies have revealed three main kinds of alarm calls used to warn about the presence of (1) terrestrial stalking predators such as leopards, (2) aerial raptors such as eagles, and (3) ground predators such as snakes (Strushaker 1967; Seyfarth et al. 1980). When a 'leopard' call is uttered, vervets escape to the top of nearby trees; 'eagle' calls cause vervets to hide under bushes, and 'snake' calls elicit rearing on the hindpaws and careful scrutiny of the surrounding terrain. Adults produce these calls only in reference to the presence of specific predators, and generate whole-group escape reactions. In contrast, infant vervets babble these calls in response to a variety of animals (predators and non-predators), as well as to inanimate objects such as falling leaves, and are paid little attention by adults. The progressive specificity of alarm-call production as vervets grow older indicates that a great deal of context learning is involved in the proper use of such calls (Cheney and Seyfarth 1990).

A Neurosemiotic Analysis of Vervet Monkey Alarm Calls

Consider two stimuli to which a vervet monkey reacts: the view of a predator and an alarm call played through a loudspeaker. The neural responses that code for the physical features of the visual image of the predator and the corresponding alarm call are iconic representations of their objects (Zaretsky and Konishi 1976; Tootell et al. 1988; Ribeiro et al. 1998), and exist within two independent modalities (visual and auditory) in a representational domain of the brain hereafter termed RD1 (see figure 1). The mere visualization of a predator must be, in principle, enough to generate an escape response via the motor system of the brain. In contrast, the physical properties of the acoustic alarm call (amplitude and frequency) do not stand for a specific predator in any intrinsic way.

In the absence of a previously established relationship between that call and the predator, the former will simply arouse the receiver's attention to any concomitant event of interest, generating a sensory scan response directed to the loudspeaker and its surroundings (Cheney and Seyfarth 1990). At least two things may happen then: if nothing of interest is found, the receiver should stay put, and therefore it can be said that the alarm call was not interpreted as anything other than an index of itself; if a predator is spotted stalking nearby, or if other vervet monkeys are observed fleeing to a neighboring refuge, the receiver should be prompted to flee. In these cases, the alarm call can be interpreted as an index either of the predator or of collective vervet monkey escape, with identical behavioral outcomes.

The experiment described above was performed by Cheney and Seyfarth (1990) in the field: predator-specific alarm calls were played from loudspeakers to groups of wild vervet monkeys, and their behaviors were carefully monitored. All individuals responded by looking around in search of a referent, and then fleeing to nearby refuges according to the specific type of call played ('leopard' calls evoked tree climbing, 'eagle' calls elicited bush hiding, etc.).

This simple but well designed experiment allows us to conclude that at least to one individual[2] in the vervet monkey group, alarm calls hold a previously established relationship to the predators they stand for, be it socially learned or genetically determined (Wilson 1975). If the alarm call operates in a sign-specific way in the absence of an external referent, then it is a symbol of a specific predator class. In other words, to say that an alarm call is a symbol of a *type* of predator is equivalent to saying that this call evokes a brain representation (of any modality) that stands for the *class* of predators represented in a specific way. This symbolic relationship implies the association of at least two representations of a lower order (i.e., indexes or icons) in a higher-order representation domain, hereafter termed RD2 (figure 1), which should be able to command escape responses through connections with the motor systems of the brain.

Sensory stimuli present in the world are *iconically* represented in the brain within a first-order domain (RD1) according to specific modalities (visual or auditory, in our example). While the view of a predator represented in RD1 is sufficient to elicit an escape response through the brain's motor system, the representation of an alarm call alone in RD1 does not evoke any predator-specific meaning, and therefore fails to cause an escape response. Presented together, the two stimuli can be interpreted in RD1 as bearing an indexical relationship, i.e., the alarm is an index of the predator's presence, generating an escape response. The existence of a higher-order domain of representation (RD2), which associates responses of both sensory modalities, enables the brain to interpret an alarm call presented alone as a *symbol* of its referent, i.e., the view of the predator, and an escape response ensues through the motor system.

In Search of the Neuroanatomical Substrates of Sign Interpretation

According to the hypothesis stated above, RD1 and RD2 should have different neuroanatomical substrates. Candidate regions to comprise RD1 are unimodal sensory ascending pathways spanning the mesencephalon, diencephalon, and early sensory neocortical areas. Candidate regions to integrate RD2 may be located

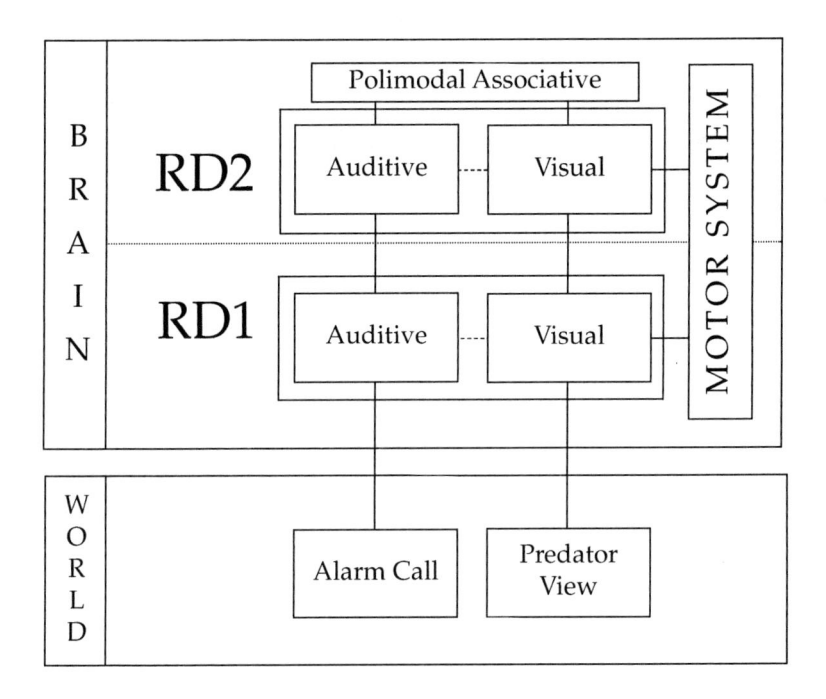

FIGURE 1 Schematic Diagram of World-Brain Interactions Involved in the Interpretation of Signs

in association areas in the parietal, temporal, and frontal neocortices, as well as the hippocampus, basal ganglia, and amygdala (Kandel et al. 1991).

We postulate that the identification of brain areas belonging to RD1 and RD2 is an empirical question that can be addressed by experiments comprising (a) specific neuroanatomical lesions of candidate regions, (b) presentation of auditory (alarm calls through a loudspeaker) and/or visual (predator view) stimuli to brain-lesioned vervet monkeys, and (c) recording of their behavioral responses so as to classify how the sensory signs were interpreted in each instance. Table 1 illustrates the behavioral analysis of one such *Gedanken* experiment.

TABLE 1 Behavioral Analysis of *Gedanken* Experiment

Site of neuro-anatomical lesion	Visual stimulus	Auditory stimulus	Post-stimulus sensory scan	Behavioral outcome	Sign interpretation
RD2	Yes	No	No	Escape	Predator icon
	No	Yes	Yes	Stay	Call index
	Yes	Yes	Yes	Escape	Predator index
RD1/Visual	**Yes**	**No**	**No**	**Stay**	**No sign interpretation**
	No	Yes	Yes	Escape	Predator symbol
	Yes	Yes	Yes	Escape	Predator symbol
RD1/Auditory	Yes	No	No	Escape	Predator icon
	No	Yes	No	Stay	No sign interpretation
	Yes	Yes	No	Escape	Predator icon
RD2 and RD1/Visual	**Yes**	**No**	**No**	**Stay**	**No sign interpretation**
	No	Yes	Yes	Stay	Call index
	Yes	Yes	Yes	Stay	Call index
RD2 and RD1/Auditory	Yes	No	No	Escape	Predator icon
	No	Yes	No	Stay	No sign interpretation
	Yes	Yes	No	Escape	Predator icon

Note: RD1 and RD2 are generic terms for brain domains related to first-order (iconic/indexical) and second-order (symbolical) levels or representation, respectively. Depending on the relationship between stimulation and behavioral outcome, brain regions can be classified as belonging to RD1 or RD2.

Conclusions

Based on the available literature and on the Peircean fundamental classification of signs (icon, index, symbol), we have presented an analysis of meaning processes underlying the interpretation of alarm calls in vervet monkeys. We have identified putative neuroanatomical constraints for these processes, which postulate the existence of at least two distinct representational brain domains underlying the interpretation of alarm calls as either iconic/indexical or symbolical signs. Current knowledge in neurobiology suggests specific candidate regions to integrate these domains. We propose *Gedanken* brain-lesion ethological experiments, which should, in principle, allow for the identification of brain regions involved in the different semiotic aspects of vervet monkey alarm call communication. Such experiments should also permit the mapping of hierarchical relations among the fundamental components of vocal signs in vervet monkeys. Finally, we suggest that certain specific behavior responses indicate the emergence of symbols in non-human primates. The transition from a sensory scan behavior after the alarm auditory perception to an escape reaction motivated solely by the call corresponds to the transition from indexical semiosis (reactive spatio-temporally) to symbolic semiosis. The object of the sign, in the latter case, is not an object but a class of objects, and therefore does not need to exist as a singular event. In other words, if there is a threshold index > symbol, then it should be possible to behaviorally identify the transition from 'object that is an event' to 'object that is a class of events', i.e., an object that does not need to be present as an external particular object. An 'ethological symptom' of this would be the failure of an adult vervet presented with an alarm call to visually scan the environment before escaping in a predator-specific way.

The argument presented above generates many questions. For instance, does the learning of vervet monkey alarm calls involve an indexical (non-symbolical) phase? The late ontogenetic maturation of this process suggests its dependency on an indexical phase. If the Peircean hierarchical model is correct (icon > index > symbol), any damage to the neuroanatomical substrate required for the indexical phase must compromise the symbolic performance at later periods, while the contrary should not be true. The analytical framework applied here to the case of vervet monkey alarm calls should permit the profitable study of many different cases of animal communication, constituting a new research program that we suggest be called 'comparative neurosemiotics'.

Catholic University of São Paulo and *Duke University Medical School*

Acknowledgments

We thank Beatriz Longo, Ivan de Araujo, and Claus Emmeche for helpful comments during the preparation of this manuscript. J.Q. (queirozj@pucsp.br) is thankful to the Institut de Recherches en Semiotique, Communication et Education (IRSCE) at Perpignan, France, in particular to its general director, Joëlle Réthoré, for her kind hosting at IRSCE. S.R. (ribeiro@neuro.duke.edu) thanks Miguel Nicolelis for his sustained support. J.Q. is funded by grant # 97/06018-4 from FAPESP, and S.R. by a Pew Latin-American Fellowship.

Notes

1. For an introduction to Peirce's theory of sign, see: Parker (1998), Liszka (1996), Santaella (1995), Fisch (1986), Queiroz (2001).
2. In the absence of further data we cannot exclude the possibility that only one individual recognized the alarm call as a sign of the predator, and all other monkeys followed the leader.

Works Cited

Bloom, P. 1999. "Evolution of language." In *The MIT Encyclopedia of the Cognitive Sciences*, ed. Robert A. Wilson and Frank C. Keil, 292–93. Cambridge, Mass.: MIT Press.

Brunning, J. 1997. "Genuine triads and teridentity." In *Studies in the Logic of Charles Sanders Peirce*, ed. N. Houser, D. Roberts, and J. Evra, 252–70. Indiana: Indiana University Press.

Burch, R. 1997. "Peirce's reduction thesis." In *Studies in the Logic of Charles S. Peirce*, ed. N. Houser, D. Roberts, and J. Evra, 234–51. Indiana: Indiana University Press.

Cheney D.L., and R. Seyfarth. 1990. *How Monkeys See the World*. Chicago: University of Chicago Press.

Darwin, C. 1859. *On the Origin of Species by Means of Natural Selection*. London: Murray.

Deacon, T. 1997. *Symbolic Species: The Co-evolution of Language and the Brain*. New York: Norton.

Fisch, M. 1986. *Peirce, Semeiotic, and Pragmatism*. Indiana: Indiana University Press.

Ghazanfar, A.A., and M.D. Hauser. 1999. "The neuroethology of primate vocal communication: Substrates for the evolution of speech." *Trends in Cognitive Sciences* 3 (10): 377–84.

Hauser, M.D. 1996. *The Evolution of Communication*. Cambridge, Mass: MIT Press.

Houser, N. 1997. "Introduction: Peirce as a logician." In *Studies in the Logic of Charles S. Peirce*, ed. N. Houser, D. Roberts, and J. Evra, 1–22. Indiana: Indiana University Press.

Janik, V.M., and P.J.B. Slater. 2000. "The different roles of social learning in vocal communication." *Animal Behavior* 60: 1–11.

Kandel, E.R., J.H. Schwartz, and T.M. Jessell. 1991. *Principles of Neural Science*. Norwalk: Appleton and Lange.

Kent, B. 1997. "The interconnectedness of Peirce's diagrammatic thought." In *Studies in the Logic of Charles S. Peirce*, ed. N. Houser, D. Roberts, and J. Evra, 445–59. Indiana: Indiana University Press

Lieberman, P. 1984. *The Biology and Evolution of Language*. Cambridge, Mass.: Harvard University Press.

———. 1998. *Eve Spoke: Human Language and Human Evolution*. New York: W.W. Norton.

Liszka, J. 1996. *A General Introduction to the Semeiotic of Charles Sanders Peirce*. Indiana: Indiana University Press.

Parker, K. 1998. *The Continuity of Peirce's Thought*. Nashville and London: Vanderbilt University Press.

Peirce, C.S. 1931–35. *The Collected Papers of Charles Sanders Peirce*. Vols. 1–6. Ed. C. Hartshorne and P. Weiss. Cambridge, Mass.: Harvard University Press [quoted as CP, followed by the volume and paragraph].

———. 1958. *The Collected Papers of Charles Sanders Peirce*. Vols. 7–8. Ed. A.W Burks. Cambridge, Mass.: Harvard University Press [quoted as CP, followed by the volume and paragraph].

———. 1976. *New Elements of Mathematics by Charles S. Peirce*. Ed. C.Eisele. The Hague: Mouton [quoted as NEM, followed by the page].

Pinker, S., and P. Bloom. 1990. "Natural language and natural selection." *Behavioral and Brain Sciences* 13: 585–642.

Queiroz, J., ed. 2001. *The Digital Encyclopedia of Charles S. Peirce.* www.digitalpeirce.org.
Ribeiro, S., G.A. Cecchi, M.O.Magnasco, and C.V. Mello. 1998. "Toward a song code: Evidence for a syllabic representation in the canary brain." *Neuron* 21 (2): 359–71.
Santaella, L. 1995. *A Teoria Geral dos Signos: Semiose e autogeração.* São Paulo: Editora Ática.
Seyfarth, R., D.L. Cheney, and P.Marler. 1980. "Monkey responses to three different alarm calls: Evidence of predator classification and semantic communication." *Science* 210: 801–3.
Strushaker, T.T. 1967. "Auditory communication among vervet monkeys (*Cercopithecus aethiops*)." In *Social Communication among Primates*, ed. S.A. Altmann. Chicago: University of Chicago Press.
Tomaselo, M., and J. Call. 1997. *Primate Cognition.* New York: Oxford University Press.
Tootell, R.B., E. Switkes, M.S. Silverman, and S.L. Hamilton. 1988. "Functional anatomy of macaque striate cortex. II. Retinotopic organization." *J Neurosci* 8 (5): 1531–68.
Wilson, E.O. 2000 [1975] *Sociobiology: The New Synthesis.* 25th anniversary edition. Cambridge, Mass.: Belknap Press of Harvard University Press.
Zaretsky, M.D., and M. Konishi. 1976. "Tonotopic organization in the avian telencephalon." *Brain Res* 111: 167–71.

Dan Nesher

How 'Our Senses as Reasoning Machines' Prove That Our Perceptual Judgments Are True Representations of External Reality

---

> It is one of the reasons for the slow progress of philosophy that its fundamental questions are not, for the most people, the most interesting, and therefore there is a tendency to hurry on before the foundations are secured. In order to check this tendency, it is necessary to isolate the fundamental questions, and consider them without too much regard to the later developments. (Russell 1910: 159)

1. Introduction: How to Reason about Reality—Hume's Problem and Peirce's Solution

The most difficult question in philosophy is how we can reason about reality to represent it truly and thus know it in order to control ourselves in our environment. In the history of philosophy, there have been two main tendencies to explain our knowledge. The first starts reasoning from some intellectual concepts and principles and infer from them our knowledge of reality, but without explaining how we reached these concepts and principles and how this knowledge can be about empirical reality being independent of its representation (e.g., Plato, Kant). The second starts reasoning about reality from some 'given' sensual experiences, but without explaining why we accept them and how they relate to reality (e.g., Hume, Russell). Therefore, the question is how to explain that our reasoning is about reality. Of course, the question is what this reality is that our cognitions are about, whether it is the reality of eternal ideas or thoughts or rather the physical reality of objects and events. But since even the most abstract ideas must have some experiential content—unless we suggest a mythology (e.g., Plato) or God's benevolence (e.g., Descartes)—our ideas are about concrete objects and events, and the meaning-contents of our reasoning with concepts and principles should be understood through the representational relations of our sensual-perceptual experience with such concrete reality.

Peirce's philosophical enterprise, as I understand it, was to solve Hume's problem of whether our impressions and ideas represent any external reality, and to discover the relation between our cognitions and reality. This problem can be solved if we can show that all of our cognitions—from the most rudimentary sensual-perceptual experience to the most abstract reasoning—are representations of some aspects of external reality that is independent from being cognitively represented by us (cf. Peirce 5.151–212). Since we cannot start reasoning from the Kantian 'empty concepts', we have to explain how our representation of reality is developing from our sensual experience into conceptual representation of reality (cf. Peirce 5.480).

> Nothing that the psychologists have since [the new experimental psychology developed from about 1860] discovered has been so surprising or so instructive [as the interpretative process of perception]; and I propose to bring out one of the lessons of these phenomena, – a lesson of practical importance, – by ranging along side of these some other facts which will show us how fine are the gradations between subconscious, or instinctive mind and our more conscious and more controlled reason. (Peirce 1900: 831[2])

> I propose to consider here only one of their [the psychologists'] lessons, a practical one for us all, by showing that instinct and reason shade into one another by imperceptible gradations. (Peirce 1900: 1101[1])

Peirce's problem is to show how we start 'reasoning' with our senses and develop our cognitions into our intellectual reasoning. But reasoning cannot operate in a vacuum (as Kant argued against Plato), and only by representing external reality (and not phenomenal reality as Kant suggested) can we reason, because in the last analysis all of our 'representations' are about external reality, some objective things independent of being represented by our cognitive minds (cf. Kant 1781–87: A4–A6; Nesher 1999c: II). Yet how is our cognition related to and how does it represent external reality? Peirce explained that already in our rudimentary perceptual operations we confront reality, learn about it, and develop our rules of habit to cope with the external reality in which we live.

In reconstructing Peirce's theory of interpretation of the perceptual signs, we can see already in such rudimentary operations an indication of the confrontation with our environment. Moreover, by analyzing these perceptual operations we can show that without going outside our cognitions (or our 'skins', in Davidson's expression) we nevertheless can feel and explain our cognitive confrontation with external reality (cf. Nesher 1998b: IV, V). This is Peirce's essential discovery—that our senses operate like 'reasoning machines' in representing external reality. But why 'reasoning machines'? Peirce suggests that even our basic sensations are neither physical machines nor computational machines but cognitive 'machines' since the other machines, which operate according to the formal-mechanical logic, cannot *discover* and *evaluate* new cognitions and thus *control their behavior* as animals and humans do (Peirce 1900: 831[10–13]; cf. Nesher 2001). Thus, relating to our senses as 'reasoning machines' emphasizes that our senses work according to the laws of our cognitive minds, similar to our conceptual reasoning. These laws of our sense-perception are basically the same laws of our reasoning, so our minds are not really machines but are only 'as' machines that can do things that real machines cannot do, namely, prove and disprove our cognitions as true or false representations of external reality. This knowledge enables us to control ourselves and behave efficiently in this reality (cf. Nesher 1997, 1998a, 1999a).

> It is necessary to arrest our attention upon this point, in order that we may be led to see how much more like reasoning the operations of our senses are than the performance of any mere machine can be. (Peirce 1900: 1101[5])

Peirce developed his theory of perceptual quasi-reasoning as 'reasoning machines' from his general understanding of the laws of mind, by analyzing the rules and the methods of scientific reasoning and comparing them with his analysis of some empirical facts concerning our perceptual experience. Peirce's enterprise is to show that the working of our senses is not a mechanical process but rather a cognitive operation according to the epistemic logic of mind, in which the formal deductive inferences are an abstraction of only partial components of the entire epistemic logic of mind (cf. Peirce 1900: 10 [4], [5]; cf. Nesher 1994b, 1998a, 1999a, 2000c: II). The pragmaticist conception of philosophy is that it is an 'observational science' in which Peirce developed the epistemic logic of human cognition (semiotics) as the logic of representation of reality (cf. Peirce 2.227, 2.65; Nesher 1997: V, 1999a: IV, 2000a: II). Peirce's essential discovery is that our senses in their perceptual operation are quasi-reasoning and quasi-proofs of the truth of our representations of external reality and that our perceptual judgments are not accepted only dogmatically as 'given' without any explanation. This is what I would like to show in this essay while dealing especially with Peirce's two manuscripts, numbered 831 and 1101, from 1900, different drafts that comprise his work "Our Senses as Reasoning Machines."

2. Instinctive 'Guess' and Rational Reasoning: How Does Our Cognition Evolve?

The Kantian conception of 'empty concepts' is itself empty since it does not have meaningful content and therefore cannot explain any human knowledge. This is so because there cannot be empty concepts, namely, concepts without meaning-contents of the sensual intuition. According to Kant, sensual intuitions must be added to 'empty concepts' in order to represent phenomenal objects, but what can the concepts be without meaning-contents: Are they concepts at all? The question is, what one can understand by 'empty concepts'? If sensual-intuition is the blind (pre-conceptual, pre-rational) contents that must combine with the empty concepts to become knowledge of phenomenal objects, then the only way to think about 'empty concepts' is that of a baby, who can hear the noises of words or see the written words without connecting them with any of her or his intuition of sensual experience. But then, the perception of words is itself a sensual experience, and without another sensual experience of any object that will become the empirical meaning-contents of the noises or the sights of the words, these noises or the sight of words themselves are just other sensual blind intuitions. In this case, the baby cannot even identify the noises or the sights as words, so the 'empty concepts' are not even empty words but only the empirical-experiential intuition of meaningless audible sounds and visual written words.

The sensual intuition of audible sounds and visual written words cannot have any conceptual meaning without the experience of an object or event that is attentively-indexically connected with these sound-words and sight-words. So the development of our cognitions cannot be explained by the Kantian unbridgeable dichotomy of two different sources of human knowledge: transcendental concepts and sensual intuitions. The question is whether our cognitions can develop, à la Plato, from transcendental concepts or rather from our sensual-perceptual experience. With a Platonic myth of eternal known ideas, or a Cartesian God endowing us with true ideas, or the Kantian faith in transcendental concepts from nowhere, we cannot explain our ideas or concepts of reality. So as Peirce suggests, we must explain our cognition as experiential representations of external reality. By rejecting Cartesian *problematic idealism* and Kantian *transcendental idealism*, Peirce leads us to inquire into the basic process of perceptual experience with which we can explain our confrontation with external reality and our rudimentary modes of representing such reality that Humean *skepticism* cannot do. As distinct from Kant's transcendental epistemology, Peirce's pragmaticist epistemology, similar to Spinoza's, is an evolutionary hierarchy of cognitive signs evolving from the **Iconic sign** to the **Indexical sign** and generalized into the **Symbolic sign-concept** as the perceptual judgment proposition:

[1] Perceptual Process of Sign Interpretations Developing the Empirical-Sensual Content of the Symbolic Sign-Concept

Relations of Interpretation

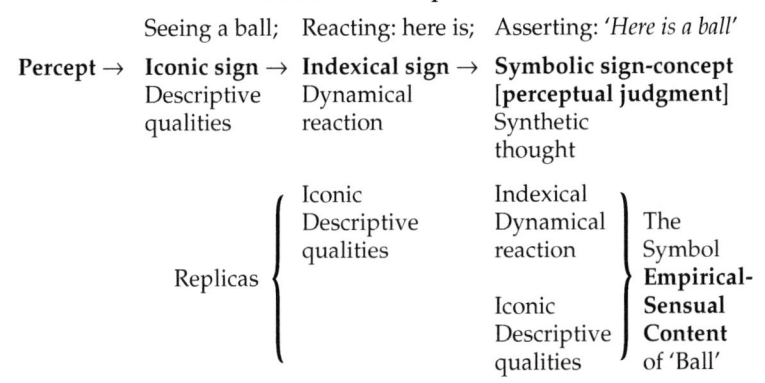

	Seeing a ball;	Reacting: here is;	Asserting: *'Here is a ball'*
Percept →	**Iconic sign** → Descriptive qualities	**Indexical sign** → Dynamical reaction	**Symbolic sign-concept** [perceptual judgment] Synthetic thought

Replicas {
- Iconic Descriptive qualities
- Indexical Dynamical reaction
- Iconic Descriptive qualities
} The Symbol **Empirical-Sensual Content** of 'Ball'

Our perceptual operations are the basic experience from which our conceptual reasoning develops. The first stage of reasoning is in our propositional perceptual judgments, the symbolic words through which we interpret and generalize our pre-verbal signs of our cognitive experience. The hierarchical relation of the meaning-contents of these perceptual stages shows that the conceptual meaning-content evolves in the perceptual process into the symbolic generalization in the form of a perceptual judgment in its propositional formulation (cf. Nesher 1987a, 1987b, 1997: I, II). This allows the perceptual judgment symbol to describe propositionally the real object, e.g., the ball. Yet the basic question is how do we know that our perceptual experiences represent external reality and not just another cognitive 'representation' as a Kantian phenomenal object? To show that external reality cannot be just the content of our modes of cognitions, namely, other Kantian 'representations', is Peirce's crucial enterprise to resolve Hume's problem. This means to move from Hume's skepticism to pragmatic theory of representation of external reality without being stuck in the Kantian phenomenalism/transcendentalism dichotomy (cf. Nesher 1999c: II).

3. How Our Senses Work in Perceptual Operations as 'Reasoning Machines' to Infer Our Perceptual Judgments

Let us analyze the structure of such perceptual operations. Beyond the scheme of the Perceptual Process of Sign Interpretations we drew above, when Peirce probed deeper into the structure of the perceptual experience and compared it with our everyday reasoning and the reasoning in scientific inquiry, he found that the entire process of perception can be analyzed into a sequence of three sub-processes having the inferential structures of the *logic of discovery* (Abduction), the *logic of consequence* (Deduction), and the *logic of evaluation* (Induction) (cf. Peirce 1900: 831[13–25], [6–9]). This entire operation is the basic structure of human cognitive interpretation and should be understood as the form of a complete proof of its results. This is so even if in formal sciences we usually consider only the formal deduction as the form of proof, since we abstract from the ways we form the premises of the formal system and evaluate its conclusions (cf. Nesher 1998a: #6). The pragmaticist conception of inquiry contains an epistemologically extended conception of logic and thus also an epistemologically extended conception of proof (cf. Nesher 1998a: ##4, 5, 6, 2000c: II.3). This is also the logic of perception and it can be shown that the sequence of this *trio*, the structure of the logical procedures of reasoning, is the enveloping of the general scheme of the perceptual process presented in [1]. However, the epistemic logic of perception differs from rational reasoning by being only instinctively and practically controlled.

> What, then, is the use of designating some formations of opinion as rational, while others (perhaps leading to the same results) are stigmatized as blind following of the rule of thumb or of authority, or as mere guesses? When we reason we set out from an assumed representation of a state of things. This I call our *premise*; and working upon this, we produce another representation which professes to refer to the same state of things; and this we call our *conclusion*. But so we do when we go irreflectively by a rule of thumb, as when we apply a rule of arithmetic the reason of which we have never been taught. The irrationality here consists in our following a fixed method, of the correctness of which the method itself affords no assurance; so that if it does not happen to be right in its application to the case in hand, we go hopelessly astray. In genuine reasoning, we are not wedded to our method. We deliberately approve it, but we stand ever ready and disposed to reexamine it and to improve upon it, and to criticise our criticism of it, without cessation. Thus the utility of the word "reasoning" lies in its helping us to discriminate between self-critical and uncritical formations of representation. (Peirce 1900: 831:10–11)

From this discussion, one might conclude that there is a strong dichotomy between instinctive operations of our sensual cognitions and genuine reasoning. This can be the case with the distinction between animal and human cognitions. Yet if with humans, genuine reasoning developed from our perceptual processes, then these processes must also have elements of self-control and criticism, though not rational but instinctive, non-rational or *'acritical inference'* through the *habitual* cognitive penetration into these processes (cf. Peirce 5.441, 5.418ff., 5.441, 5.445, 2.175). Such perceptual processes are quasi-inferences and only instinctively self-controlled and self-criticized, as are also the change of their methods and rules of habit as Peirce argues (cf. Peirce 1900: 831[10–13]; Nesher 1994b, 1999a). Moreover, as we have already seen in the analysis of our perceptual cognitive operations, the rationality of our symbolic thought in perceptual judgment is based on pre-rational sensual contents without which no conceptual reasoning is possible. This is also the case "when we apply a rule of arithmetic the reason of which we have never been taught" as Peirce presents our mathematical intuition (cf. Wittgenstein 1953: ##180–207; Nesher 1994b, 1998a, 2000a, 2001). The instinctive penetration into our low levels of self-conscious cognitive processes is the basis of animal and human evolutionary self-control, enhancing the change and the evolution of cognition.

> When the mind of the lower animals first began to be studied, it was the unchangeableness of animals' methods that led observers to draw a sharp line of demarcation between Instinct and Reason. But facts subsequently came to light showing that that fixity was only relative, that bees in a clime of perpetual summer, after some generation, give up storing vast quantities of honey; that beavers, provided with new material, gradually evolve new styles of architecture; that sheep, carried to valleys where poisonous hellebore grows, learn not to eat it; that birds sometimes take to unaccustomed food, and come to prefer it.... Such phenomena evince an element of self-criticism, and therefore of reasoning. (Peirce 1900: 831[12–13])

The perceptual process is primordial and rudimentary, and its sub-processes operate only as quasi-inferences when the relations of interpretation of their components are only quasi-purposed and quasi-controlled (cf. Peirce 5.441; Nesher 1982: 80–82, 1994b: II.2). Therefore, we can know about the nature of such processes only from our instinctive penetration into them that allows the instinctive self-control and our strong feeling of assurance about our perceptual judgments, and also from their consequences in our practical and rational behavior (Peirce 7.444–450; Nesher 1997: V, 2000c: IV). The very process of perception can be seen as a sequence of the trio of *quasi-inferences* to infer the perceptual judgments as the conclusions from the various assumptions of the perceptual operation. The question that I will deal with later concerns the states of things that the perceptual process is about and whether the inferred and asserted perceptual judgments are basically true and *positive knowledge* of external reality. In the analysis of the perceptual process the first sub-process is the Abductive procedure of discovery in which the percept is identified by its sensual qualities in the perceptual cognizance:

[2.1] Abductive Cognizance: $Ab((C, A \rightarrow C) \Rightarrow A^{Ab})$

where C is the percept, and $A \rightarrow C$ is the interpretation of the Percept C by a structure of qualities of *feeling*, in a form of the iconic-pattern

A. This subconscious quasi-inference operates by comparing the *similarity* of the qualities of the percept C with already cognized qualities of some iconic-pattern A. When the most similarity is detected between the percept and some general iconic-pattern A, the chosen A is inferred by the *plausibility* connective ⇒ as the suggested iconic interpretation of the percept C (cf. Nesher 1997: IV.2, 2001: VI).

> [The Abductive or Hypothetical inference] consists in the introduction into a confused tangle of given facts [C] of an idea not given [A] whose only justification lies in its reducing that tangle to order. This kind of inference is little subject to control, and so not highly rational [even as a component of rational reasoning]; and one reason for this is that when once the facts have been apprehended in the light of the hypothesis [A], they become so swallowed up in it, that a strong exertion of intellect is required to disembarrass them from it, and to recall them in their pristine nudity [C]. (Peirce 1900: 831[13–14])

What Peirce calls here the "given facts" should be understood in the perceptual operation as the original percept that becomes the sensual meaning-content of the perceptual hypothesis. The Deductive quasi-inference follows the Abductive inferential stage to elaborate the anticipation of the perceiver to interpret and apprehend C as A:

[2.2] Deductive Anticipation: $Dd(((A \rightarrow C)^{Ab}, A^{Ab}) \rightarrow C^{Dd})$

where C^{Dd}, which is inferred by the *necessity* connective →, is the abstract object deduced by the mind from the iconic-pattern A of Abduction and thus has the sensual qualities of feeling of the original percept that might fit different perceptual objects. It presents all of the abstract qualities of the anticipating perceptual object whose sensual qualities have been perceived. However, the Deductive sub-process of perception is not cognitively penetrable, except for the feeling of low awareness of the abstract object C^{Dd} that presents our anticipation (Peirce 1900: 8–17, 22–29). Yet in rational Deduction, the imaginary states of things, which we formulate, are lying quite open to our observation and controlled operation.

> Deductive inference is peculiar in the following respect, namely, that its premise may represent a purely imaginary state of things and in any case it is treated as if it were of that character [an ideal or abstract state

of things]. This imaginary state of things, being of our creation, lies quite open to our observation. We remark some feature of it, and then we easily satisfy ourselves that this feature will remain unchanged, however the imaginary state of things is altered, so long as a certain condition is fulfilled.... Thus, it is the characteristic of deductive reasoning that when it is applied to experience it makes anticipations, and declares that this or that shall be and must be. (Peirce 1900: 831[15–16])

The last sub-process of the perceptual process is the Inductive evaluation of the hypothesis A, from which the abstract iconic sign C^{Dd} is inferred to be anticipated if its qualities will reappear in the actual evaluative perceptual experience. The inference is by the *probability* connective ≈>, which measures the ratio of coherency between the anticipated perceptual iconic sign C^{Dd} (presented by the general iconic-pattern A^{Ab}) and the actual perceived indexical sign C^{In}:

[2.3] Inductive Evaluation: $In((A^{Ab}, C^{In}) \approx > PRm/n(A^{Ab} \to C^{In}))$

In perception, the evaluation is made through the strong feeling of the coherency or incoherency we experience in the Inductive stage of perception. This evaluation is accomplished by *comparing* the sensual qualities of the iconic-pattern A^{Ab} (by which the percept C^{Ab} was first cognized in Abduction) with the reacting indexical sign C^{In} in this continuous perceptual process. The result of this comparison is either a *positive* or a *negative* evaluation of the respectively *coherent* or *incoherent* relation between these two signs, according to the proportion of the concordance between A^{Ab} and C^{In}.

> Inductive inference finds, running through a fragment of experience, some features, which it extends to a larger experience embracing that fragment as a part of it. Whether the Globe geodetic measures have been made, the sea-level has been found approximately to coincide with the surface of a certain ellipsoid; whence we inductively infer that the same thing will hereafter be found approximately true of that much larger part of the earth's surface where no geodetic operations have yet been conducted. (Peirce 1900: 831[17])

The following is the general scheme of the perceptual process and the inferential 'mechanism' of our senses as 'reasoning machines' with its triple logical operations of Abduction, Deduction, and Induction that comprise the *quasi-proof* of our *perceptual judgments*.

[3] The Structure of Perception and the Mechanism of Our Senses as Reasoning Machines

The quasi-proof of our perceptual judgments

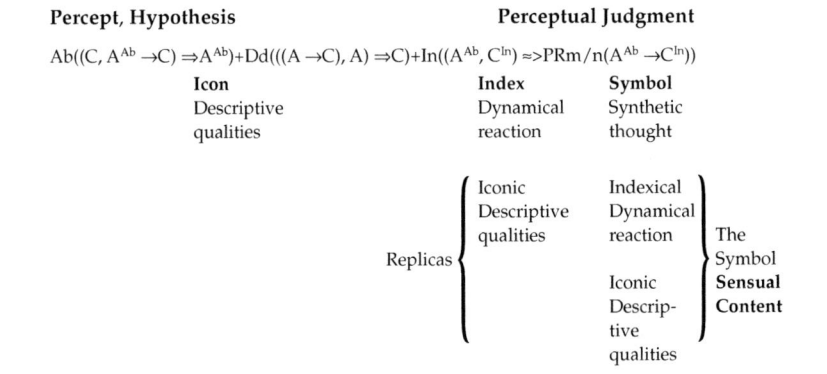

Ab((C, A^{Ab} →C) ⇒A^{Ab})+Dd(((A →C), A) ⇒C)+In((A^{Ab}, C^{In}) ≈>PRm/n(A^{Ab} →C^{In}))

Icon	**Index**	**Symbol**
Descriptive qualities	Dynamical reaction	Synthetic thought

Replicas { Iconic Descriptive qualities / Indexical Dynamical reaction / Iconic Descriptive qualities } The Symbol Sensual Content

Peirce's dynamical conception of mind operation as reflected in his writings adheres to evolutionary epistemology. The question is how the Peircean evolutionary epistemology can explain our representation reality external to our cognitive modes and their evolutionary relations.

In analyzing Kant's epistemology we can show that he could not overcome Hume's skepticism about our knowledge of external reality because both have the same epistemological theory of perception that we can only know objects as *immediately* or *directly* perceived by us, and these phenomenal objects are nothing but our modes of cognitions. The difficulties of Kantian philosophy are still alive in the positions of his followers in our contemporary philosophy and it seems that Putnam's 'direct realism' has the same difficulty (cf. Nesher 1999a: III, 1999c: II).

Peirce agreed with the Humean-Kantian tradition that the relations to the phenomenal object, as it is presented in the different signs interpretational stages—the different interpretants of the Percept, the Emotional [Feeling] Interpretant, the Dynamical [Indexical] Interpretant, and the Logical [Symbolic] Interpretant— are indeed the *immediate, direct,* and *familiar* relations respectively (cf. Peirce 8.349ff., 5.473, 2.230). But Peirce also rejected the notion that our cognitive modes can represent only cognitive modes. These interpretational cognitive modes are at the same time *indirect* representations of the Real Object that is external to our cognitive processes (cf. Nesher 1990: 10–24, 1997: III, IV, 1999a: III.3).

This is the distinction between two kinds of referential relations, the relation of presentation of the phenomenal object and the representation of the real objects, which can be explicated differently, namely, respectively as the 'Anaphoric-Referential-Relation' to the *phenomenal object* and the 'Representational-Referential-Relation' to the *real object* (Nesher 1997: III, 1999c: III.1).

The following scheme presents the Pragmaticist theory of cognitive *interpretation* and *representation*, and in it we can see that the Kantian phenomenalist-internalist concept of reference, in which the Symbol refers to the intuited Empirical Content as the phenomenal object of Perception, is a partial component only. Kant's Perceived Phenomenal Object is the Iconic and Indexical meaning-contents of Perceptual Experience.

[4] Perceptual Process of Sign Interpretations and Their *Immediate, Direct,* and *Familiar* Relations

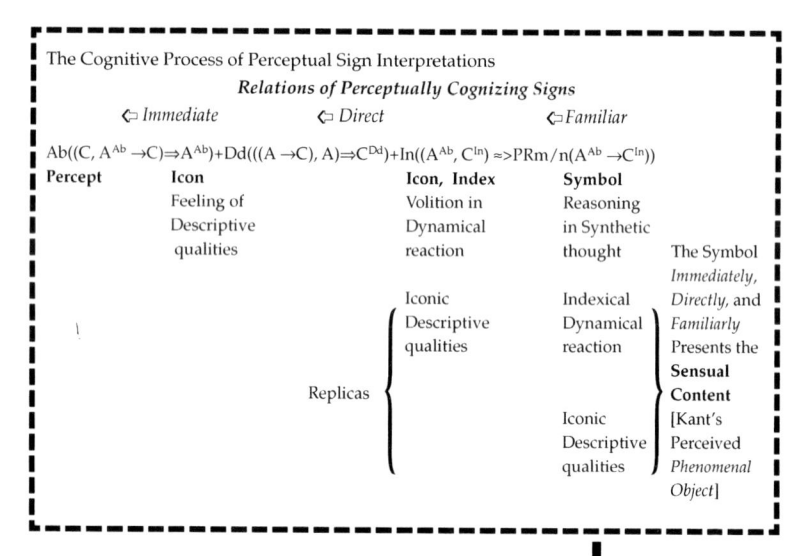

```
The Cognitive Process of Perceptual Sign Interpretations
              Relations of Perceptually Cognizing Signs
         ⇐ Immediate         ⇐ Direct              ⇐ Familiar
```

$Ab((C, A^{Ab} \to C) \Rightarrow A^{Ab}) + Dd(((A \to C), A) \Rightarrow C^{Dd}) + In((A^{Ab}, C^{In}) \Rightarrow PRm/n(A^{Ab} \to C^{In}))$

Percept	Icon	Icon, Index	Symbol	
	Feeling of Descriptive qualities	Volition in Dynamical reaction	Reasoning in Synthetic thought	The Symbol *Immediately, Directly,* and *Familiarly* Presents the **Sensual Content** [Kant's Perceived *Phenomenal Object*]
		Iconic Descriptive qualities	Indexical Dynamical reaction	
		Replicas		
			Iconic Descriptive qualities	

Indirect Representation of External Reality

↓

[Peirce's Represented **Real Object**]

In the Cognitive Process of Perceptual Sign Interpretations (in the frame), the relation of the **Iconic sign** (A^{Ab}) to the initial **Percept** (C) is *Immediate*, since the Percept is 'swallowed up' by the Iconic sign; the relation of the **Indexical sign** (C^{In}) to the **Iconic sign** (A^{Ab}) is a *Direct* reaction to the sensual image of the object; and the relation of the **Symbolic sign** ($A^{Ab} \rightarrow C^{In}$) to the **Indexical sign** (C^{In}) is *Familiar*, because the Iconic and Indexical experiential contents are already cognized as the internal replica, the phenomenal object of the Symbol. Thus, all of these interpretants interpret at different levels the sign-Percept and represent the same Real Object (cf. Peirce MS 517, 2.230).

But why cannot the object of our semiotic-cognitive interpretation be the internal phenomenal object contained in the perceptual signs, which is itself only a kind of Kantian 'representation' (cf. Kant 1781–87: B:236; Nesher 1999c: II.2)? If it is an internal object, namely, the 'sum' of the meaning contents of one's private sensual experience, then the Wittgensteinian question arises: How do we know that this is an object common to different people's experiences and even of different experiences of the same person or also common to all phases of the same perceptual operation process (e.g., Wittgenstein 1953: ##258, 293)? This is a question for the hermeneuticians: Is there any objectivity in our interpretational operations, or are they only contingent, subjective, and 'haphazard or arbitrary' interpretations, changing from person to person and situation to situation? Indeed, if there is no restriction external to the interpretive operations, as it is with the 'inner experience' for Wittgenstein, then there is no unity to our cognition and no way to distinguish between right and wrong, true or false interpretations. This is so since even the public language-game and the common 'inherited background' must be developed and accepted through the experience of the individuals, which is, in the last instance, an inner experience. Without any external restriction, there is no unity in individual cognition, let alone any possible unity of cognitions of different individuals, which is required for the acceptance of a common practical and linguistic convention (cf. Wittgenstein 1969: #94). This impossibility of having a personal experience without an external restriction was Kant's motivation for looking at least for a *negative conception of external reality* in the form of the 'transcendental object', without which he could not explain the 'synthetic unity' of human consciousness or, in Peirce's terms, the empirical unity of the semiotic process of interpretation (Kant 1781–87: B307; Peirce 1.284, 1.42–43, 2.273, 5.554; cf. Nesher 1997: I, II).

> Now we find that our thought of the relation of all knowledge to its object carries with it an element of necessity; the object is viewed as that which prevents our modes of knowledge from being haphazard or arbitrary, and which determines them a priori in some definite fashion. For in so far as they are to relate to an object, they must necessarily agree with one another, that is, must possess that unity which constitutes the concept of an object. (Kant, 1781–87: A104–105; cf. A250–251)

So Kant *inevitably* had to accept this bizarre, unknowable external transcendental object to hold the entire possibility of knowledge of empirical phenomenal objects (e.g., Kant 1781–87: Bxxviiff., A103–110; cf. Nesher 1999c: II.2). The crucial question is, how do we know, as we commonsensibly believe, that our perceptual judgments represent Real Objects? Can we show that our perceptual processes with their trio of inferences as 'reasoning machines' are the quasi-proofs of our perceptual judgments and at the same time an indication of our representation of external reality? Should we show it by analyzing linguistically the perceptual judgment propositions as Ramsey thought, or rather by analyzing epistemologically the entire perceptual process in which we confront reality (cf. Ramsey 1927: 39; comp. Nesher 2001: I, II.2, III)? In most perceptual processes, the perceptual judgments are usually potential, implicit, and practically only optional: I am just sitting on a chair, and usually I do not accompany it by saying, "I am sitting on this chair." Therefore, our interest now is mainly in the analysis of the prepropositional perceptual process to find in it the indication for our confrontation with external reality. The question is, how do we know that our perceptual experience and the perceptual judgments represent external objects and not only phenomenal ones?

4. How Perceptual Inferences Are Quasi-proofs of Our Perceptual Judgments as True Representations of External Reality

In *direct* perception, the dynamic *duality* of consciousness between the **iconic feeling** and the **indexical reaction** to it (as the component of the triadic process) appears forcefully and beyond our control and criticism. This is (as in scheme [4]) the duality between our feeling of the *anticipated percept* with the perceptual Descriptive

Qualities (C^{Dd}) presented by (A^{Ab}) and the Dynamical Reaction of the *actual Percept* (C^{In}) to (A^{Ab}), in the duality (A^{Ab}, C^{In}), which is forced upon us by something independent of us interjected by the actual percept (C^{In}).

> A duality is thus forced upon him: on the one hand, his expectation which he had been attributing to Nature, but which he is now compelled to attribute to some mere inner world, and on the other hand, a strong new phenomenon which shoves that expectation into the background and occupies its place. The old expectation, which is what he was familiar with, is his inner world, or Ego. The new phenomenon, the stranger, is from the exterior world or Non-Ego. (Peirce 5.57; cf. 1.431)

The clash between the anticipated Percept and the actual one is "the momentary direct dyadic consciousness of an *ego* and a *non-ego* then and there present and reacting each upon the other" (Peirce 1.334). This clash cannot be explicitly realized in the stage of Feeling, "since feelings in themselves cannot be compared" (Peirce 1.383); but in Volitional Reaction of the indexical sign to the iconic one, we are internally compelled to react differently to two different feelings: one is of the past, the feeling of the anticipated percept (C^{Dd}); the second is of the present, the feeling of the actual percept (C^{In}) that operates as the indexical reaction and frustrates our expectation (cf. Peirce 8.87). In this case, the Sign of the past, the first Percept in Abduction, when it has been interpreted *erroneously* is identified with the Self. Hence, the present actual Sign is separated from and antagonizes the past Sign, the Self, and compels the person to accept the actual Sign as representing the Other, an external Reality:

> In the idea of reality ... the real is that which insists upon forcing its way to recognition as something other than the mind's creation.... The real is active; we acknowledge it, in calling it actual. (Peirce 1.325)

Thus we find that through *error*, we first become conscious of reality different from the Self. This is our *negative* cognition of *reality*, in which we cognize the existence of something contradicting our expectation, but we still do not have a *positive* true description of such external reality. Peirce continued to argue that the phenomenon of surprise cannot come from the person's inner world, since he himself cannot play a trick upon himself. We know *habitualiter* the hidden springs, the working laws or rules in our behavior. Through their effects on our behavior we know our inborn and acquired rules of habits (cf. Peirce 5.441, 5.504, 8.18, 5.492). Moreover, the person does not conclude from the unexpected perceived object that he has been surprised; on the contrary, the person generalizes about the unexpected object from his surprise, namely, from the strong experience of duality—the clash between his expectation and its failure. This cognitive stage of the dual action and reaction between the mind and the stimulus of the object Peirce calls Volition (cf. Nesher 1990: 17–27).

> Volition is through and through dual. There is a duality of agent and patient, of effort and resistance, of active effort and inhibition, of action on self and on external object. Moreover, there is active volition and passive volition, or inertia.... That shock which we experience when anything particularly unexpected forces itself upon our recognition ... is simply the sense of the volitional inertia of expectation, which strikes a blow.... Low grades of this shock doubtless accompany all unexpected perceptions; and every perception is more or less unexpected. Its lower grades are, as I opine,... that sense of externality, of the presence of a non-ego, which accompanies perception generally and helps to distinguish it from dreaming. (Peirce 1.332, comp. 1.334; cf. 2.142, 2.143)

Thus, inside our cognitive processes in the "duality of agent and patient, of effort and resistance, of active effort and inhibition, of action on self and on external object" we can distinguish dreaming from reality without any need for the help of the Cartesian God (cf. Descartes 1641: 13–14, 48–49, 61–62). Volition, therefore, is the signaling (pre-symbolic, or pre-propositional) cognitive reaction of the organism to its actual perceptual Feeling, and this reaction takes the form of either active or passive volitional efforts. The active efforts are based on fulfilled expectation, and operate and act on the relevant object, while the passive efforts are intended to criticize and replace the erroneous expectation by a new one (cf. Peirce 5.510, 1.321, 1.332–334, 8.315).

> But though the sense of effort is thus merely a sensation, like any other, it is one in which the duality which appears in every sensation is specially prominent. A sense of exertion is at the same time a sense of being resisted. Exertion cannot be experienced without resistance, nor resistance without exertion. It is all one sense, but a sense of duality. Every sensation involves the same sense of duality, though less prominently. This is the direct perception of the external world of Reid and Hamilton. (Peirce 5.539)

The indexical volitional reaction to the iconic feeling qualities is also a reflexive comparison between these two cognitive signs to evaluate their relations. The last stage of the perceptual process is the interpretation of the Percept with Symbolic Reasoning as the Synthetic thought, the explicit Perceptual Judgment. This judgment is a proposition asserting the relation between the percept interpreted in the iconic sign of feeling of an object, **a Stove**, and the indexical sign of reaction, ☛ **a Stove**, to the same object, e.g., the asserted proposition "This is a Stove."

Now, I would like to suggest that at the stage of Volition at which the indexical reaction takes place, the *evaluation* of the perceptual cognition as accepted or rejected, its *True* or *False* representation of reality is determined. This is processed in a quasi-inductive evaluation of the concordance or non-concordance between the *expected perceptual sign* and the *actual perceived sign* (cf. Nesher 1990: 20–24, 1994b: 154–56, 1997: V; 2000b: V, VI). This is the origin of *Truth* in our cognitive behavior, and it is clear why Peirce calls this perceptual *evaluation* 'the natural instinct for truth' (Peirce 7.220 [1903]; cf. 7.77ff., 2.176, 5.212, 5.551ff.). This is so since the level of our self-consciousness in the perceptual process of evaluation is very low, and our self-control is only an instinctively 'associational suggestion of belief' in the perceptual judgment; this can be understood in contrast to the rational reasoning inferences with propositions, over which we have critical self-control and, therefore, rational criticism and correction (cf. Peirce 1900: 831[12–14], 2.141, 5.151–157, 5.418–421, 5.440–442, 7.615–636; Nesher 1994b: II.2, IV.1, V.1). The semiotic cognitive process consists of relations among signs, but in contrast to the philosophical phenomenologists and metaphysical realists, the pragmaticist shows that *inside* this process we can detect the interaction of humans with their *external* environment and the representational function of their cognitive minds (comp. Davidson 1986a: 312; cf. Nesher 1998b: IV, V). For a recent misunderstanding of Peirce's pragmaticist epistemology see Meyers, 1999: III; comp. Nesher 1997: V).

> Now thought is of nature of a sign. In that case, then, if we find out the right method of thinking and can follow it out—the right method of transforming signs—then truth can be nothing more nor less than the last result to which the following out of this method would ultimately carry us. (Peirce 5.553 [1906]; cf. 5.286; 1.339; 1.538)

It can be shown that 'the last result to which the following out of this method would ultimately carry us' is the end of a *specific* process of inquiry that is an experiential or experimental concrete proof and not an ideal limit as expressed in Peirce's early writings and accepted by the interpreters as pragmatic theory of ideal truth (cf. Nesher 1994b: IV, 1997: V, 1998a: #5; comp. e.g., Quine 1992 [1995: 67]; Putnam 1981: 49–56; and recently also Meyers 1999: 649). The 'last result' of the inquiry in Peirce's theory of scientific inquiry is a 'local truth', but not a 'local convergence' as an isolated relativistic result of a Kuhnian scientific paradigm, which cannot be compared with more or less comprehensive truths, as Rorty understands Peirce. The pragmaticist 'local truth' is a relative truth only as a component of a *continuous convergence* of an unending inquiry, and according to Peirce's fallibilism, without being 'a final convergence' (cf. Rorty 1991: 129–32; comp. Hausman 1993: 214–24; Nesher 1994a: 170–74, 1997: IV). However, the source of this 'local truth' is the perceptual process in which the pragmaticist detects the quasi-reasoning mechanism of positive evaluation of the empirical contents of our perceptual judgments as true assertions.

Let us analyze the structure of such an operation in the cognitive process of perception. The indexical volitional reaction to the iconic feeling qualities is a reflexive comparison between these two cognitive signs to evaluate inductively their concordance (coherency) or non-concordance (incoherency). The result can be either a coherent or incoherent relation between the two signs that in the first case, in regular perception, render true beliefs; in the extreme case, when we do not have assurance in our perception, we express it by doubt. (I will not deal here with cases of illusions, which arise when we do not have proper instinctive self-control of our perceptual processes) (cf. Hume 1739: 84, 132, 217; Peirce 5.570–571). Thus, without going outside our cognitive skins we instinctively feel the duality in the meaning-content of our perceptual process, and accordingly we either assert our perception by the propositional judgment or hold it, in the case of strong surprise about our perception that has caught us in doubt about the perceived object. Yet how do we explain that in this specific sign-stage of the perceptual process we detect the representation of external reality? The logical structure of such representation is the structure of the perceptual process, which is similar to the structure of our rational reasoning that developed from it. This primordial perceptual process is called by Peirce "quasi-reasoning," which is the sequence of the trio of inferences "quasi-abduction," "quasi-deduction," and "quasi-induction" (cf. Peirce 1900: 831[21–22], 1101[7–9]). They are called quasi-inferences because of their instinctive and practical low levels of self-consciousness and self-control in comparison with the rational levels of our reasoning.

> There are three kinds of reasoning, the Inductive, the Deductive, and the Hypothetical [Abductive]. The last consists in the introduction into a confused tangle of given facts of an idea not given whose only justification lies in its reducing that tangle to order. This kind of inference is little subject to control, and so not highly rational.... (Peirce 1900: 831[13–14])

What is our justification of our perceptual judgments? Must justifications be rational, as the Wittgensteinians think? I would like to argue that if the pragmaticist conception of truth as the result of the human proof operations holds for our first and simple truths of perception upon which all of our reasoning is based, then it also holds for the complex truths of our reasoning and scientific theories. What should be shown is that the results of our perceptual processes are not just 'given' but must be mainly 'veridical', as Davidson also suggested (cf. Davidson 1986b: 332). For this, we have to show that the basic structure of our perceptual process is a quasi-proof procedure like the proof structure of our reasoning, and that they all have true conclusions in their representational functions (cf. Nesher 1997: V, 1998a: ##5, 6; Bohm 1977: 374). According to the pragmaticist conception of human cognition, our rational reasoning and logical proof procedures develop from our instinctive and practical mental quasi-proof operations, in contrast to the dichotomy between logic and psychology. Since Frege maintained the dichotomy between logical proofs and mental processes, he could not think that our mental processes are the basic proofs, or quasi-proofs, of the truth of our asserted perceptual judgments.

> And so one might come to believe that logic deals with the mental process of thinking and the psychological laws in accordance with which it takes place. This would be a misunderstanding of the task of logic, for truth has not been given the place which is its due here. Error and superstitions have causes just as much as genuine knowledge. The assertion both of what is false and of what is true takes place in accordance of psychological laws. A derivation from these and explanation

of a mental process that terminates in an assertion can never take the place of a proof of what is asserted. (Frege 1918: 85–86)

Thus, if our logical proofs did not develop according to psychological laws, including the laws of logic, then they must exist independently of our thinking, and the question is, even if we do not formulate them with our thinking, how can we grasp them without thinking about them? At any rate, Frege cannot explain why the assertive force of some of our propositions forces us to accept them as true assertions, because formal logic as the theory of truth cannot explain psychological events like true assertions. But this real assertive force is the reason to accept the truth of our experiential propositions and, at the last analysis, also our formal logic intuition. This is the Peircean explanation that we quasi-prove our perceptual judgments in the perceptual process, though sometimes we also can err in such proofs and in our assertions.

The result of Peirce's analysis of the working of human minds is that the entire procedure sequence of the three sub-processes of the *logic of discovery* (Abduction), the *logic of consequence* (Deduction), and the *logic of evaluation* (Induction) is the basic inferential structure of all human cognitions. Yet only through our perceptual processes do we confront reality, and the perceptual triadic sequential procedure should be understood as the form of a complete quasi-proof of our perceptual judgments as our basic truths (cf. Nesher 1997: V&[14], 1998a: ##4, 5, 6). The perceptual process is primordial, and its sub-processes operate only as quasi-inferences when the relations of interpretation of their components can be considered quasi-purposed and quasi-controlled (cf. Peirce 5.441, 1900: 831[20–25, 6–9]; Nesher 1982: 80–82, 1994b: II.2). Therefore, we can know about the nature of the perceptual processes only from our *instinctive penetration* into them from our *strong feeling of assurance* about our perceptual judgments and from their consequences in human behavior (cf. Peirce 7.444–450; Nesher 1997: V, 2001: I, II, V). The very processes of perception are *quasi-proofs* of the perceptual judgments that when asserted are our basic true propositions—*positive knowledge* of external reality.

The perceiver learns whether he or she has perceived the object of the percept correctly or not, and *in this evaluative comparison the basic simple perceptual truth emerges*. If it is found that the interpretation of the indexical sign C^{In} (as is expected in C^{Dd}) by the iconic-pattern A^{Ab} continues to hold *coherently*—namely, the probability of the interpretation of C^{In} by A^{Ab} is close to 1—then the expectation has not vanished and a *propositional judgment* is concluded: $A^{Ab} \to C^{In}$, e.g., "This is a table." Yet if the actual perceived indexical sign C^{In*} is *incoherent* with, and thus cannot be recognized by, the iconic-pattern A^{Ab}, when $PRm/n(A^{Ab} \to C^{In*}) < X$ (X is the parameter of acceptance by assurance), then the expectation of C^{Dd} vanishes (Peirce 7.210). Then C^{In*} is the unexpected percept that causes the perceiver's surprise. When the incoherence arises and the conflict between the expected C^{Dd} and the actual perceived C^{In*} forces the perceiver to feel doubt, then usually he or she refrains from asserting a perceptual judgment. Here the distinction between being true and not being so is expressed in assertion or hesitation and changing one's mind in the perceptual situation. When one evaluates positively a perceptual process, one continues to act with this perceptual knowledge, either on objects or by asserting one's judgment. Otherwise, one should act to reinterpret one's percept, namely, act passively to change one's mind (Peirce 5.510). The following is the general scheme of the perceptual process, on whose logical structure we can explicate *our strong feeling of perceptual assurance as the source of the true representation of the confronted reality*). This is the source of the concept of truth that Dummett is looking for (Dummett 1990).

[5] The Structure of Perception and the Mechanism of True Representation of Reality

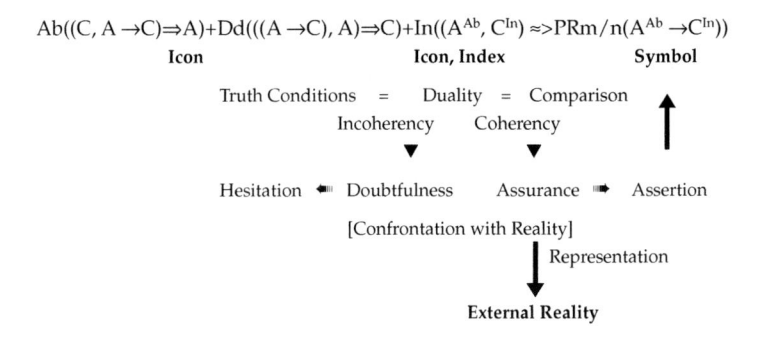

$Ab((C, A \to C) \Rightarrow A) + Dd(((A \to C), A) \Rightarrow C) + In((A^{Ab}, C^{In}) \approx > PRm/n(A^{Ab} \to C^{In}))$

      Icon   **Icon, Index**   **Symbol**

         Truth Conditions = Duality = Comparison
                       Incoherency   Coherency
                        ▼   ▼   ↑

        Hesitation ← Doubtfulness   Assurance → Assertion

                [Confrontation with Reality]
                             ↓ Representation

                         External Reality

This is our instinctive quasi-proof operating like a 'reasoning machine' of human perceptual cognition that enables us to gain true perceptual knowledge of reality (cf. Peirce 1900: MSs). The perceptual judgments are only *instinctively proved,* and as such they are the 'simple truths' distinct from the 'logical truths' of propositions and theories that are *rationally proved or disproved* to be true or false (Peirce 5.570–571). The *instinctive truths* of the perceptual judgments are due to the resulting *coherency* among components of the perceptual process.

When the coherent structure is formed and *instinctively evaluated positively* and we feel its 'assertive force', then the perceived empirical content is generalized and interpreted in the propositional form of perceptual judgment (cf. Peirce 5.119, 2.254–2.265, 2.337, 5.571, 5.553; Nesher 1997: IV). Here we can see that the *truth-conditions* of the *perceptual judgments* are the *duality* in which the *instinctive comparison* of the interaction between the *icon* and *index* is *evaluated* in the stage of *induction*. The positive evaluation is our *feeling of assurance* of *representing veritably external reality*, and upon such feeling we assert our perceptual judgments as true. This basic 'mechanism' of proof, which is based on our 'natural instinct for truth', is comparable to Quine's 'mechanism' of assenting to and dissenting from sentences, though for Quine this is a physical and not a cognitive mechanism.

Russell was wrong when he separated the truth of our perceptions from the truth of our perceptual judgments (Russell 1910: 155–59). Russell's theory—that perception cannot *err* and is always true, but the truth of perceptual judgments, and all other propositional judgments, is independent from their being proved and known—is based on two wrong philosophical-cognitive assumptions. The first is that our perception is about *subjective-phenomenal sense-data* immediately perceived as a single whole and therefore always *correct* and *true*; that perceptual judgments, linguistically articulated into different terms, refer to separated *physical objects* and therefore can be *true* or *false*. The second is that truth is eternal—the metaphysical realist position; that judgments are about *physical reality*, and their truth or falsity is from God's point of view or the eternal perspective and independent of our knowledge. For Russell, the truth conditions of our judgments are existing facts and events that we cannot perceive immediately; we therefore cannot know them and can only assume their existence —but then how can we know the truths of our judgments (cf. Russell 1910: 157–59)? Therefore, we can see that the metaphysical realists confuse and confound the truth of our cognitions with reality independent of being cognitively represented (cf. Russell 1910: VII, 1940: chaps. 20, 21; comp. Nesher 1998a: ##4, 5, 8, 1999a: #V). As we analyze the perceptual process, we can see that its pre-propositional inferences and the inferred perceptual judgment are components of the same concatenated cognitive process. As will be shown below, the truth of the proved perceptual judgment in the perceptual process depends on the efficiency of its self-control, and it is always in respect to its specific [quasi-]proof-conditions (cf. Nesher 1998a: #8).

As to the truth-conditions of our perceptual judgments, we have seen, as explained above, that the *duality* in the perceptual process is the *truth-conditions* that 'hook' our cognitions and their linguistic expression in the perceptual judgment to 'the world'. However, the relation of these *truth-conditions* to our perceptual judgments is not *physical causation* but *cognitive causation* of interpretation in the perceptual process that is the quasi-proof process in which we assert the perceptual judgments that are our basic true propositions, our basic facts (cf. Peirce 5.440, 2.141, 7.616–636; Nesher 1990: 20–21, 2001: IV). The question as to what the *factors* or the *quasi-facts* are upon which the perceptual judgment is quasi-proved can be answered directly; namely, they are the *truth-conditions* embedded in our perceptual experience. With this Pragmaticist's epistemological theory of truth, we can show that *we can know external reality with our proved truths*.

5. Conclusion: 'Our Senses as Reasoning Machines' Quasi-proves Our Perceptual Judgments as Our 'Simple Truths' and the Basis of All of Our Knowledge

I would like to claim that if the pragmaticist conception of truth as the conclusion of the human proof operations holds for our quasi-proofs of first and *simple truths* of perception upon which all of our reasoning is based, then it also holds for complex truths of our reasoning and scientific theories. This can be explained since the problem of human truth lies in our ability to represent 'correspondingly' segments of external reality, and this can be done, according to the pragmaticist epistemology, by our first and basic confrontation with reality that can only occur through our perceptual process (comp. Putnam 1999: 9–12, 100–102; cf. Nesher 1999b). What has been shown is that our perceptual processes are the quasi-proofs of the perceptual judgments as true representations of reality (cf. Nesher 1997: V, 1998a: ##5, 6).

This is our instinctive proof operating like a 'reasoning machine' of human cognition that enables us to gain true perceptual knowledge of reality. This basic 'mechanism', called by Peirce "the natural instinct for truth," is similar in its observed facts to Quine's described mechanism of assenting to sentences, but Peirce analyzes the cognitive perceptual operation and not just the listener's behavioral reaction to sentences (Peirce 7.220; cf. Quine 1960: chap. 2). I believe that the above analysis of the perceptual components that determine the truth of our assertions somehow also fits Davidson's intuition that "the sort of assertion that is linked to understanding already incorporates the concept of truth" (Davidson 1996: 275). We can see that what I consider the *feeling of assurance for our assertion* is considered by Davidson the "belief [that] the sentence we use to make the assertion is true" (ibid.). But as it can be understood from the above analysis, this "belief" about the truth of a sentence precedes our assertion of the perceptual judgments and is a *pre-propositional* belief that contradicts Davidson's requirement that belief must be *propositional* (cf. Nesher 1998b: VII). As to the truth-conditions, we have seen, as explained above, that the *duality* between the indexical volitional reaction and the iconic feeling qualities embedded in the perceptual process is the truth-conditions that 'tie' our cognitions and their linguistic expression in the perceptual judgment to the world.

The question is whether we can generally identify *truth-conditions* with *facts*, because if we identify facts with the truth-conditions upon which general propositions or theories are proved, then what are the truth-conditions of these factual truth-conditions? But what are facts? Some philosophers tried to define *facts* and *true propositions* such that a *fact* is "what true a proposition corresponds to," and a *true proposition* is "what corresponds to a fact" (cf. Russell 1912; Wittgenstein 1921; Austin 1950; Brandom 1994: 327–33; comp. Nesher 2001: IV). This inconvenient circularity is probably the reason that some philosophers, such as Davidson, try to avoid the term 'fact' or 'states of affairs' (cf. Davidson 1996: 266, 277; comp. Nesher 1998b: IV–IV). However, if following Peirce we identify 'perceptual facts' with 'true perceptual judgments', we can see that these 'facts' are not the truth-conditions of the perceptual judgments themselves but of other propositions and theories of our reasoning. The "facts" upon which the true perceptual judgments were quasi-proved are those *pre-propositional truth-conditions*, the *duality* between the indexical volitional reaction and the iconic feeling qualities embedded in the perceptual process. Thus, the *truth-conditions* of our perceptual judgments are the cognitive components embedded in our perceptual experience, which can be considered only as the *quasi-facts* upon which the perceptual judgments are *quasi-proved* without eliminating them as "pseudentities" as Strawson did, and then we can settle the paradoxical problem of how to define 'facts' and 'true propositions' (cf. Strawson 1950: 41; comp. Nesher 2000c: II).

With the above analysis of the instinctive perceptual process we can explain why the foundationalists accept this 'given' perceptual judgment as the bedrock of our knowledge. They think about truth only in terms of rational justification from other 'given' propositions, and cannot conceive the function of the non-propositional instinctive processes of quasi-proof as the 'justification' of such 'given' perceptual judgments (cf. Nesher 1997: IV&[8], [9]). Owing to the *instinctive* low level of self-consciousness and self-control of the feeling of truth in our perceptual judgment, it is no surprise that Davidson took the concept of *truth* to be primitive and built upon it his theory of meaning. However, in the above analysis of the cognitive stages of perceptual interpretation, we found that our *natural instinct* of *truth* consists in our awareness of the *indexical reaction* to the *iconic feeling*, which is indeed quite primitive, but not the most primitive because it is located between the stage of *feeling* of *iconic qualities* and of *symbolic propositional judgment* (cf. Nesher 1990, 1997: V, 1998b: VII). This perceptual situation, which misled Davidson in his theory of meaning, was observed by Peirce: "We often derive from observation strong intimations of truth, without being able to specify what were the circumstances we had observed which conveyed those intimations" (Peirce 7.46; cf. 7.48, 7.77, 1.635, 1.14, 5.571).

Therefore, Davidson is wrong about *truth* being the most primitive relation preceding *meaning*, perhaps because he considers only the *meaning* of the propositional language. Davidson's mistake in this regard is probably due to his not being aware of the entire cognitive process of perception and its pre-propositional meaning components (cf. Davidson 1967, 1986a: 308, 312; Nesher 1998b: VII).

We have seen that the strong intimation of *truth* is a very primitive stage of our cognitive representation of external reality. This might be the source of Ramsey's feeling for the *redundancy* of specifically emphasizing the truth of propositions, if we already know their truth instinctively (cf. Ramsey 1927: 39; Nesher 2000c: II.2, III). Nevertheless, if being proved or quasi-proved makes our cognitions *true*—as distinct from being unproved and thus *doubtful* cognitions—then the *ascription of truth* to our proved propositions is not redundant but crucial for our knowledge of external reality. According to Peirce's explanation, proof is

> [a]n argument which suffices to remove all real doubt from a mind that apprehends it. It is either mathematical demonstration; a probable deduction of so high probability that no real doubt remains; or an inductive, i.e., experimental proof. (Peirce 2.782; cf. 2.663)

Yet there is a seeming paradox if we understand beliefs as cognitions proved true. If we accept different kinds of proofs, ranging from perceptual quasi-proofs to logical formal proofs, then actually all human cognitions should be true because otherwise we would not hold them. This is basically Davidson's intuition, and it could be right if human cognition were not a dynamic and continuous process of inquiry that replaces relatively weaker true cognitions by relatively stronger ones. Through repeated proof procedures of confirmation and refutation, we limit the truth of previously proved propositions and theories and prove the more comprehensive truth of the new ones. Thus, we find in the entire human cognitive processes *true, false*, and undecided *doubtful* cognitions as essential components of the dynamic and continuous evolution of human knowledge (cf. Nesher 1998a: ##4, 5, 6).

Our 'simple truths' are the true conclusions of the quasi-proof operations from which we proceed to infer the axioms by non-formal non-demonstrative (ampliative) inferences. Thus, the entire procedure of proof is a combination of the quasi-proof of the 'simple truths' and the entire rational and scientific proofs with the non-formal inference of the axioms, the formal inference of the theorems of the axiomatic-deductive system, and their non-formal inductive evaluation. Therefore, Peirce lay the epistemological foundation to solve Hume's problem by showing that 'our senses as reasoning machines' quasi-prove our perceptual judgments as the basis for the formation of all of our knowledge of reality.

University of Haifa

Works Cited

Austin, J.L. 1950 [1964]. "Truth." In *Truth*, ed. G. Pitcher, 18–31. Englewood Cliffs,: Prentice-Hall, Inc.
Bohm, D. 1977. "Science as perception-communication." In *The Structure of Scientific Theories*, ed. F. Suppe, 374–91. Urbana: University of Illinois Press.
Brandom, R. 1994. *Making It Explicit: Reasoning, Representing, and Discursive Commitment.* Cambridge Mass.: Harvard University Press.
Davidson, D. 1967 [1984]. "Truth and meaning." Reprinted in idem, *Inquiries into Truth and Interpretation*, 17–36. Oxford: Clarendon Press.
———. 1986a. "A coherence theory of truth and knowledge." In *Truth and Interpretation: Perspectives on the Philosophy of Davidson*, ed. E. LePore, 307–19. Oxford: Blackwell.
———. 1986b. "Empirical content." In *Truth and Interpretation: Perspectives on the Philosophy of Davidson*, ed. E. LePore, 320–32. Oxford: Blackwell.
———. 1996. "The folly of trying to define truth." *The Journal of Philosophy* 93 (6): 263–78.
Descartes, R. 1641 [1985]. "Meditations on the first philosophy." *The Philosophical Writings of Descartes*. 2 vols. Translated by J. Cottingham et al., 1–62. Cambridge: Cambridge University Press.
Dummett, M. 1990. "The source of the concept of truth." In *Meaning and Method: Essays in Honor of Hilary Putnam*, ed. George Boolos, 1–15. Cambridge: Cambridge University Press.
Frege, G. 1918 [1999]. "The thought: A logical inquiry." In *Truth: Oxford Readings in Philosophy*, ed. S. Blackburn and K. Simmons, 85–105. Oxford: Oxford University Press.
Hausman, C.R. 1993. *Charles S. Peirce's Evolutionary Philosophy.* Cambridge: Cambridge University Press.
Hume, D. 1739 [1978]. *A Treatise of Human Nature.* Edited by. L.A. Selby-Bigge; 2nd ed. by P.H. Nidditch. Oxford: Clarendon Press.
Kant, I. 1781–87 [1965]. *Critique of Pure Reason.* Translated by N.K. Smith. New York: St. Martin's Press.
Meyers, R.G. 1999. "Pragmatism and Peirce's externalist epistemology." *Transactions of Charles S. Peirce Society* 35 (4): 638–53.
Nesher, D. 1982. "Remarks on Peirce's pragmatic theory of meaning." *Transactions of Charles S. Peirce Society* 18 (1): 75–90.
———. 1987a. "Remarks on Spinoza's philosophy, its consistency, and its evolutionary character." *Iyyun: A Hebrew Philosophical Quarterly* 36 (2): 83–123. [Hebrew]
———. 1987b. "Epistemological investigations: Is metalanguage possible? Evolutionary hierarchy vs. logical hierarchy of language." In *Development in Epistemology and Philosophy of Science*, ed. P. Weingartner and G. Schurz, 72–80.Vienna: Holder-Pichler-Tempsky.
———. 1990. "Understanding sign semiosis as a self-conscious process: A reconstruction of some basic conceptions in Peirce's semiotics." *Semiotica* 79 (1–2): 1–49.
———. 1994a. "Spinoza's theory of truth." In *Spinoza: The Enduring Questions*, ed. G. Hunter, 140–77. Toronto: University of Toronto Press.

———. 1994b. "Pragmaticist theory of human cognition, and the conception of common-sense." In *The Peirce Seminar Papers II*, ed. M. Shapiro, 103–64. Providence: Berghahn Books.
———. 1997. "Peircean realism: Truth as the meaning of cognitive signs representing external reality." *Transactions of Charles S. Peirce Society* 33 (1): 201–57.
———. 1998a. "The pragmaticist conception of truth with a 'bold solution' to the liar paradox." Manuscript.
———. 1998b. "In spite of Davidson's arguments for 'the folly of trying to define truth', truth can be defined." Manuscript.
———. 1999a. "Peirce's theory of signs and the nature of learning theory." In *The Peirce Seminar Papers IV*, ed. M. Shapiro. Providence: Berghahn Books.
———. 1999b. "Putnam on truth: Can we know reality with a big 'R' with proved truths with a small 't'?" Manuscript.
———. 1999c. "Pragmaticist realism: The third philosophical perspective as the 'intermediate point' between 'metaphysical realism' and 'internal realism.'" *Journal of Speculative Philosophy* 13 (4): 257–93.
———. 2000a. "Spinoza's epistemology of freedom." The International Conference: Spinoza 2000. Ethics V: Love, Knowledge and Beatitude. Jerusalem, Hebrew Union College, June 16–21, 1999 (forthcoming in the Proceedings of the Conference).
———. 2000b. "How to explain our knowledge of external reality: The controversies about 'facts,' 'true propositions' and 'truth-conditions' and the pragmatist solution." Presented in the Center of Philosophy of Science, the University of Pittsburgh, February 15, 2000.
———. 2000c. "Pragmatic theory of truth: Are Frege's and Ramsey's equation 'p is true = p' And Tarski's equivalence 'X is true if, and only if, p' true?" Read at the Fifth International Bariloche Colloquium of Philosophy, Argentina, June 27–29, 2000.
———. 2001. "Peircean epistemology of learning and the function of abduction as the logic of discovery." *Transactions of Charles S. Peirce Society* 37 (1): 23–57.
Peirce, C.S. 1900. "Our senses as reasoning machines." Manuscripts 831+1101. Cambridge Mass.: Houghton Library, Harvard University.
———. 1931–58. *Collected Papers*. Vols. 1–8. Edited by. C. Hartshorne, P. Weiss, and A.W. Burks. Cambridge Mass.: Harvard University Press.
———. 1857–1913. Manuscripts. Cambridge Mass.: Houghton Library, Harvard University. In Robin, R.S. 1967.
Putnam, H. 1981. *Reason, Truth and History*. Cambridge: Cambridge University Press.
———. 1999. *The Threefold Cord: Mind, Body, and World*. New York: Columbia University Press.
Quine, W.V. 1960. *Word and Object*. Cambridge, Mass.: The MIT Press.
———. 1992 [1995]. *Pursuit of Truth*. Rev. ed. Cambridge Mass.: Harvard University Press.
———. 1995. *From Stimulus to Science*. Cambridge Mass.: Harvard University Press.
Ramsey, F.P. 1927 [1990]. "Truth and probability." In *F.P. Ramsey: Philosophical Papers*, ed. D.H. Mellor, 52–110. Cambridge: Cambridge University Press.
Robin, R.S. 1967. *Annotated Catalogue of the Papers of Charles S. Peirce*. Amherst: University of Massachusetts Press.
Rorty, R. 1991. *Objectivity, Realism, and Truth: Philosophical Papers*. Vol. 1. Cambridge: Cambridge University Press.
Russell, B. 1910 [1994]. *Philosophical Essays*. London and New York: Routledge.

———. 1912 [1973]. *The Problems of Philosophy*. Oxford and New York: Oxford University Press.
———. 1940 [1965]. *An Inquiry into Meaning and Truth*. London: Routledge.
Strawson, P.F. 1950 [1964] "Truth." In *Truth*, ed. G. Pitcher. Englewood Cliffs: Prentice-Hall, Inc.
Wittgenstein, L. 1921 [1961]. *Tractatus Logico-Philosophicus*. London: Routledge and Kegan Paul.
———. 1953 [1958]. *Philosophical Investigations*. Oxford: Basil Blackwell and Mott, Ltd.
———. 1969. *On Certainty*. New York: Harper Torchbooks.

Michael Shapiro

Aspects of a Neo-Peircean Linguistics: Language History as Linguistic Theory

1. Introduction

This essay is an attempt to capitalize and improve on earlier work of mine (esp. 1983 and 1991) aimed at founding what I have variously called a (neo-)Peircean or neo-structuralist linguistics, the main conceptual cast of which is semeiotic or sign-theoretic. In sketching just what Peirce's whole philosophy, but particularly his theory of signs, contributes to the modern study of language structure, perhaps a useful heuristic is the comparison of crucial differences between Peirce and Saussure, as in the following table (cf. Short 1989).

	SAUSSURE	PEIRCE
1.	'semiology': the study of "the life of signs within society" [man-made signs]; language as a model for other sign systems	'semeiotic': the study of all sign phenomena [signs of all sorts, including natural signs]
2a.	sign: union of material signifier and the concept it signifies [signified is essential to signifier only by being *part* of signifier]	sign: signifier and sign are identified [object is not part of sign, no more than a mother is a complex of woman + child]

SAUSSURE	PEIRCE
2b. denial of logic of relations; return to scholastic metaphysics of substance and attribute	something can be what it is because of its relation to *another*
3. only one sign: material signifier—a general type of articulated sound (*not* concrete use in speech)	legisign: not only sign; also qualisign and sinsign, i.e., qualities and singular entities that are signs
4. signified = concept [Cartesian inheritance, i.e., every sign must be associated with a mental entity]	signified = sign requiring interpretation, i.e., interpretant rather than conceptual content
5. dyadism, with 'sign' as basic concept of theory	triadism, hence 'semeiosis' not 'sign' as basis of theory
6. change is "fortuitous and blind"; synchrony is severed from diachrony	change is an aspect of continuity (growth); all synchrony is dynamic product of end-directed processes

While this is not the place to explain in detail the basic principles of Peirce's theory of signs, the right-hand column of the above table can be amplified by the following main points.[1] Significance is a triadic relation of sign, object, and interpretant. A sign is something non-arbitrarily interpretable as signifying an object (real or unreal). A sign has two objects, one immediate and the other dynamic. The immediate object is the object as the sign (rightly or wrongly) portrays it as being. The dynamic object is that same object as it is, independent of how it is signified (even a fiction or a dream can be misrepresented). So far as the sign does not misrepresent its dynamic object, its immediate object IS its dynamic object, though it will normally not be the whole of it. A sign has two interpretants that can remain unactualized potentialities; in addition, it can—but need not—have one or more actual interpretants. The immediate interpretant is the way a sign would be interpreted by anyone who understands it: it apprehends the sign's immediate object. Dynamic interpretants are the ways a sign is actually interpreted. These are actualizations of the immediate interpretant, with such additions and qualifications as are suggested by the collateral experience of the sign's dynamic object. A dynamic interpretant can include a correction of the sign if the sign misrepresents its dynamic object. No dynamic interpretant need be formed at all, and in most cases any number of dynamic interpretants may be formed. Some or all of these may incorporate errors; normally, all fall short of the full truth about the sign's dynamic object. The final interpretant is the ideally complete and accurate interpretant to which inquiry (collateral experience of the dynamic object) would eventually lead interpreters were they to continue this process long enough. In some cases, the final interpretant is an ideal that may be approached but never reached; in other cases, it is within reach, i.e., it can be actualized in a dynamic interpretant. Interpretants themselves can be signs, and the dynamic object of a given sign is the immediate object of that sign's final interpretant.

Peirce's semeiotic is unintelligible without a knowledge of his phenomenological categories—his phaneroscopy, i.e., with Firstness, Secondness, and Thirdness. With the application of Peirce's semeiotic to linguistic structure in mind, his categoriology can be used to clarify the relation between the three levels of patterning in language. Applying Peirce's terms to those used so productively by Coseriu, they are:

FIRST   **system**, i.e., everything functional that is productive in the language, including usage that exists *in potentia*;
SECOND **norms**, i.e., usage that is historically realized and codified in the given language community;
THIRD   **type**, i.e., the specific Bauplan or underlying design of a language.

This scheme is coordinate with the categories expressed as modes of being, which in the case of language are expressed not in the familiar, dyadic form of *langue* and *parole*, but expanded to reflect their proper triadic form (Andersen 1991:291):

FIRST   **grammar**—language as TECHNIQUE (*dúnamis*)
SECOND **speech**—language as ACTIVITY (*enérgeia*)
THIRD   **text**—language as PRODUCT (*érgon*).

I want to shift now from preliminaries and generalities to the main point of my presentation, namely, the matter of language history as linguistic theory (a topic developed at greater length in Shapiro 1991), specifically as it involves TELEOLOGY and the formation of ICONS OF RELATION, or DIAGRAMS.

2. The Telos of Linguistic Change

It may be difficult, or even wrong, to speak of *the* telos of linguistic change: teleological behavior usually encompasses several goals at once because of its complexity. Furthermore, there are short-term and long-term goals (cf. Itkonen 1982); and there may be minor goals which conflict with each other and stand to be eliminated or subordinated in favor of one or more major goals.

Long-term teleology is what Edward Sapir called 'drift'. Since drift (as we shall see in greater detail below) is an end-directed process spanning generations, centuries, and even millennia, it is not easy to identify the goals precisely. It has been suggested, moreover, that drift differs from short-term teleology in having goals that are specific to individual languages or language families, rather than an overarching or universal goal (Itkonen 1982: 97). But as we shall see, this is not so: all tele of linguistic change are of the same type; hence all teleological change in language, whether long- or short-term, conforms to the same principle.

It is not at all clear, actually, how short is short. Diachronic changes that are clearly more pronounced than mere tendencies can go on for hundreds of years. When the history of whole language families is involved, the seeds of change may be isolable at a given historical point, but the growth of the individual daughter languages may proceed at different rates and with diverse geographical extension. Moreover, a language may be of a specific type which predisposes it to develop in a certain direction. But the structural traits that manifest themselves subsequently may "not necessarily [be] directly reflected in the overt categories or surface regularities of a given language state" (Andersen 1978: 2). Also, these traits are liable to be evaluated in different ways by different segments of a speech community; in effect, they "determine what possible deviations from the norms will be acceptable to the members of the speech community and, hence, what innovations will occur" (ibid.).

In order to assess how the issues of teleology, drift, and type are interrelated, let us begin by considering how drift was construed by Sapir in the context of his far-ranging investigations of language and culture. This procedure will give us a quick entree to the entire range of questions associated with the goals of change.

The word 'drift' seems to have originated in Sapir's writings as a term of linguistics and cultural anthropology (see Malkiel 1981). A modern textbook of historical linguistics defines drift "in language change [as] an observable tendency toward a goal" (Anttila 1988: 194). Sapir used drift in this general sense, as applied to cultural history rather than to language specifically, as early as 1917 (Malkiel 1981: 537). Of course, the locus classicus within Sapir's whole oeuvre is chapter 7 of his book *Language*: "The drift of a language is constituted by the unconscious selection on the part of its speakers of those individual variations that are cumulative in some special direction" (1921a: 155). Rather less well known is Sapir's later (1933) reformulation of the definition as it appeared in his entry on "Language" in the *Encyclopaedia of the Social Sciences* (reprinted in Sapir 1949: 23):

> The enormous amount of study that has been lavished on the history of particular languages and groups of languages shows very clearly that the most powerful differentiating factors are not outside influences, as ordinarily understood, but rather the very slow but powerful unconscious changes in certain directions which seem to be implicit in the phonemic systems and morphologies of the languages themselves. These "drifts" are powerfully conditioned by unconscious formal feelings and are made necessary by the inability of human beings to actualize ideal patterns in a permanently set fashion.

Although language is certainly the chief focus of Sapir's remarks involving the concept of drift, it is clear that he thought of this process as informing *all* behavior over the long term; witness the following excerpt (1931) from his entry on "Fashion" in the *Encyclopaedia of the Social Sciences* (reprinted in Sapir 1949: 376): "Under the apparently placid surface of culture there are always powerful psychological drifts of which fashion is quick to catch the direction. In a democratic society, for instance, if there is an unacknowledged drift toward class distinctions fashion will discover endless ways of giving it visible form." All of these Sapirian loci taken together contribute to the notion that has arisen about drift as tantamount to what Itkonen calls "long-term teleology" (1982: 85) and distinguishes from "short-term teleology." The sorts of goal-directed changes that may have a very long run were also singled out by Meillet, for instance, the tendency in the Indo-European languages for inflection to be reduced, if not lost (Meillet 1921: 28). Meillet's actual attempts to work out the mechanisms by which drift is effected (1938: 110–11) are not convincing, and in fact bear out Sapir's assessment (1921a: 183) that "these psychic undercurrents of language are exceedingly difficult to understand in terms of individual psychology, though there can be no denial of their historical reality."

Although there appears to be no cross-fertilization between Peirce and Sapir, Sapir (1927) sees the action of teleology and final causation in a way that is eminently compatible with Peirce's thought: "[S]ocial behavior is merely the sum or, better, arrangement of such aspects of individual behavior as are referred to culture patterns that have their proper context, not in the spatial and temporal continuities of biological behavior, but in historical sequences that are imputed to actual behavior by a principle of selection" (reprinted in Sapir 1949: 545).

The mention of final causation now requires some special consideration of its role in semeiosis.

3. Semeiosis and Linguistic Change (Efficient and Final Causation)

Peirce's distinction between legisigns and replicas can be used to good account in lifting some of the confusion that surrounds linguistic change, which is the end-directed evolution of a system of legisigns.[2] Replication is the end-directed use of already developed legisigns. In this process, the legisigns (or rules of replica-formation) do not function as efficient causes precisely; indeed, it is doubtful whether a rule or general type could ever be an efficient cause. But neither are they tele of replication. The purpose of replication is communication (conveying information, issuing commands, expressing emotions, etc.). Thus, legisigns are not replicated simply for the sake of being replicated. They could be efficient causes of acts already explained by final causes—except for one thing. They could be efficient causes because final causes require the cooperation of efficient causes. Suppose I want Jones to close the door. I look around for means to do so. One means is replicating the English sentence, "Jones, close the door!" If that were the only means, then, given my purpose, one can suppose that the availability of that legisign causes me (like a mechanical push) to replicate it. (But this is wrong—why in a moment.) However, the availability of alternative legisigns (e.g., "For God's sake, Jones, close the door!" or "Jones, dear fellow, I feel a draft.") means I must *choose*, and so those legisigns are not efficient causes. Legisigns cannot be efficient causes at all. In the first place, the efficient causes that must cooperate are those motor reflexes, etc., that make my tongue wag, my mouth open and close, or my hand type these words. Second, legisigns are general types and hence can never be efficient causes. The upshot of this is that legisigns both exist for a purpose (they have evolved to make communication possible or to facilitate communication that was already possible) and are *used* when *we act* for the purpose of communicating. Thus, already existing legisigns are subsidiary final causes: we make such-and-such sounds or marks *in order to* replicate certain legisigns, and we replicate those legisigns *in order to* communicate something.[3] There is, therefore, an important difference between (1) legisigns developing and (2) legisigns being used.

Talk about final causation is often accompanied by contrasting references to efficient causation. An efficient cause is a particular event or condition that compels its effect. The effect follows the cause in accordance with a general law (a law of efficient causation). A final cause is not a particular event or condition and does not compel its effect. Suppose a man is seen bounding down a steep incline. Why? Possibly because the man was pushed. That would be an efficient cause. But perhaps the man acted in order to catch a goat. 'To catch a goat' is the final cause; it is not a particular event and did not compel the behavior.

Final causation is consistent with efficient causation—indeed, requires it. Men cannot bound goat-wards if their muscles do not relax and contract, compelling movement of limbs. Presumably, then, the two types of cause explain different phenomena—or complementary aspects of the same phenomenon.

To explain something by a final cause is teleological explanation. Teleology is the doctrine that teleological explanations are sometimes legitimate, that some phenomena can only be explained teleologically, and that final causes exist. Teleological explanation was introduced deliberately by the Greek philosophers, primarily Plato and Aristotle, in explicit contrast to already well-established conceptions of causation—those that Aristotle identified as 'efficient' and that we can identify as 'mechanistic'. And already with Plato, it was recognized that this new form of explanation would be rejected by those who think (a) that everything can be explained by causes that compel or (b) that nothing that does not compel its effect could explain it.

In particular, what teleology was invented to explain is the existence of order—in human affairs, in individual actions, in plant and animal life, in the cosmos—wherever that order is inexplicable mechanistically. The point of teleology is to explain the emergence of order out of chaos. By contrast, the mechanistic world-view of modern science admits none but efficient causes. However, not all forms of explanation in modern science conform to the mechanistic idea, even in its broadest and most up-to-date sense, but do approximate to the Aristotelian idea of explanation by final causes. Teleological theories are thus the best, or only, explanations of certain important classes of phenomena. Hence, we have good reason to suppose that final causes exist.

If this sounds too apodeictic for every reader's taste, it is evidently due to the fact that teleology is poorly understood.[4] An aid in dispelling some of the mist surrounding teleology is Peirce's idea of certain processes as 'finious', a neologism he coined for fear that "teleological is too strong a word to apply to them" (7.471).[5] These are non-mechanistic processes that "act in one determinate direction and tend asymptotically toward bringing about an ultimate state of things" (ibid.). The importance of non-teleological finious processes is that they explain how teleological phenomena are possible. One might say that they remove the mystery from teleology. Operating with the notion of finiousness imposes an obligation on the analyst—a hierarchical ordering of non-mechanistic explanations, some of which are merely finious and some of which are teleological.

If one is to arrive at such an ordering following Peirce's conception, then it will be necessary to take into account his definition of final causation: "[W]e must understand by final causation that mode of bringing facts about according to which a general description of result is made to come about, quite irrespective of any compulsion for it to come about in this or that particular way; although the means may be adapted to the end. The general result may be brought about at one time in one way, and at another time in another way. Final causation does not determine in what particular way it is to be brought about, but only that the result shall have a certain general character" (1.211; cf. 1.204).

Any finious process is the result of fortuitous variation plus a principle of selection. These processes are everywhere observable in populations of individuals, whether molecules or living things. Other processes, equally finious, might be found within the actions of a single individual (not necessarily human).[6] It is the nature of finious processes that their particular outcomes cannot be predicted; all that we can predict is their general tendency.

4. Diagrams and Diagrammatization in Language

Sapir's treatment of drift does not include a discussion of explicit goals and ends, but actually, there is one extended passage in Sapir (1921b) that seems to indicate a nexus of thoughts along explicitly teleological lines: "As one passes from ideographic system to system and from alphabet to alphabet perhaps the thing that most forcibly strikes one is that each and every one of them has its individual style. In their earlier stages there is a certain randomness.... The historian has no difficulty in showing how a starting-point gives a slant or drift to the future development of the system.... Wherever the human mind has worked collectively and unconsciously, it has striven for and often attained unique form. The important point is that the evolution of form has a drift in one direction, that it seeks poise, and that it rests, relatively speaking, when it has found this poise" (reprinted in Sapir 1949: 382).

Sapir goes on (383) to mention the Chinese writing system as one which "did not attain its resting-point until it had matured a style, until it had polished off each character into a design that satisfactorily filled its own field and harmonized with its thousands of fellows." Although writing systems may not seem to be of central importance to a consideration of drift, they actually provide ample evidence that changes in writing (like those in spoken language) "are in a sense prefigured in certain obscure tendencies of the present and that these changes, when consummated, will be seen to be but continuations of changes that have been already effected" (Sapir 1921a: 155).

It is useful to juxtapose Sapir's ideas with those of Peirce and see how they converge. For instance, take the following passage from the *Collected Papers*: "[U]nderlying all other laws is the only tendency which can grow by its own virtue, the tendency of all things to take habits.... In so far as evolution follows a law, the law or habit, instead of being a movement from homogeneity to heterogeneity, is growth from difformity to uniformity. But the chance divergences from laws are perpetually acting to increase the variety of the world, and are checked by a sort of natural selection and otherwise ..., so that the general result may be described as 'organized heterogeneity,' or, better, *rationalized variety*" (6.101; emphasis added). The idea of a "rationalized variety" is supported by Peirce's comments about the foundational role of diagrams: "A concept is the living influence upon us of a diagram, or icon, with whose several parts are connected in thought an equal number of feelings and ideas. The law of mind is that feelings and ideas attach themselves in thought *so as to form systems"* (7.467; emphasis added).

Given enough time to work itself out, even an apparently arbitrary system (such as an orthography) will tend toward diagrammatization. Its drift is, in other words, determined by a movement with an explicit telos. In Sapir's words (1921a: 150, 155): "Language moves down time in a current of its own making. It has a drift.... The linguistic drift has direction. In other words, only those individual variations embody it or carry it which move in a certain direction, just as only certain wave movements in the bay outline the tide."

When the question of the reality of tendencies (drift) is raised, it is often cast in terms of predictability; but the focus on prediction might be misplaced, at least in part. Linguistics has taken over from the philosophy of science a preoccupation with predictability (of linguistic rules, particularly), forgetting that in the case of language (as in all human domains) the best we can do is to assert an overarching rationality and constrain the range of possibilities as much as we can based on our empirical knowledge of actual changes. The explanation of change as an instantiation of drift is, therefore, retrodictive, not predictive, in the time-honored manner of all philological (read: hermeneutic) explanations. We make sense of accomplished cognitions ("re-cognize"). Nothing follows from this understanding of change as a matter of necessity. Of course, since drift involves the immanent or inherent structure of the language, further instantiations of this structure will be favored and those that go against it will not.

A priori one could, of course, make the claim that a trend once started could simply continue of its own accord, that the drift itself is the ultimate fact. A riposte to this would be to claim (with Aristotle) that every working out or process is a working out of something else—that "something else" being an *arche* or organized whole. Plot is the working out of character; the speech chain is the elaboration of the simultaneously given phonological system; drift is a process by which the type manifests itself gradually over time.

That still leaves the question: How does type determine drift? The answer suggested by the discussions in my earlier work (1991) is unequivocal: type determines drift by diagrammatization. When a language changes in a direction that demonstrates its conformity to type, it achieves a higher degree of diagrammatization than it had before the drift was completed. If this line of thinking is correct, then drift is explained by a kind of goodness (of fit). When the cumulative result of a series of changes makes a vocalic language more vocalic or a consonantal language more consonantal, the developments are teleological in that the goal is greater diagrammatization between the facts of the language and the type of language that it is. The type is the ideal for that of which it is a type. Being vocalic is no "better" than being consonantal, or vice versa, but conformity to type is a better realization of structure and the changes it comports than disconformity. We might say that each type of language reveals new values, to be fully realized in the further drift of that language toward a fuller realization of those values, i.e., of its type. The only overarching value, then, is fuller realization (alias diagrammatization) of the values specific to one's type. This is evidently what is meant by the genius or 'beauty' of a language. If we use some of the same words to describe values specific to different types, e.g., the 'beauty' of French and the 'beauty' of English, we have only to admit the caveat that 'beauty' does not mean the same thing in the two cases.

Apart from some such notion as diagrammatization (= goodness of fit), type would not explain drift. Talk of type would not seem to add much by way of explanation except to provide terms for the classification of drift: this language changes in that direction (type), that one in another direction (type). If, on the other hand, type explains drift because of its goodness, then even if type is evident only in drift, the mention of type helps us understand why drift occurs. The explanation in that case may fall short of the scientific ideal of predictive power, but it would still be like any other historical explanation, i.e., be couched in terms of circumstances that made the actual outcomes plausible as against alternative possibilities.

Conscious choice or preference is not involved here. When diagrammatization occurs over long stretches of historical time, we cannot talk about the intent or desires of language users, because of the discontinuity of the generations that all participate serially in the drift. Here we are face to face with the less familiar, Peircean kind of final cause, not with final causes that are purposes. The final causes that are operative in long-term drift are the kind that influence human choices but are not conscious (or are consciously made but not for reasons of which one is conscious; cf. Keller 1985).

Pushing diagrammatization this way to account for drift is to move the sense of the concept in the direction of the crystallization of values. Although it might seem that as far as language is concerned, the crystallization of values might be just one kind, evidence from the way that synchronic rules cohere as the historical tendencies that underwrite such coherence make isomorphism the most likely goal of change. Specifically, the isomorphism is between markedness values as the epitome of diagrammatization. It is to a discussion of this point that we can now proceed.

Diagrammatic correspondences between form (expression) and meaning (content) are instantiations of the principle of isomorphism. There is another, equally fundamental sense in which isomorphism can be said to pervade the structure of language, namely, the sense in which rules at the core of grammar are not merely statements of regularities but are coherent. The notions associated with the terms 'rule' and 'coherence' need to be discussed separately. Although the concept of rule was not prominent among the theoretical advances of the early European structuralists, it is nonetheless clear that its ubiquitousness today owes much to an understanding of grammatical relations as patterning and regularity that goes back to pre-war discussions (principally in Prague and Copenhagen) of the foundations of linguistic theory. What is missing from both pre- and post-war theorizing, however, is the notion of the coherence of linguistic relations, and as a corollary, the precise means whereby coherence is to be expressed in the practice of linguistic description.

All along, the potential for making coherence an explicit principle in the understanding of language structure existed unexploited among the many overt achievements of early structuralism, specifically in the idea of *markedness*. Coherence obtains when rule relations signify the mirroring of markedness values across content and expression levels, or between different aspects of expression (as in the case of some morphophonemic congruences). The latter case—an *automorphism*—will once again be the focus here. Since patterning is present at all levels of grammar, to the extent that the rules of language structure expressing this patterning reflect congruences of markedness values, we can attribute their coherence (their raison d'être) to such cohesions. What is more, we can do this uniformly in virtue of the isomorphism of grammar. Nothing proves the validity of this universal notion of coherence better than the evidence of linguistic change. The drift of a language involves the actualization of patterns that are coherent in just this sense and the rejection of those that are not (Andersen 1980: 203 and 1990: 13ff.).

Rules are more than mere generalized formulas of patterns when they embody specifications of coherence between linguistic elements, namely, cohesions between units and contexts. This criterion of rule coherence remains true and valid but practically vague without the necessary involvement of markedness because it is markedness that provides the explicit means of expressing coherence.

While there may be several goals of language change, I wish to argue (anew) that the overarching telos of linguistic change is the establishment of a pattern—not just any pattern but specifically the semeiotic kind Peirce called a 'diagram'.[7] Since diagrams are panchronic signs, it is not surprising that they subtend both linguistic synchrony and linguistic diachrony. Diagrammatization can be seen as one species of the process by which unconformities in language are reduced or eliminated over time. These dynamic tendencies can be couched in Coseriu's terms: system is brought into conformity with type, while norms are brought into conformity with system.

Diagrams and diagrammatization in language are states, resp. processes, whereby relations mirror relations, as between form and content (isomorphism) or between form and form (automorphism). They are states in synchrony and real tendencies in diachrony. As a corollary, I am claiming that all language states are the cumulative results of preceding states (ontogeny recapitulating phylogeny?). Moreover, there is no telos in language 'beyond' diagrammatization: (1) conformity to a pattern is diagrammatic in itself; and (2) language conforms to nature by diagrammatizing content in form. (These two positions effectively put an end-stop to the Cratylistic debate.)

In expanding on these postulates, it will be useful first to outline some familiar types of diagrammatization in language history:

I. **Synaesthesia**: Phonological oppositions in their perceptual dimensions are associated with and diagram other perceptual dimensions.

II. **Onomatopoeia** and **Ideophones**: Similarities between phonological perceptual dimensions and other experiential dimensions can be utilized to form iconic lexical signs.

III. **Word Affinities**: Direct association between phonological signs and lexical content is effected through diagrammatization of partial identity between signifiers and signifieds.

IV. **Morphophonemic Alternations**: Diagrams involve indexing signifiers and/or signifieds of contiguous morphemes; or suprasegmentals (prosody).

Here are some examples of the fourth category, drawn from languages of which I am a native/near-native speaker.

1. Morphophonemics of composition (compounds), incl. prosody:

Russian

	króv̱'	'blood'	krov̱-o-podt'ók	'bruise'
			krov̱-o-smeßénie	'incest'
			krov̱-o-Ωádnij	'bloodthirsty'
cf.	grúḏ'	'chest'	gruḏ-o-br'úßnij	'thoraco-abdominal'
	kúdṟ'i	'tresses'	çern-o-kúdṟij	'black-tressed'
	bróv̱'	'eyebrow'	gust-o-bróv̱ij	'beetle-browed'

Japanese

fúufu + ḵenka	fuufugénka	'husband & wife + fight' / 'family quarrel'	
ánpo + jooyaku	anpojóoyaku	'security + treaty'	'security pact'
mé + ṯátu	meḏátu	'eye(s) + stand'	'stand out'

		VERBAL	NOMINAL
English		rént a cár	rént-a-càr
		fíll ín	fíll-in
	cf.	frequént	fréquent
		envélop	énvelope
		rejéct	réject

In the case of the Russian compound adjectives, the constituent with a palatalized (= marked) stem-final segment in its uncompounded form appears in the compound with a non-palatalized (= unmarked) stem-final segment. I interpret this as an unmarking. The unmarked alternant is to be explained as a sign of the subordination of both constituents to the marked compound; hence the compound appears with reversed markedness values.

In the Japanese case, assuming (contrary to the standard treatment; see Shapiro 1974) that protensity is distinctive in Japanese rather than voicing, the tense (marked) stem-initial segment of the second constituent is replaced by its lax (unmarked) counterpart.[8]

English nominalization and verbalization are typically accompanied by a shift of stress. In the first case, the nominalized form retracts the stress to the initial—unmarked—syllable, mirroring the unmarked status of nominals vis-à-vis marked verbals. In the second case, stress shifts from the unmarked initial syllable of the nominal form to its rightmost neighbor, the marked syllable of the verbal form.

2. Formal vs. informal style (honorific language in Japanese):[9]

	INFORMAL	FORMAL	
Verb	yobu	o-yobi ni náru	'call'
Verbal noun	soodan suru	go-soodan ni náru	'consult'
Adjective	isogasíi	(o-)isogasikute irassyáru	'busy'
Adjectival noun	génki da	(o-)génki de irassyáru	'is well'
Precopular noun	byooki da	(go-)byooki de irassyáru	'is ill'
Noun	senséi da	senséi de irassyáru	'is a teacher'

The diagrammatization here is between the markedness values of grammatical complexity, on one hand, and stylistic level, on the other: in each example, marked grammatical complexity is coordinate with marked stylistic level.

4. Conclusion

Peirce understood a final cause as being a possibility—sometimes he said "idea," but that is not to be understood in a subjective sense as existing in some person's thought—that has a tendency to become actual, one way or another: "[E]very general idea has more or less power of working itself out into fact; some more so, some less so" (2.149).

It is in this sense that markedness must be viewed as a final cause in linguistic change.[10] When the question of causation is posed in terms of efficient and final causes—and teleological processes distinguished from finious—then the claim that, rather than markedness principles, it is "perceptual factors and processing strategies [that] may influence the development of linguistic structures" will be seen for what it is—a category mistake.

This mistake results from the apriorism that underlies how contemporary linguists commonly understand markedness (e.g., in Optimality Theory, but not only). On this view, markedness is simultaneously conflated with and pitted against notions like 'sentence processing' or 'perceptual strategies', as if markedness were an efficient cause, i.e., categorically of a piece with the latter. Lending support to skepticism regarding the relevance of markedness (and emanating directly from what I would now call the Apriorism Fallacy) is the perceived difficulty of assigning universal or immutable markedness values, even though markedness is invariably context-sensitive and dependent on the existence of choice between variants.

The question Why? as applied to linguistic change does not have a homogeneous answer. The problem of assigning markedness values is not solely the burden of linguists; it falls on language users, as well. Linguistic data always contain the germ of ambiguity, of differing interpretations, and it is only by trial and error that the finious process of reaching a definitive markedness assignment proceeds. This process is necessarily always historical and not given a priori because at any given time linguistic habits, like all other habits, have a structure, and this structure is always *in statu nascendi*. But the important thing is that *an assignment will be reached*.

Language users do not need to wait for linguists to decide what is marked and what unmarked in order to be influenced by markedness considerations in making innovations and (tacitly) agreeing that some innovations qualify for the (social) status of full-fledged changes: they do it willy-nilly because they are impelled to by the power of the idea. Or as Peirce put it: "[I]t is the idea that will create its defenders and render them powerful" (1.217).

Brown University

Notes

1. In this résumé, I follow T.L. Short's interpretation of Peirce's semeiotic, as set forth in numerous publications, e.g., (most recently) Short MS. See also the concise characterization of the flaws of Saussure's semiology by comparison with Peirce's semeiotic set out in Short 1996: 511–12.
2. Conceptual change is the end-directed evolution of the rules of interpretation of symbols, sometimes with concomitant changes in the symbols themselves. Conceptual change then determines linguistic change, but in general this is not necessary to linguistic change.
3. Notice that when we say things just for the sake of saying them, then legisigns may be truly final causes. But we need to distinguish three cases. The availability of certain meanings (= rules of interpretation of symbols) might intrigue me: so I want simply to express those ideas. Or it might be the legisigns themselves that intrigue me: poets (like the Russian futurist Mayakovsky)

and composers (like Mozart) are said to be fond of repeating certain (nonsense/foreign-language) words simply for the sake of their sound rather than their sense. Or it might be the truth we wish to state for *its* own sake, and in that case the final cause is the *agreement* of certain legisigns with an independent reality. In any case, replication of legisigns can be an end in itself, and in that case the legisigns are essential to one's ultimate purpose in speaking. That is to say, we would have a different purpose or none at all if we did not have those legisigns.
4. Perhaps especially by linguists—like Lass (1997) and Labov (1994); see Short 1999 for a demolition of the former's anti-teleological stance. As for the latter, his "Plan of the Work as a Whole," set out on the book's very first page, already betrays a fundamental misunderstanding of causation: it presents the organization of a projected three volumes into (respectively) "Internal factors," "Social factors," and "Cognitive factors—as if these "factors" were categorically distinct from each other (they are, of course, all "internal").
5. Citations in this form (volume and paragraph separated by a dot) are to Peirce's *Collected Papers*.
6. With respect to the deliberate conduct of human beings, the principle of selection is a type of outcome they have in mind and which they consciously apply in choosing among the alternatives available to them. In other words, what we have in this case is purposefulness. Since an analysis of purpose would take us even farther afield, I refer the reader to the admirably clear exposé in Short 1999.
7. Here I part company with Short 1999.
8. Here is a literary parallel from Italian. In Giorgio Bassani's *Gli occhiali d'oro* (from his *Storie ferraresi*) the very name of the hero, Dr. Fadigati, connoting *(af)faticat(i)* 'tired', evokes an age-old tiredness, a lurking familiarity with the perennial 'question' to be faced atemporally by homosexuals vis-à-vis heterosexuals, and in Bassani's analogy, by Jews vis-à-vis non-Jews in a Fascist society. Fadigati's name otherwise contains his fate: the lenition of the consonants *t* and *c* (*k*) to *d* and *g* shows an unmarking (as regards Standard Italian) that corresponds to or diagrams the gradual unmarking of his personality and the disintegration of his being. [NB: In a language like Italian, with phonemic tenseness in the system of obstruents, tense consonants are marked and lax consonants unmarked.] I am indebted for this example to my wife, Marianne Shapiro.
9. The acute designates high pitch.
10. In the event, I understand Andersen's conception of markedness to be compatible with this view. For a discussion of final and efficient causes in linguistic change that takes part-whole relations into account, see Shapiro 1991: 16ff.

Works Cited

Andersen, Henning. 1978. "Vocalic and consonantal languages." In *Studia Linguistica A. V. Issatschenko oblata*, ed. H. Birnbaum et al., 1–12. Lisse: Peter de Ridder Press.

———. 1980. "[Summarizing Discussion:] Introduction." In *Typology and Genetics of Language*, ed. T. Thrane et al., 197–210. Travaux du Cercle Linguistique de Copenhague, 20. Copenhagen: Linguistic Circle of Copenhagen.

———. 1990. "The structure of drift." In *Historical Linguistics 1987*, ed. H. Andersen and K. Koerner, 1–20. Amsterdam: John Benjamins.
———. 1991. "On the projection of equivalence relations into syntagms." In *New Vistas in Grammar: Invariance and Variation*, ed. L. R. Waugh and S. Rudy, 287–311. Current Issues in Linguistic Theory, 49. Amsterdam: John Benjamins.
Anttila, Raimo. 1988. *Historical and Comparative Linguistics*. Current Issues in Linguistic Theory, 6. Amsterdam: John Benjamins.
Itkonen, Esa. 1982. "Short-term and long-term teleology in linguistic change." In *Papers from the 3rd International Conference on Historical Linguistics*, ed. J. P. Maher et al., 85–118. Amsterdam: John Benjamins.
Keller, Rudi. 1985. "Towards a theory of linguistic change." In *Linguistic Dynamics: Discourses, Procedures and Evolution*, ed. T. Ballmer, 211–37. Berlin: Walter de Gruyter.
Labov, William. 1994. *Principles of Linguistic Change*. Vol. 1: *Internal Factors*. Oxford: Blackwell.
Lass, Roger. 1997. *Historical Linguistics and Language Change*. Cambridge: Cambridge University Press.
Malkiel, Yakov. 1981. "Drift, slope, and slant: Background of, and variation upon, a Sapirian Theme." *Language* 57: 535–70.
Meillet, Antoine. 1921. *Linguistique historique et linguistique générale*. Vol. 1. Paris: Champion.
———. 1938. *Linguistique historique et linguistique générale*. Vol. 2. Paris: Klincksieck.
Peirce, Charles Sanders. 1965–66, *Collected Papers*. Vols. 1–8, 2nd printing. Edited by C. Hartshorne et al. Cambridge, Mass.: Harvard University Press.
Sapir, Edward. 1921a. *Language: An Introduction to the Study of Speech*. New York: Harcourt, Brace and World.
———. 1921b. "Writing as history and as style." *The Freeman* 3: 68–69.
———. 1927. "The unconscious patterning of behavior in society." In *The Unconscious: A Symposium*, ed. E. Dummer, 114–42. New York: Knopf.
———. 1931. "Fashion." *Encyclopaedia of the Social Sciences*. Vol. 6, 139–44. New York: Macmillan.
———. 1933. "Language." *Encyclopaedia of the Social Sciences*. Vol. 9, 155–69. New York: Knopf.
———. 1949. *Selected Writings*. Edited by D. Mandelbaum. Berkeley: University of California Press.
Shapiro, Michael. 1974. "Tenues and mediae in Japanese: A reinterpretation." *Lingua* 33: 101–14.
———. 1983. *The Sense of Grammar: Language as Semeiotic*. Bloomington: Indiana University Press.
———. 1991. *The Sense of Change: Language as History*. Bloomington: Indiana University Press.
Short, T.L. 1989. "Why we prefer Peirce to Saussure." In *Semiotics 1988*, ed. T. Prewitt et al., 124–30. Lanham, Md.: University Press of America.
———. 1996. "Interpreting Peirce's interpretant: A response to Lalor, Liszka, and Meyers." *Transactions of the Charles S. Peirce Society* 32: 488–541.
———. 1999. "Teleology and linguistic change." *The Peirce Seminar Papers* 4: 111–58.

Tony Jappy

Indication, Iconicity, Grammaticalization, and the Categories

0. Introduction

In 1937, William Edward Collinson, a professor of German at the University of Liverpool, and Alice V. Morris, wife of a one-time U.S. ambassador to Brussels, founder members of the association for the promotion of the artificial international language Interlingua, jointly published a *Language* monograph entitled *Indication: A Study of Demonstratives, Articles and Other 'Indicaters'* (Collinson 1937), with Collinson as author and Morris as 'editor'. Over and above its intrinsic merits as an exhaustive early discussion of a subject that has stimulated much subsequent research, the text is of interest for at least three further reasons.

Firstly, it takes up and considerably extends the list of indices and subindices discussed briefly by Peirce in paragraphs 2.283–291 of the *Collected Papers*. Secondly, although the book's index contains numerous references to authorities on the subject, for example the lexicographer Roget and the philosopher Bertrand Russell, it makes no reference to Peirce.[1] Finally, like Peirce's, the list of expressions studied, e.g., demonstratives, pronouns of various sorts, prepositions, etc., nearly all relate to the noun phrase. With the exception of one chapter, entitled "Indication applied to occurrents" (1937: 69–73), in which he investigates the relation between verb form and determiners, Collinson has little to say of the verb phrase, which suggests that his conceptions of the index are referent- or entity-oriented. Now it is clear, to use his rather ugly neologism, that 'indicaters' such as demonstratives relate at least as much to the speaker as to the entity denoted, not least because the speaker is a decisive contributor to the determination of the linguistic sign, and hence a vital constituent of an utterance's dynamic object.

Although not formulated in quite the same manner, this is basically the framework within which Roman Jakobson advanced his innovative ideas on shifters as forms of verbal indication in the 1950s (1971 [1957]: 130–47). But whereas Jakobson was primarily interested in shifters as cases of 'overlapping' where items of the code refer to the message, my concern here will be primarily with indication as a function of the relation between the speaker, the utterance and, above all, the medium. In view of this, then, the present highly speculative study will engage with the following:

- an investigation of verbal indication, namely, of certain features of the English verb phrase that reveal or indicate the speaker's personal implication in his utterance;
- an examination of the relation between indication and grammaticalization, the general assumption being that grammaticalized items are indices of various sorts;
- an assessment of the way that the categories—Secondness, in particular, as the category of existence and therefore of speech —contribute to our understanding of both indication and grammaticalization, most notably in determining how symbols can degenerate into indices, and how, conversely, icons cannot accrete to 'indexhood'.

1. Indices, Subindices, and Grammaticalization

Consider, to begin with, Collinson's definition of indication (1937: 17):

> Before we can deal with anything whether physically or mentally, we must detach it or at least distinguish it from the other things with which it is surrounded. A uniform background from which nothing emerges or is made to emerge, one in which no points or regions are distinguishable, cannot be treated except as a whole. Hence the first

condition of all thinking and judging is the emergence of some object or objects or regions from a whole situation and the separate presentment of this or that item within a given context.

The simplest and most universal form of communication is gesture and the simplest kind of gesture is the act of pointing. We use it before we have acquired speech and we fall back on it after we have lost the use of speech.

This constitutes a regression from the way Peirce had earlier defined the basic functor of such processes, the index. Nevertheless, Collinson draws attention to the importance of ostension in his definition, this being typically enacted by the index finger. Now, it is a truism that the pointing finger has an entity of some sort to which it directs attention at one end of it, but it is less often noted that it has a 'possessor' at the other. The act of pointing involves a relation between two relates, entity denoted and possessor, and operates for the benefit of a third, the addressee. At no point does Collinson consider the implications of this situation.

As a corrective to this rather conventional view of indication, consider now the distinction Peirce draws between indices, which are genuine, and subindices, or hyposemes, which are in some way degenerate. What distinguishes them, he states, is the fact that the former are individuals, whereas the latter, in spite of the fact that they enter a real relation ("actual connection") with their objects, are not. In paragraphs 2.283 and 2.284, and in a manner reminiscent of the famous division of the icon into the three 'subicons' (hypoicons)—image, diagram and metaphor—according to the nature of the Firstness of which they partake, Peirce defines and illustrates such genuine and degenerate indices, in this case, in terms of the type of Secondness of which these partake:

> 2.283. An *Index* or *Seme*†1 ({séma}) is a Representamen whose Representative character consists in its being an individual second. If the Secondness is an existential relation, the Index is *genuine*. If the Secondness is a reference, the Index is *degenerate*. A genuine Index and its Object must be existent individuals (whether things or facts), and its immediate Interpretant must be of the same character. But since every individual must have characters, it follows that a genuine Index may contain a Firstness, and so an Icon as a constituent part of it. Any individual is a degenerate Index of its own characters.
>
> 2.284. *Subindices* or *Hyposemes* are signs which are rendered such principally by an actual connection with their objects. Thus a proper name, personal demonstrative, or relative pronoun or the letter attached to a

diagram, denotes what it does owing to a real connection with its object but none of these is an Index, since it is not an individual.

Thus for Peirce, genuine indices could be illustrated by an airsock, a pointing finger, even the situation of utterance, "the environment of the interlocutors" (*CP* 2.330), while the demonstratives, etc., are defined as subindices, whose common function is to supply "such indexical directions of what to do to find the object meant" (*CP* 2.284). The list Peirce gives is short but quite comprehensive—pronouns of various kinds, adverbs of place and time, prepositions and prepositional phrases—and Collinson's monograph very thoroughly discusses them all. Now, the important feature of such a division for linguistic purposes is that the classes of words Peirce advances concern, as mentioned earlier, entities denoted by noun phrases. Nevertheless, in a brief discussion of the acts of describing and referring, Peirce adds the following comment: "[W]hen [prepositional phrases] refer, as they do oftener than would be supposed, *to a situation relative to the observed, or assumed to be experientially known, place and attitude of the speaker relatively to that of the hearer*, then the indexical element is the dominant element" (*CP* 2.290, emphasis added). Thus, not only does he present us with a brief catalogue of reference-based indexical expressions, but, in explicitly acknowledging both ends of the finger, so to speak, with the pointing end identifying an entity and the possessor end constituting in some way an expression of the speaker, he also specifies an important dyadic characteristic of indication: "A possessive pronoun is two ways an index: first it indicates the possessor, and, second, it has a modification which syntactically carries the attention to the word denoting the thing possessed" (*CP* 2.287).[2]

For present purposes, the most significant feature of the extract from 2.290 is the reference to "attitude." In the case of the extended principle of indication that I am suggesting here, it will be more appropriate to speak of 'stance'. This is a term with a long history in rhetoric, the *ethos* of Aristotle, signifying the arguments by means of which the orator seeks to project his sincerity and honesty vis-à-vis the issue at hand and, concomitantly, to adapt to the communal character of his listeners—to identify with them, as the modern idiom would have it—generally to promote an atmosphere of confidence and trust. By 'stance' here, however, I mean a far more restricted concept, namely, a framework and a set of expressions by means of which the speaker can indicate his position or viewpoint with respect to the addressee, to the latter's speech and/or to the topic under discussion. It is my contention that such a function is performed not only by the indices mentioned by Peirce and discussed extensively by Collinson, but also by the various types of auxiliary, periphrastic or otherwise, to be found in the English verb phrase. For a neutral but far-ranging description of the phenomenon, consider this extract from Biber et al. (1999: 966):

> In addition to communicating propositional content, speakers and writers commonly express personal feelings, attitudes, value judgments, or assessments; that is, they express a 'stance'.... Stance meanings can be expressed in many ways, including **grammatical** devices, word choice and **paralinguistic** devices. To some extent, personal stance can be conveyed through paralinguistic devices such as loudness, pitch, and duration, as well as non-linguistic devices such as body position and gestures. Such expression of stance is not linguistically explicit, and as a result it can be unclear just what attitudes or feelings a speaker is intending to convey. Further, in writing there are few non-linguistic or paralinguistic devices available for the expression of stance.... For these reasons, both speakers and writers commonly express stance meanings overtly, using either grammatical or lexical means.

Among the expressions of stance cited by these authors is one example of the sort of linguistic forms I am interested in, namely, the epistemic modals (ibid.: 972–75). And what is true of these modals is equally true, I maintain, of the other auxiliaries. In short, I am suggesting that certain expressions of stance are, in addition to the lexical devices described by Biber and his colleagues, indexical: certain grammatical expressions of stance are a form of indication.

Consider at this point the concept of grammaticalization. This is generally defined as the way languages derive new grammatical material from established lexical sources (Hopper and Traugott 1993: xv). In other words, it is one of the processes involved in language change, and has given rise to a vast literature, in which, incidentally, certain authors prefer the term 'grammaticization' in order to avoid confusion with a stage in the ontogenetic process of acquiring one's mother tongue (cf. Hopper and Traugott 1993: xvi, for a discussion). Obviously, it would be beyond the scope of the present article to review the field, but, in order to prepare the ground for the case studies to come, I should like to illustrate briefly the broader concept.

Consider, for example, the following utterances:

(1) *Hunting with hounds always procures a strong feeling of revulsion*

(2) *Hunting with the hounds, Mary experienced a strong feeling of revulsion*

(3) *Mary was hunting with the hounds when she experienced a strong feeling of revulsion*

The *be* + *ing* 'progressive' auxiliary form illustrated by (3) is an interesting—because unresolved—case of grammaticalization. Denison (1993: 397–412) reviews a number of theories of the origin of the progressive form, some of which are 'polygenetic', i.e., claim that the form is the product not of a single source but the coalescence of several including the gerundive and participial forms illustrated by (1) and (2). If we are to believe Jespersen (1969 [1933]: 263), for example, the form was originally gerundive in nature, and, since prepositions always govern nominals in English, he claims that it derived originally from an expression such as *The king was on hunting* or (1a) below, in which the preposition *on* meant something like 'in the middle of' (cf. the following expressions in PDE: *on holiday, on the prowl, on a binge, on the game*, etc.) rather than the more punctual meaning it has today, and in which *be* (from OE *beon/wesan*) had, in addition to the expression of identity, a locative meaning similar to that of contemporary Spanish *estar*. The form is thought subsequently to have reduced to *I was a-hunting* through phonetic attrition of the preposition until finally the proclitic *a-* was dropped altogether, leaving the modern expression of imperfective aspect illustrated by (3) above.

However, two other possible sources are *be* plus the present participle with adjectival force, and *be* plus an appositive participial phrase. These are illustrated respectively by (2a) and (2b).[3]

(1a) *ac gyrstandæg ic wæs on huntunge*
but yesterday I was at/in the middle of hunting

(2a) *he is feohtende* = he is fighting

(2b) *he wæs on temple lærende his discipulas*
He was in the temple, teaching his disciples
Compare PDE: *She was in the kitchen, making a cup of tea*
And *She was making a cup of tea in the kitchen*

What makes the polygenetic thesis plausible is the fact that the gerundive ending -*ung(e)* and the participial ending -*ende* both reduced to -*ing* in the Middle English period, in other words, coalesced, rendering identification difficult and a straightforward theory of the development of the PDE form a matter of speculation. What we do know is that, whatever its origin and subsequent development, the *be* + *ing* form had become fully grammaticalized by the end of the eighteenth century (Denison 1993: 407).

This returns us to the problem of indication. Just what, it might be asked, has the use of imperfective aspect come thus to indicate? Obviously, unlike the demonstrative *that*, for example, the *be* + *ing* auxiliary cannot 'identify' or denote a process, even less an entity. But if we consider the definition of aspect as the representation by the speaker of the degree of completion of a process *with respect to some reference point*, then it becomes clear that *be* + *ing* is the expression of a viewpoint adopted or 'constructed' by the speaker (the need for a reference point is obvious, since nothing could be measured without one). And choosing a reference point and using it to focus, in the case of *be* + *ing*, the post-inception phase of the process represented by the verb must surely be seen as one realization of stance as defined above. Another important feature of this type of stance indication, namely, presupposition of the speaker's prior knowledge of an event, is illustrated by the following:[4]

(4) *If you're coming tomorrow, I'll get in some beer* (as opposed, for example, to *If you come tomorrow, I'll get in some beer*)

(5) *I won't be able to watch* Loft Story *tonight—I'm dining in town with my wife*

2. Methodological Considerations

Support for the observations to follow will draw on what, for most semioticians, would be considered a most improbable source: corpus linguistics. Given the qualitative nature of semiotics—a theory of reasoning and the cognitive processes in general—it might at first sight seem irrelevant to adduce quantitative data in defense of a theoretical claim. To take a simple example, it is not the wealth of data in Collinson's monograph that determines what indication is, but rather the definition given by Peirce, who arrived at it by working precisely from first principles within his semiotic model.

Furthermore, the kind of macroscopic linguistic analysis characteristic of corpus linguistics in no way obviates the close attention to detail that is the strength of traditional microscopic investigations: without these, there would be no way of knowing the purpose to which a given expression may be put or of discovering its range of meanings. Nor is it the sheer weight of the evidence offered by corpus linguistics that is relevant in this case. The use of large bodies of data is, of course, not new: at the beginning of the century, in his seven-volume *Modern English Grammar on Historical Principles* (1909–49), Otto Jespersen provided a voluminous bibliography of the sources he quotes from (the first volume of part II *Syntax:* xiii–xxvii). Unfortunately, close inspection reveals them to be 'monotype'—they are virtually all imaginative texts, e.g., works of fiction or plays—and any examples of conversation or dialogue, such as they are, are perforce scripted, and consequently not natural.

However, what corpora, especially modern electronic corpora containing components of the spoken language, can uniquely provide is reliable information concerning the distribution of linguistic forms. The corpora available today not only present a wide variety of written registers other than fiction, but also provide transcriptions of oral data of varying degrees of spontaneity, and while no corpus could ever claim to be exhaustive or fully representative of the features of a language such as English, this variety, as will be seen below, yields important information concerning the distribution of the linguistic forms I shall be examining. In short, where traditional research was restricted to quasi-idealized discussions of the functions performed by a given linguistic form—imperfective aspect in English, for example—it is now possible to specify whether the form in question is a written or an oral phenomenon. In what follows, therefore, I shall be drawing on information obtained from my own research across two particular genre categories of the 100-million-word World Edition of the British National Corpus (BNC).

First published in 1995, the BNC contains approximately 90 million words of written texts, which, following the conventions first established in the Brown corpus, are divided into two major categories: imaginative prose (e.g., fiction, poetry, etc.), and informative texts (written expository discourse), of which there are eight subcategories amounting to approximately 70 million words. The oral component comprises two main types of speech: context governed and demographic. The first is made up of transcriptions of scripted speech—news bulletins, documentaries, films for television, etc.—while the second, amounting to approximately 4.2 million words, contains the transcriptions of spontaneous conversations recorded by means of the hidden microphone technique. Over and above the intrinsic interest for the linguist of such data, the speakers are classified by age, sex, social class, and the region where the recordings were made, whence the label 'demographic'. The oral texts have additionally been classified according to interaction type—whether monologues or dialogues. Naturally, all the texts of spontaneous speech are dialogues, while some of the context-governed recordings are monologues. All of this information is available in the header associated with each text, thereby providing the researcher with a valuable breakdown of the circumstances surrounding the linguistic activities that it records.

In the work reported below I have restricted the searches to what I consider to be the two 'polar' categories, i.e., those that correspond most closely to their respective situations of production. First are the informative written texts, since any dialogue to be found in them is incidental and probably reported, whereas it is an organic and therefore major constituent of the fiction genre of the imaginative component. Second are the oral demographic texts, since these, unlike their context-governed counterparts, are comparatively free from constraint, and any 'noise' from the situation of utterance is most likely to be at its lowest.

3. Case Studies

3.1 gonna

The first study concerns the English semi-auxiliary *going to* and its companion form *gonna*, textbook cases of grammaticalization (cf. Traugott 1993; Hopper and Traugott 1993) for the evolution of which we now have very plausible accounts. As an introduction to the wider problem, consider the following remarks by Biber et al. (1999: 488–90):

> It is not surprising that the most recently developed semi-modals-(*had*) *better* and (*have*) *got to*-are common in conversation, but virtually non-existent in written exposition. Interestingly, BrE has been more innovative recently in the use of semi-modals than AmE. While the older semi-modal forms, such as *have to* and *be going to* are considerably more common in AmE, the more recent semi-modals (*had*) *better* and

(*have*) *got to* (also transcribed *gotta*) are more common by far in BrE conversation.

> You **better** go. (conv)
> We**'ve got to** leave that till later on. (conv)
> I **gotta** read this. (conv)

The lower frequency of modals with obligation/necessity meanings probably has two sources. First, this relative rarity reflects a general tendency to avoid the face threatening force of expressions with an obligation meaning (cf. 6.6.4.2.). In addition, semi-modals have become better established in this semantic domain, apparently replacing the modal verbs to a greater extent. Six different semi-modal verbs are used to express obligation/necessity (including all semi-modals first attested after 1650).

It is already clear from this passage that there is a close relation between linguistic form and medium: the semi-auxiliaries (or "semi-modals" as Biber et al. call them) are far more frequent in spoken discourse than in writing. With this in mind, we turn to the examination of *going to* and *gonna*.

According to the *Oxford English Dictionary* (henceforth *OED*), entry 47b of the verb *go*, *going to* first came to function as a semi-auxiliary toward the end of the fifteenth century:

> **47.** Uses of the pr. pple. *going*.
>
> **b.** *going to* (with active or pass. inf.): on the way to, preparing or tending to. Now used as a more colloquial synonym of *about to*, in the auxiliaries of idiomatic compound tenses expressing immediate or near futurity. Cf. F. *je vais*. (***to be*) *just going to***: (to be) on the point of (doing so and so).
> **1482** *Monk of Evesham* (Arb.) 43 Thys onhappy sowle..was goyng to be broughtene into helle for the synne and onleful lustys of her body

In view of the (necessarily written) evidence, the more colloquial form *gonna*, on the other hand, would appear to be a more recent phenomenon:

> **gonna** ('gɒnə),
> colloq. (esp. U.S.) or vulgar pronunciation of *going to* (see go *v*. 47 b). [Cf. the earlier Sc. *ganna, gaunna*: see Eng. Dial. Dict. s.v. *Go*, quots. 1806, etc.]
> **1913** C. E. Mulford *Coming of Cassidy* ix. 149 Yo're gonna get a good lickin'.
> **1929** E. W. Springs *Above Bright Blue Sky* 136, 5684 has a busted cylinder. Gonna put a new motor in it.

1952 A. Baron *With Hope, Farewell* 56 Put 'em all in clover, that's what I'm gonna do.
1967 M. Shulman *Kill* 3 ii. iv. 81 I'm gonna keep on yelling tell you let me out.

The two forms can be analyzed as follows: *be* + *ing* with the pre-suppositional character very much in evidence in (4) and (5) above, signaling the speaker's awareness of some event or datum antecedently perceived or mentioned, or of some decision already taken; the lexical verb *go*, which, according to the *OED*, etymologically signified 'walk', as in 'go alone' meaning 'walk unsupported', or *walk*, as opposed to *run, creep, fly*, etc., an evolution paralleled by French *aller*, from Latin *ambulare*, 'walk'.

According to Bybee and Dahl (1989: 91), *be going to* first began to express futurity when it was used with purposive, directional constructions with a non-finite complement, as in (8) below, expressing the idea of 'movement toward a goal', or 'some agent is on a path toward a goal', i.e., has already been seen setting out toward the goal. Compare

(6) *I'm going to London* [*to visit the Queen*]

(7) *I'm going there* [*to visit the Queen*]

in which the locatives *to London* and *there* are present, with (8), which has no locative, and where the preposition *to* is consequently interpreted as a sign of purpose:

(8) stage 1 *I'm going* [*to visit the Queen*]

Subsequently, the expression was reanalyzed as a semi-auxiliary, as indicated by the brackets, with the preposition *to* 'demoted', so to speak, to an enclitic with *going* as its host:

(9) stage 2 [*I'm going to*] *visit the Queen*

This evolution was deemed complete when the purpose involved not only dynamic processes, such as *visit the Queen*, but also stative ones not involving directionality, such as *like the Queen*:

(10) stage 3 [*I'm going to*] *like the Queen*

The final stage, according to most descriptions (cf. Hopper and Traugott 1993 for a more comprehensive discussion), is assumed to have occurred when the auxiliary function came to be signaled by the phonetically impoverished form *gonna*, in which the morpheme *going* and the enclitic *to* have become fused into a new, opaque form that coexists with the more formal *going to*.

As seen in the *OED* entry, the first attested written form is an extract from a Hopalong Cassidy novel, although occurrences of *ganna* and *gaunna* have been found in early-nineteenth-century Scottish texts. To my mind, the presentation of the evolution of the semi-auxiliary as given above is problematic in that, like the *OED* entry, it suggests, or at least gives the impression, that *gonna* is the more recent, American form, and that the 'full form' *going to* in its semi-auxiliary function is somehow earlier. We return to this point below.

The exact meaning of the expression is the subject of much debate, surely a sign of our difficulty in pinpointing the expressive nature of stance indices, but most authorities agree that *going to* has come now to express a complex type of future reference or orientation.[5] It is also the case that in a given situation *going to* can have an inferential value (*Look at those clouds, it's going to rain*), whereas in cases not oriented toward some future situation, the expression reports a decision already taken that the speaker knows of but which the addressee is assumed to be ignorant of as with examples (4) and (5) above—in other words *going to/gonna*, too, can express speaker presupposition. The most important feature of the evolution of *be going to* seems to have been the shift of viewpoint from the agent in the original verb-of-motion case, e.g., utterances (6) and (7) above, where the purpose complement obviously concerns the agent of the movement, to the expression by the semi-auxiliary of the viewpoint of the speaker. This process, known as subjectification (Langacker 1991: 330–33; but cf. Traugott 1995, for a conflicting and perhaps intuitively more convincing view of the problem), is the expression of the subjectivity of the speaker rather than that of the agent of the verb, and seems to have been responsible for the evolution of the entire English auxiliary system, most notably in the case of the epistemic modals.

Table 1 presents the data concerning the distribution of *gonna* and *going to* together with the three forms of the modal *will* (*will*, *'ll* and *won't*) across the two categories of the BNC described above: raw totals first, followed by the frequencies normalized to occurrences per 1000 words. If we allow for the fact that no attempt was made to weed out cases where the expression *going to* occurred as part of the lexical verb (spot checks showed a rate of

TABLE 1 Distribution of *Going to*, *Gonna*, and *Will* across Two Registers

	Tokens	going to	per 1000	gonna	per 1000	will	per 1000
Demographic	4,206,058	4,898	1.2	8,071	1.9	30,995	7.4
Informative	70,900,479	10,725	0.2	231	0.003	221,248	3.1

about 5 percent, but this is not a reliable figure), these data obviously tally with the statements by Biber et al. quoted above. The semi-auxiliary is relatively infrequent in comparison with the modal *will*, in British English at least. Nevertheless, it is many times more frequent in the demographic component than in the informative; as for *gonna*, it is all but non-existent in written discourse, and far more common than its more formal alternative *going to* in the oral component. Finally, although more frequent than the other two forms, the difference between the written and spoken scores for *will*, it should be noticed, is much smaller, showing just how marked *going to* and *gonna* are in the written language. In view of the descriptions of these forms given by the *OED*, there are a number of related issues that require discussion.

Firstly, to what extent can *gonna* be considered a later evolution, indeed an Americanism, as the editors of the *OED* deem possible? The answer to this obviously depends crucially upon timing. We note that the first attested occurrence of the form is given in the oft-quoted extract from the *Monk of Evesham* (and contains the *be + ing* form mentioned above). Now this dates back some century and a quarter before the first permanent settlements at Jamestown. If *gonna* is simply an Americanism, then the phonetic attrition of the enclitic *to* would have had to have occurred after that date. If we refer to descriptions of the evolution of the semi-auxiliary given in the literature, *gonna* is always represented, as in (6) to (10) above, as the most recent stage in the process, and it is difficult not to interpret this diachronically as the most recent stage, too. However, in view of the phonetic instability that has always been a characteristic of the auxiliary function in English, this seems highly improbable, and the two Scottish reduced forms are proof that representations of this phonetic attrition predate the 1913 cowboy novel by over a century. It seems reasonable to suppose, therefore, that the early settlers took some form of reduced pronunciation of *going to* to America with them, for how else would they have signaled the semi-auxiliary function?

Secondly, is *gonna* a case where phonetic reduction threatens to bring about the ultimate disappearance of the auxiliary? This is, of course, possible, but as shown by two of the examples given by Biber et al. in the second extract quoted above, it is the *be* and *have* tense-supporting forms that are the more unstable (e.g., *You better go*, *I gotta read this*). If it is possible to project future developments at all, it is surely *gonna*, the stance marker, which will remain, since it alone permits stance distinctions, while the tense-supporting elements of this and the other semi-auxiliaries are susceptible to omission or deletion as a consequence of their superfluity: such is the nature of the medium and hence the situation of utterance that such deictic elements as present tense markers are surely not strictly necessary.

Finally, from a semiotic point of view, the case of *going to/gonna* is of considerable interest in that in addition to a full lexical form, a symbol whose meaning has to be learned, we also have a derived indexical expression: while the lexical verb continues to function as a genuine symbol, *go* has also undergone a process of categorial degenerescence, evolving from the category of Thirdness to a form intimately associated with that of Secondness, the category of existence. In other words, while continuing to be legisigns dependent upon law and convention but independent of any particular situation, and whose meanings have to be learned, the derived forms *going to/gonna* signal a new, degenerate function that depends entirely upon the existential character of the situation of utterance. This degenerescence has resulted concomitantly in a broadening of the extension of the original lexical verb—for *go* is now the superordinate of all English verbs of motion—and a narrowing of its intension, an instance of semantic bleaching.

As table 1 clearly shows, the use of the indexical expression is largely confined to spoken discourse, as is the case with most, if not all, of the emerging periphrastic auxiliary forms. With respect to this point, it is generally argued that written language is more conservative, no doubt as a result of printing conventions and the formality norms that attend written discourse generally. For this reason, informal *going to/gonna* are deemed incompatible with written registers. Nevertheless, another explanation for the rarity of semi-auxiliaries in writing is that relations to the speech act itself, to the addressee, and to what one is talking about are essentially deictic and expressive. Given the circumstances in which the activity of informative writing is pursued, the use of such deictic relations is inappropriate and, indeed, generally inaccessible. It is only in the existential 'crucible' of the speech act that indication can find a medium, and such indications and stance indications as are necessary are performed by means of deictics—both nominal and verbal.

3.2 that

We turn now to a discussion of demonstratives. What makes these important is that they call into question one of the basic tenets of grammaticalization theory, namely, the condition that new grammatical material should emerge along prescribed grammaticalization channels from necessarily pre-existent *lexical* material. Such a condition, we shall see, is highly problematic from a semiotic point of view.

Consider, to begin with, the following extract from oral demographic text KCE, in which two teenage girls are talking about a third. Successive portions of speech in brackets indicate turns that coincide and are therefore difficult to transcribe; <1> and <2>, for example, identify the two speakers, while text between the delimiters <...> and </> represents some particular paralinguistic feature. The complete text constitutes some five hours and forty-eight minutes of recorded conversation, while the transcription occupies 368 pages in a Word file.

<2> No I don't hate her she just annoys me badly!
<1> [<laughing>That's all!</>]
<2> [She made] ... she made Heather a birthday cake the other day ... and I, I've got say actually this cake was pretty good ... but like, she had to take it to school!... I mean, the girl is sad! If you're gonna take a birthday cake to school ... I mean, that is sad isn't it?
<1> My brain's <laughing> just died</>!
<2> But that is very very sad! But like er, she took it sch= to school ... and Scott was giving us a lift to school ... so she didn't have to walk ... and she's in the car and she's going if this gets ... if this gets all smashed up Scott I hope you realise I'm blaming you! And she was serious! I was thinking
<1> I would've turned round and ge= [get out]
<2> [I did]
<1> get out the fucking car! [<nv>laugh</nv>]
<2> [I sa=, I said ... I just went] ... I just said to her look ... Hannah you don't have to come in the car! And like, I said it jokingly but wi= [with]
<1> [Mm.]

```
<2> with that sort of hint
<1> <laughing>with that sort of </> ... with that sort of ... I'm
    dying to stick this knife [<laughing>in your back</>]
<2> [<nv>laugh</nv>] Yeah
<1> Oh!
<2> Oh, did you see Inspector Morse last night?
<1> No I saw the very end bit.
<2> Did you see the ... where's she ... where that girl stabbed er ...
    her ... what was that girl in? I was sat there, me and my dad
    going, <laughing>what has she been in</>?
<1> She was in erm
<2> Got a really irritating voice hasn't she?
<1> You know where there was that ... there was the young girl ...
    and there was the old wo=, oldish woman who was supposed to
    be a film star or something?
<2> Oh yeah! That thing where erm ... she, she worked for him
    [didn't she]
<1> [Yeah.]
<2> she lived in that hotel.
<1> Mm.
<2> Oh yes, I remember ... [Oh that thing that was supposed to
    be funny]
<1> [It was crap wasn't it!]
```

The extract illustrates admirably the distribution of the English demonstratives *this* and *that*. There are 12 cases of *that* to four of *this*, a ratio that corresponds closely to the data provided by the entire BNC-World corpus, as table 2 indicates.

The so-called 'distal' form *that* is the infrequent and hence marked case in the informative texts, while its 'proximal' counterpart *this* is marked in the demographic. What is interesting is that *that* is 10 times more frequent in the oral component than in the written, whereas the difference between the respective frequencies for *this* in either component is barely significant. We infer from this that indication by means of the former is a more widespread and perhaps more fundamental characteristic of speech. Now, historically, pronominal *that* has given rise to a relative pronoun and a

TABLE 2 Distribution of *This* and *That* across Two Registers

	Tokens	this	per 1000	that	per 1000
Demographic	4,206,058	23,927	5.7	68,252	16.2
Informative	70,900,479	341,617	4.8	110,845	1.6

complementizer, while the English definite article evolved from its adnominal equivalent. Such is the importance of demonstratives generally that it has even been argued that they are the origin of gender systems (Greenberg 1978). Thus, given that it is *that* which has undergone polygrammaticalization in English, the distributions evidenced by table 2 suggest that the existential status of the speech act is once more the decisive factor (cf. Diessel 1999: chap. 6). With this in mind, what follows is a necessarily brief examination of the complex relation between distribution, function and the medium.

It has been suggested that in Old English the pronoun *that* carried definite reference, whereas *this* had an emphatic function (Millward 1996: 100; cf. also the OED entry for *this*, which shows how the form is a coalescence of the simple demonstrative *that* and the suffix *se, si* signifying 'see', 'behold'). The preponderance of adnominal (9) and pronominal (3) occurrences of *that* in the extract suggests a partial explanation for the enormous disparity in the scores for the two demonstratives across the BNC. We see that most cases of *that* are 'recognitional', i.e., occurrences where "the intended referent is to be identified via specific, shared knowledge rather than through situational clues or reference to preceding segments of the ongoing discourse" (Himmelmann 1996: 230). From the reference to Inspector Morse on, all occurrences of *that* are both adnominal (I am assuming that the case of *that* followed by an ellipsis eight lines from the end is adnominal) and recognitional. Moreover, the three occurrences in the first part of the text, two of which refer to alter's speech, are instances of discourse deixis (ibid.: 224–29). This distribution would account for the extreme rarity of *that* in the informative texts: reference to information shared with alter in the ongoing situation of utterance is generally unavailable to the writer of informative prose, as is the possibility of referring to alter's speech. In short, the recognitional and hence presuppositional function of *that* is logically restricted to situations in which participants can readily identify those with whom they presume shared knowledge.

On the other hand, the introductory and continuative functions of *this*, where the demonstrative signals a shift of entity or focus of attention to a new focus, or maintains an entity as focus of attention (cf. McCarthy 1994: 273), are entirely compatible with the 'situation of writing', so to speak. There are nevertheless two occurrences of *this* that are not available to the writer of informative prose (though they would be possible in fiction): on two occasions the speakers 'exit' from the current situation of utterance, or deictic center, to refer to a deictic center determined by their narrative, typical cases of *deixis am phantasma* (Bühler 1990) or 'deictic projection'. The first is when speaker <2> quotes Hannah's words to Scott in the car: "if this gets ... if this gets all smashed up Scott ..."; the second when speaker <1> says, "I'm dying to stick this knife...." In neither case does the referent of *this X* bear any relation to the general situation of utterance, and it would appear that this and the discourse-pragmatic recognitional function examined above are now overriding the traditional spatial distinctions to which each demonstrative owes its name, namely, proximal *this* supposedly referring to an entity close to the speaker, and distal *that*, to an entity close to alter.

From a semiotic point of view, we see that the evolution of *that* toward new grammatical material—new hyposemes, to use the Peircean expression—runs counter to that of *going to/gonna*: *that* is a presuppositional linguistic form rooted in the existential world which has not only persisted in its demonstrative function, but has also been the source of new indexical material. That there should be a certain degenerescence, bleaching even in the case of the new material involved in this evolution, seems normal, and the relatively degenerate status of the relative pronoun, the complementizer and the definite article with respect to the parent demonstrative *that* is signaled by an iconicity phenomenon: the first three are phonetically reduced while the demonstrative retains its strong, diagnostic form /ðæt/ at all times.

To return to the problem of grammaticalization, we note that in their discussion of the origin of *that* and of the Indo-European root *to-* from which it is derived (cf. too, Christophersen 1939), Hopper and Traugott (1993: 129) maintain that ultimately *to-* itself must have derived from some as yet unidentified lexical material: "Among the highly stable grammatical items with no known lexical origin is the Indo-European demonstrative *to-*. Given the unidirectionality hypothesis, we must hypothesize that *to-* originated in some currently unknown lexical item. We do not know at this stage what that item was. But neither do we know that there was none, or indeed that there might theoretically have been none. We must leave for future empirical study the question whether grammatical items can arise fully formed, and if so under what circumstances." From a semiotic point of view again, this hypothesis is untenable: there is no reason to suppose that such subindices as demonstratives should necessarily evolve from lexical items.

Indication is a basic, not a derived, semiotic function, and is rooted in an existential environment. There must have been hyposemes in semiosis from the start—hyposemes that occurred "fully formed," as Hopper and Traugott put it, both phylogenetically and ontogenetically. Were this not the case, we should have to posit some Adamic evolutionary stage in which people grunted nouns at one another until some inaugural moment when the indices finally emerged—a fanciful supposition, for we know that were no indexical expressions available, it would be impossible to specify what one was talking about and communication could never be initiated. Indeed, more spectacularly, there could be no situation of *utterance* in the first place.

Peirce's answer to this dilemma is to suggest that not all symbols are necessarily lexical in nature: "There are words, which, although symbols, act very much like indices. Such are personal, demonstrative, and relative pronouns, for which A, B, and C, etc., are substituted" (*EP2*: 307). In other words, while the linguist has to work with a distinction between lexical and grammatical, Peirce's definition of the sign accommodates a less constraining and reductionist view of the constituents of communicative activity, and while many if not all of the stance indicating expressions of English, such as *going to/gonna*, for example, are of lexical origin, there is no semiotic reason to extend the principle to every grammaticalized item. To be a symbol, a sign must be general, must function by convention, and needs to be learned. These are virtually the only conditions of symbolhood that are relevant to a discussion of indication and grammaticalization, and they apply to expressions other than the purely lexical material—e.g., nouns, adjectives, verbs, and adverbs—that seems to exercise the imagination of the grammarians. As it happens, Peirce suggests a more radical form of linguistic evolution in the same text, whereby many symbols can be shown to have evolved from indexical expressions: "A simple symbol is interpreted to signify what it does from some accidental circumstance or series of circumstances, which the history of any word illustrates" (ibid.: 317). The process of accidental generalization and, ultimately, the process by which symbols emerge can be seen in the origin and development of the English common noun *coach*, derived by metonymic association from the Magyar *Kocsi*: "For example, in the latter half of the fifteenth century, a certain model of vehicle came into use in the town of Kots (pronounced, *kotch*) in Hungary. It was copied in other towns, doubtless with some modifications, and was called a *kotsi szeker*, or Kots cart. Copied in still other towns, and always more or less modified, it came to be called, for short, a *cotch*. It thus came about that *coach* was used ... [for] any large vehicle for conveying passengers at a fare by the seat from one town to another" (ibid.).

3.3 Metaphor

Finally, there are aspects of linguistic and cognitive activity, often classified as figurative language, which do not grammaticalize in any known language, in other words, which are not marked formally, and to that extent are syntactically indistinguishable from their 'non-figurative' counterparts. One such case is metaphor. The reader will note immediately that as far as metaphor is concerned, there is no table of frequencies to be drawn from the BNC, for there is no reliable way of trawling through a corpus to find instances of it. This is because metaphor, from a Peircean point of view, is a property of utterances, not an overt grammatically or morpho-syntactically identified marker. In short, it is one of a number of features of language use which, as John Haiman puts it, "have never achieved ritual grammatical canonization" (1995: 329).

For example, if we compare the following:

(11) *Here in Venice, buses, taxis and cars are all boats*

(12) *Here in London, lawyers, bankers and insurers are all sharks*

we find that while (11) is a relatively straightforward descriptive statement, (12) is clearly a metaphorically informed, but highly underspecified, judgment.[6] To understand just how this should be, we need to review Peirce's theory of the icon and iconicity, his 'logic of the icon'.

By iconicity is meant the set of qualitative, and principally formal, properties inherited by signs from their dynamic objects. In a sentence, this might typically, but not exclusively, be word order; in a photograph, it is that disposition of color and form that enables the viewer to recognize the model. These qualitative, formal properties are not some random collection, but an organized hierarchy, the hypoicons, whose description is most conveniently undertaken with reference to the definitions. In his introduction to the concept, for example, Peirce offers the following informal account: "Any material image, as a painting, is largely conventional in its mode of representation; but in itself, without legend or label it may be called a hypoicon" (*CP* 2.276). Emphasizing the material qualities of the sign, Peirce is here assimilating the hypoicon to a painting without a caption: a sketch of Canet-Plage, for example, without the name beneath. However, after beguiling the reader by this rather straightforward account into thinking that the matter is a simple one, Peirce continues in the immediately following paragraph with the initially forbidding formulation that constitutes, to the best of our knowledge, the only full definition of the hypoicons, one in which he subjects the icon to the familiar categorial analysis: "Hypoicons may be roughly divided according to the mode of Firstness of which they partake. Those which partake of simple qualities, or First Firstnesses, are *images*; those which represent the relations, mainly dyadic, or so regarded, of the parts of one thing by analogous relations in their own parts, are *diagrams*; those which represent the representative character of a representamen by representing a parallelism in something else, are *metaphors*" (CP 2.277).

It is by means of this terse and uncompromising statement that Peirce scholars and linguists at large are invited to investigate the nature and function of the hypoicons. The paragraph records the deduction of the three possible formal configurations characterizing any (pictorial or linguistic) sign's representative quality, and as such constitutes an important theorem of iconicity theory: since at different removes both an index and a symbol involve some form of icon, it follows that both index and symbol will involve one or other of the three increasingly complex 'subiconic' configurations defined in paragraph 2.277.

We can take for granted a straightforward one-to-one relation between the nominals in (11) above and their respective referents, which, for the sake of argument we assume to be entities in the extralinguistic world. In (12), however, a parallelism is drawn between the violent, predatory behavior of sharks toward other animals on the one hand, and the equally predatory behavior of lawyers, bankers and insurers on the other, a situation we can represent schematically as a parallelism between two domains—a base domain that serves as a yardstick by means of which to describe a certain pattern of behavior, and the target domain we are trying to come to grips with. The formal relations involved are illustrated in figure 1.

In the figure, the mediate determination of the interpretant by the object is represented by the arrows. Within the object, the indices *shark* and *prey* represent respectively the sharks and the other animals of the base domain, for these constitute the experiential basis

Indication, Iconicity, Grammaticalization | 147

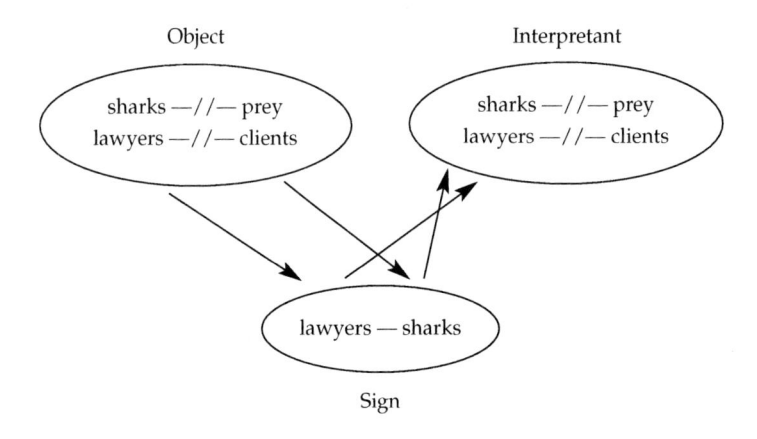

```
        Object                        Interpretant
   ⎛ sharks —//— prey ⎞         ⎛ sharks —//— prey ⎞
   ⎝ lawyers —//— clients ⎠     ⎝ lawyers —//— clients ⎠

                  ⎛ lawyers — sharks ⎞

                         Sign
```

FIGURE 1 The Hypoiconic Structure of Sentence (12)

of this particular judgment. In the target domain—the new area of experience we are attempting to integrate and judge—the index *lawyers* stands for the lawyers, bankers, and insurers, and *clients* their respective clients. We see, however, that the sign itself simply establishes an inclusive relation between the class of lawyers, etc., and the class of sharks, which it represents simply as (*lawyers — sharks*): there is no parallelism in its structure. The interpretant, however, reproduces the original parallelism in the object. This is meant to signify that if the judicative inference represented by utterance (12) has itself been correctly interpreted, in spite of the relative poverty of the information available, the original parallelism has been successfully reconstructed by the interpreter. In view of the underspecified nature of (12), and the fact that formally, i.e., morphologically or syntactically, it is no different from (11), it is patent that metaphor is not, and cannot be, grammaticalized.

As before, we find that this is a category problem, for iconicity theory deals exclusively with Firstnesses, as paragraph 2.277 clearly states. It is important to note that the inescapably existential medium in which the metaphorical utterance is communicated constrains the latter's structure, determining it to underrepresent an object informed by a two-tiered configuration far more complex than its own. As a consequence of this 'flattening' and linearizing influence of the existential medium, the parallelism in the object in figure 1 has been 'reduced' to a vectorial, dyadic structure in the sign. Moreover, none of the three hypoicons is eligible for promotion to the function of indication, since collectively they constitute the qualitative, non-existential and non-substantial aspects of linguistic expressions. More simply put, within iconicity theory they are defined as formal and immaterial phenomena, and as such are incapable of supporting reference. Nor is there any process of accretion by which they could ever attain to the existential status of an index.

4. Discussion and Conclusion

The three case studies have, in their different ways, illustrated how an existential medium such as that through which speech is 'transmitted' determines and indeed constrains the function of indication. It was seen that the conditions in which the semantics of a genuine symbol like the verb *go* are such as to make degenerescence to the status of stance indication possible, not only in English, but in other, non-Germanic languages as well; it was asserted, too, that irrespective of linguistic conventions, there is no semiotic reason why a subindex such as the demonstrative *that* should not have originated as such, while continuing to evolve phonetically and functionally, even providing new grammatical material; finally, in the case of metaphor, the existential character of both spoken and written 'channels' was observed to function as a phenomenological 'funnel' causing the formal complexity of the sign's object to be 'collapsed', so to speak, into a far simpler, essentially dyadic representation. Such is the categorial status of the medium that this characteristic underspecification of metaphorical signs can be correctly interpreted only by inference on the part of an experienced interpreter, for this much impoverished structure is indistinguishable from that of a diagrammatic sign such as (11) above, and consequently can never be indicated formally as metaphorical—proof that metaphor can neither grammaticalize nor attain to the function of indication. As all three cases studies show, indication as the expression of the speaker's point of view makes it possible to overcome the severe limitations imposed on certain legisigns by the medium: *be + ing, going to/gonna, that*, and even metaphorical form have a strong presuppositional potential that is absent from purely symbolic lexical items, and are able to suggest more than they appear to indicate.

The category of Secondness is thus crucial to the function of indication. It is the category of individuals, facts, contrasts, and oppositions, in which seconds are defined in relation to firsts. It is the only universe or medium in which ostension can operate, in which entities can be seen and separated from one another, in which relations to the speech act, to the addressee, and to what one is saying can be signaled and indeed expressed directly. More importantly, perhaps, such a restricting environment has brought about the emergence of term-level presupposition, the presumption of knowledge shared with one's addressee, a characteristic that appears to be shared by many grammaticalized items, and which seems unavailable to strictly lexical resources.

Secondness is also a defining characteristic of a medium in which error is possible, and without the possibility of error, misinterpretation, reanalysis, and evolution—as evidenced by such a simple lexical process as folk etymology, for example—would be impossible. Each speaker brings to the speech act his unique experience of the world and tries as best he can to make sense of what the other is saying. This suggests that language is an aggregate—indeed, a ragged aggregate—not an inviolable, perfect system waiting to be discovered by the diligent linguist, even less a pre-existent, universally shared whole that speakers carry around in their heads. It is surely an aggregate that each of us infers differentially from the imperfect data—as the extract from the BNC shows— to which we are perforce exposed. Given this situation, it is understandable that grammatically marked stance indication of the type discussed above should be volatile and constantly changing, while entity indication of the sort performed by the demonstratives should persist and endure: expression is variable, ostension, if it is to function correctly, must presumably be stable. In a universe other than the existential, neither would be possible.

University of Perpignan

Notes

1. This is not really surprising as the *Collected Papers* were just being published and were no doubt known only within philosophical circles. Note that following a longstanding tradition, references to the *Collected Papers* are by paragraph number, while *EP2* refers to the second volume of *The Essential Peirce*, edited by the Peirce Edition Project.
2. Which is not to deny the triadic nature of their function as signs, of course.
3. Examples (1a) from Dennison (1993: 387), and (2a) and (2b) from Traugott (1992: 188 and 190).
4. Cf. Wright (1995: 153–57) for a discussion of literary examples of this sort of usage.
5. Often referred to as the 'immediate future', though this is really a misnomer, since in the utterance *It appears that the sun is going to explode in 300 million years' time* the projected event is patently far from immediate.
6. For a discussion of the underspecified nature of metaphorical expressions and their relation to inference in general, see Jappy 2001.

Works Cited

Biber, Douglas, Stig Johansson, Geoffrey Leech, Susan Conrad, and Edward Finegan. 1999. *The Longman Grammar of Spoken and Written English*. London: Longman.
Bühler, Karl. 1990. *Theory of Language*. Trans. D. Goodwin. Amsterdam: Benjamins.
Bybee, Joan, and Östen Dahl. 1989. "The creation of tense and aspect systems in the languages of the world." *Studies in Language* 13 (1): 51–103.
Christophersen, Paul. 1939. *The Articles: A Study of Their Theory and Use in English*. Copenhagen: Munksgaard.
Collinson, William Edward. 1937. *Indication: A Study of Demonstratives, Articles and Other 'Indicaters'*. The Linguistic Society of America. Baltimore: Waverley Press.
Denison, David. 1993. *English Historical Syntax*. London: Longman.
Diessel, Holger. 1999. *Demonstratives: Form, Function and Grammaticalization*. Amsterdam: Benjamins.
Greenberg, Joseph. 1978. "How does a language acquire gender markers?" In *Universals of Human Language*, ed. J. Greenberg, 48–82. Stanford: Stanford University Press.
Haiman, John. 1995. "Moods and metamessages. Alienation as mood." In *Modality in Grammar and Discourse*, ed. Joan Bybee and Suzanne Fleischman, 329–45. Amsterdam: Benjamins.
Himmelmann, Nicholas. 1996. "Demonstratives in narrative discourse: A taxonomy of universal use." In *Studies in Anaphora*, ed. Barbara Fox, 205–54. Amsterdam: Benjamins.
Hopper, Paul, and Elizabeth Traugott. 1993. *Grammaticalization*. Cambridge: Cambridge University Press.

Jakobson, Roman. 1971 [1957]. "Shifters, verbal categories and the Russian verb." In R. Jakobson. *Selected Writings*. Vol. 2, 130–47. The Hague: Mouton.

Jappy, Tony. 2001. "Iconicity, hypoiconicity." *On-line Peirce Digital Encyclopedia*, http://www.digitalpeirce.org/jappy/hypjap.htm.

Jespersen, Otto. 1969 [1933]. *Essentials of English Grammar*. London: George Allen and Unwin.

———. 1909–49. *A Modern English Grammar on Historical Principles*. 7 vols. London: George Allen and Unwin.

Langacker, Ronald. 1991. *Concept, Image, and Symbol: The Cognitive Basis of Grammar*. Berlin and New York: Mouton de Gruyter.

McCarthy, Michael. 1994. "*It, this* and *that*." In *Advances in Written Text Analysis*, ed. M. Coulthard, 266–75. London: Routledge.

Millward, C.M. 1996. *A Biography of the English Language*. 2nd ed. Fort Worth: Harcourt, Brace and Company.

Peirce, Charles Sanders. 1931–58. *Collected Papers*. 4 vols. Edited by C. Hartshorne, P. Weiss, and A. Burks. Cambridge, Mass.: Harvard University Press.

———. 1998 [1893–1913]. *The Essential Peirce: Selected Philosophical Writings*, ed. Peirce Edition Project. Bloomington: Indiana University Press

Stein, Dieter, and Susan Wright, eds. 1995. *Subjectivity and Subjectivisation*. Cambridge: Cambridge University Press.

Traugott, Elizabeth. 1992. "Syntax." In *The Cambridge History of the English Language*, ed. R.M. Hogg, 168–289. Cambridge: Cambridge University Press.

———. 1993. "Grammaticalization and lexicalization." In *Encyclopedia of Language and Linguistics*, ed. R.E. Asher, 1481–86. Oxford: Pergamon Press.

———. 1995. "Subjectification in grammaticalization." In *Subjectivity and Subjectivisation*, ed. D. Stein and S. Wright, 31–54. Cambridge: Cambridge University Press.

Wright, Susan. 1995. "Subjectivity and experiential syntax." In *Subjectivity and Subjectivisation*, ed. D. Stein and S. Wright, 151–72. Cambridge: Cambridge University Press.

Joëlle Réthoré

The Sense of Language (as *Langage*) versus the Nonsense of Languages (as *Langues*): Iconicity versus Arbitrariness

---

Thus my language is the sum total of myself; for the man is the thought. (Peirce CP 5.314)

De tous les ouvrages accomplis au cours de son passé—spatial et temporel—par l'homme pensant, il n'en est aucun qui soit pour l'anthropologie un document comparable à l'ouvrage que fut en lui, lieu de l'édifice et architecte de l'édifice, la causation et l'édification du langage.
    Réalité linguistique et causation du langage sont, en étendue, des équivalents. Le réalisme, conséquemment, suppose qu'on sait voir l'entier de celle-ci, et c'est y manquer que d'avoir des yeux pour ce qui, survenu en elle en second, y est causé construit et causation déverse, et de n'avoir point d'yeux pour ce qui, survenu en premier, y est causation obverse. (Guillaume 1994: 327)

Such a possibly provocative title only serves to hide the seriousness of a purpose, which is to see the question of language (as *langage*) debated following the lines and constraints of the hierarchical frame of the phenomenological categories of C. S. Peirce. Friendly critical comments have already been proposed on a few related published papers (Réthoré 2000a, 2000b). I shall certainly keep them in mind, while further arguing that *langage* might not merely or solely be a biological or innate capacity to speak or write a language, or be reduced to being the sum total of *langue* plus *parole*,[1] or *langue* plus *discours*,[2] but that it could also well be the third missing phenomenological universe of representation, which would, along with the other two (*discours* and *langue*), help complete the range of possible categories, while not being restricted, as the other two are, to verbal representation. I have thus devoted the first part of my essay to a new illustration of the categories with *langage* as first, *discours*, second, and *langue*, third, which all have a specific part to play in our perceptual and cognitive processes. This conception entails that *langage*, among other functions, be seen as a condition of possibility of the other two, as well as providing human beings with the qualitative and tonal foundations of their signs, both public and private.

Preceding research (Réthoré and Paucsik 1998–99) had already led me to suggest that there might be more 'sense' to *langage* than to the morphemes of *la langue*, because the signs of *langage* are mostly qualitative. For that reason, they are described either as qualisigns (or tones) or as icons. I make a point of distinguishing between signs that are properly called icons and mere iconic signs that would, in themselves, be qualisigns. To perceive a qualisign as iconic is to be conscious of its being a sign, i.e., as representing an object, which is not the case when a sign is perceived as an icon. On the contrary, signs known by the interpreter to belong to *la langue*, i.e,. to be entities of *la langue*, are all symbols and hence types within culturally identified repertoires.

In this essay, I shall attempt to show that it is the category of feeling, or quality, that is attached to *le langage*, while I shall consider cognition as the category relevant to *la langue*. And although I do not share Katz's Platonist conception of natural languages, be it a realist one, I find some possible agreement, through my focus on a relative specificity of *langage*, with Katz's statement (1981: 8): "Whether language is biological, social, or a mixture, there is a feeling that we are *more intimately* related to our language than we are to mathematical entities or truths" (emphasis added).

The opposition that will here be made between arbitrariness and iconicity will certainly be based on a somewhat different approach from that adopted in iconicity theory. I do not so much intend to defend the idea that *langage* is iconic of reality as I want to show that it is the ground upon which rests our knowledge of *la langue*, a ground that is a structured mesh of icons—the images that have been awakened in our minds whenever we have interpreted an assertion and that give form to our linguistic competence, while providing the spatio-temporal stage on which all of our emotions have been acted in the continuous chain of our semioses. According to Peirce's semiotic theory, it is these very icons that enable us to communicate and have direct access to the meaning of any assertion, provided we forget that we are dealing with signs in the course of our interpretation. It is clear that such an approach to meaning is radically different from the commonly accepted symbolic approach to the sense of words, which is given or checked in their dictionary definitions.

The Three Categories Newly Illustrated

Since the advent of generative-transformational grammar and N. Chomsky's nativism, we seem to have generally accepted the view that language is an innate capacity that humans are born with—an exclusive sign of humanity.[3] For that reason, Chomsky and his followers declared grammars and linguistic theory to be components of psychological theories. Innate schemata were the answer given to the question of knowing where our grammatical knowledge came from, while they also served to reject the view that "the speaker's knowledge of the grammar of a language can be acquired on the basis of inductive generalizations from linguistic experience" (Katz 1981: 4).

I have often expressed the view[4] that if it were possible to prove without question that language is innate, one possible argument in favor of this theory would be to evoke the capacity that humans and, to some extent, the higher primates have of making and understanding sentences as propositional, rather than to define verbal language as mere strings of rules and symbols. I have interpreted what I consider the major role played by the immediate interpretant as that of the copula of assertion,[5] itself a symbol, according to Peirce. It is the copula of assertion that identifies the various types of signs in any assertion and enables us to recognize, although generally subconsciously,[6] their differential semiotic function: that of the predicate as interpretive of the relation, thus iconic because dreamlike, imaging, as verbs[7] are; and that of the nominal(s)[8] as partly indexical,[9] i.e., referring to the dynamical object (single or plural, depending on the presence of one or several subjects in the utterance).

My (partial) dissatisfaction with Saussure's or Guillaume's (and their followers') equations of *langage* with *langue* + either *parole* or *discours* has probably arisen from untouched aspects of *langage* that

I feel may belong to the realm of Firstnesses. I am thus proposing to add it to the fairly rich list of typical ideas[10] of Firstness, namely, indeterminacy, indefiniteness, quality, creativity, originality, spontaneity, orience. I highlighted supra[11] parts of the explanations given by Peirce to explain his conception of the copula of assertion: "The assertion represents a compulsion, which experience, meaning *the course of life*, brings upon the deliverer to attach the predicate to the subjects as a sign of them taken in a particular way. This compulsion strikes him at a certain instant; and *he remains under it forever after*.... It is ... a permanent conditional force, or *law*" (emphasis added).[12]

I suppose this deserves at least one comment on my part, and especially so because we are clearly dealing here with assertions and law, i.e., Thirdnesses, not Firstnesses. Moreover, the very concept of compulsion striking at a certain instant is typical of the Secondness of the experience of shock, of interaction between the ego and the non-ego. Notwithstanding these two counterarguments, I insist on conceiving of *langage* as a first, different from both the actuality of *discours* and the rules of *langue*. The phenomena of what I call *langage* are essentially made of feelings, "comprising all that is immediately present.... A feeling is a state of mind having its own living quality.... Or is an element of consciousness which might conceivably override every other state [of mind] until it monopolized the mind" (Peirce: 6.18).

Habit, by contrast, is what the Thirdness of *langue* is about, and it enables us to become "conscious that a connection between feelings is determined by a general rule" (Peirce: 6.20). My intention is not to deny *langage* the capacity of turning into a conscious activity, whenever a habit forces us to produce a general conception (ibid.). It is for that very reason that I see *langage* as capable of evolving from Firstnesses into Thirdnesses. But when it is a mere feeling of recognition of the meaning of a perceptual judgment, or even a sign, I call it *langage*, reserving the concept of *langue* to the recognition of a specific rule (or set of rules).

Wittgenstein (1958: 491), when looking for the primary purpose of language (which I think should be here taken to refer to *langage*), offered a pragmatic view of it in stating that the purpose of language was neither comprehension nor even representation, but the exercising of our influence on others. He claimed it would be better to say that "without language we cannot influence people" than to say that "without language we could not communicate with one another."

If it should be accepted that the communicative intention that produces a particular effect on somebody is not directly linked to the content of the assertion (its *dictum*), then this would be a good reason for claiming that the pragmatics of assertion should definitely be kept separate from its semantics. Our experience, i.e., the continuous course of our lives, is a witness to the pragmatic consequences of all the assertions we have more or less consciously heard or made since infancy.[13] This experience has developed on a territory that was for months void of any recognized symbols, but it coincided in time with the gradual forming of a mesh of icons with a myriad of indexical connections, of which, as speakers of *la langue*, we gradually grew aware. It is because the weaving of this fabric was chronologically first in the ontogeny of language that I consider it as the structuring primary diagram, or metaphor, on which *la langue*, as a specific set of rules and relations, could be learned, i.e., both spoken and written.[14]

Jacques (1983: 49) has proffered a criticism of Wittgenstein's language games for being essentially public, ahistorical and neutralizing verbal interaction in the genesis of meaning. It might be of interest to recall here that Wittgenstein (1958: 492) thought these language games similar to the process of inventing a language. This, I think, is itself close to what I imply when I say that *langage* is that perceptible qualitative area of the private experiences of humans as social beings. I must insist, however, on the embedding of this individual *langage* into public language: our individual rules, far from being totally private, are selected by each of us, though subconsciously, in the encompassing system that feeds, questions, and modifies them in the course of our lives. The presence of such an individual system within the larger one of *la langue*, however, is well accepted in linguistic theory, and is referred to as idiosyncratic language. I would go as far as saying that the more public a language becomes, the more it tends to develop into, or to become part of, *la langue*, while the fate of individual language, because it is so closely dependent on our life experiences, is either to expand or to shrink[15] as *langage*. So it is some phenomenon akin to the creativeness of *langage* that is here alluded to when I choose to classify it amid the phenomena of Firstness.[16] Contrastingly, *la langue* is a phenomenon of Thirdness because it has far more extended scope, in terms of its sub-systems (phonological, syntactic, and semantic), historicity, and distinctiveness in the sense of being autonomous relative to comparable data (other languages), and also greater systematicity. *La langue* is made of symbolic representamina, which answer abstract and general definitions[17] apt at ensuring communication between individuals. They are necessary to maintain the cohesiveness of the system, but they cannot pretend to bring existence, quality, or feeling to what is being said. Our consciousness of *la langue* is founded on a more or less long process of iterated instances of symbols in the Secondness of discourse, which, at some point in the ontogeny of language, produces a judgment of identity between two or more signs of the same object, thus leading us to linguistic competence.

There is, unfortunately, a limit to the capacity that humans have to communicate through a common language (*langue*), due, mainly, to the presence of icons in it. Peirce believed that it is because the quasi-utterer is convinced that the quasi-interpreter shares the same icons as he does when he talks that he troubles at all to address the other. And, mostly, he thought communication was based on this resemblance between one and the other's icons as diagrammatic correspondants of dictionary definitions. Recent viewpoints in the domain of the philosophy of language, as represented by Jacques, for instance, have offered a less idealistic conception of the way we communicate our meanings to others. If misunderstandings are not quite the rule of all communication, Jacques says (1979: 136), it is because we sometimes notice our disagreements and then engage in overcoming them. We are as far from Peirce, here, as we are from the prevailing conception that communication has become global, thanks to the Internet and other technological media. I must admit I feel rather inclined to share Jacques's moderate pessimism.

A spatio-temporal approach to semiosis, which implies taking into consideration the *hic et nunc* of all assertion and the necessary contextualization of the pragmatic data attached to the sign, is the lesson to be drawn from adopting the Peircean viewpoint. Our inferential processes are always unique in time, and they occur chronologically. There cannot be any a priori order or any kind of interpretation (immediate, dynamical, or final). Things happen the way they do, both qualitatively and quantitatively, regardless of the verbal or non-verbal character of the sign. We each have a different story to tell in *la langue* that is common to both speakers. And that is what Peirce founds his logical theory of communication on: it is because we dispose of *la langue*, thanks to the iterative nature of the representamina of *la langue*, that we can hope that the icons which spring to our mind are similar to those evoked in the other's mind. It is certainly the only serious logical foundation of a theory of communication. But empirical experience, that of teaching, for instance, shows that it is rarely successful and that the chance of getting the pupils or students to provide an immediately correct interpretation of the same signs as those intended and produced by their teachers is minimal. If we attribute any validity to the notion of 'generation gap', it seems to point in the same direction, namely, to the difficulty that the older generation has in establishing a satisfying relationship with the younger one. The source of such a phenomenon can be found in our *collateral experience* of the objects of the signs we have interpreted since we were born in all of the communicative situations we have been engaged in. Each of us has interpreted the signs he was capable of dealing with in a constantly changing and unique context, so that, for any given communicative situation in which signs are exchanged, it would be quite unrealistic to expect the same symbolic meanings to emerge in the minds of all at the same time. The qualities and indices present in the signs asserted over the course of our lives give each assertion a *sui generis* touch that colors all of the subsequent evocations or uses of the words employed in the assertion: "[T]he impressions of any moment are very complicated—containing all the images (or the elements of the images) of sense and memory, which complexity is reducible to mediate simplicity by means of the conception of time" (Peirce: 5.223).

The Sense of *Langage* and the Nonsense of *Langues*

This might only be a play on words, based on the ambiguity of the word 'sense', which means not only 'meaning' but also 'sense-feeling', 'sensation'. It is, indeed, thanks to our senses that, as infants, we grow capable of registering the data of language (both as *langage* and as *langue*), in their verbal and non-verbal pragmatic manifestations. This capacity develops coincidentally with the neural and psychic connections that later enable us to become more and more active as participants in our linguistico-cultural community.

P.D. Eimas recalls an experiment, devised by P. K. Kuhl at the University of Washington, in which a baby showed his ability to distinguish contrasting phonemes (in that case, o/i as in *pop/peep*) from acoustically varied instances of the same phoneme. In the case of a vocalic change, the infant turned his head toward the loudspeaker from which the sounds were issued, while if the same word was repeated, he ignored its variations in volume or pitch and let his attention be held by a toy in a direction opposite to that of the loudspeaker. Another experiment showed that "if an infant grows familiar with one stimulus and then encounters a stimulus it perceives as different, its rate of sucking ordinarily increases" (Eimas 1985: 37). The conclusion of the author was that "categorization occurs because a child is born with perceptual mechanisms that are tuned to the properties of speech. These mechanisms yield the forerunners of the phonemic categories that later will enable the child unthinkingly to convert the variable signal of speech into a series of phonemes and thence into words and meanings" (ibid.). Eimas entertains little doubt as to the innate character of the perceptual mechanisms of infants, though these are necessarily affected by environmental factors to the point that the child loses his "ability to detect distinctions that do not occur in [his] native language" (ibid.: 40).

The purpose of this brief comment on the ambiguity of the word 'sense', meaning both 'signified' and 'sensed' (or 'perceived'), was to state some of my reasons for defining *langage* as a cognitively primitive system capable of providing the baby with modes of access to the signs of *la langue*. In order to be experienced, the latter, obviously, has to be mediated by discourse in Secondness—first, that of the other individuals making up the child's environment, then his own as well. This access is based on perceptual mechanisms of verbal and non-verbal data of the native tongue(s) and culture(s) that are specific to a region or country. The sensitivity of individuals to those mechanisms unfortunately seems to grow less as the child becomes a teenager and approaches adulthood.

This system is not only primitive, but also chronologically first in the child's apprehension of language as *langue*; further, it is categorially first in being based on sense-data that are qualities or qualities of feeling. Of these, we have direct knowledge, and we later learn to extend them to innumerable characters of which we do not even have an immediate consciousness. My belief is that the sum of all the characters met in our life experience shapes a certain identity that I call our personal *langage*. Peirce (6.197) states that we can hardly but suppose that those sense-qualities that we now experience—colors, odors, sounds, feelings of every description, loves, griefs, surprise—are but the relics of an ancient ruined *continuum of qualities*.

In earlier stages of their development, when the relations of their dimensions are not yet definite and contracted (see Peirce: 6.195), forms have a vaguer being. Acquiring language as *langue* can be understood as the very emergence of definite potentiality from the indefinite potentiality of *langage* as an (open) set of qualities of feeling based on its "own vital Firstness and spontaneity."[18] Such a long and arduous process takes place in Secondness, at each single stage of its development: "Existence is a form of evolution," says Peirce (6.195).

Now the question that remains to be answered is the following: Is it a fair conclusion to draw from what precedes that *la langue* is senseless? I accept the prevailing view that *la langue* is a symbolic system, a model. A symbol is "adapted to fulfill the function of a sign simply by the fact that … it is so understood" (Peirce 1976: 255), i.e., that it is a sign of its object. Clearly, this states that the symbol has nothing to do with our senses.

Moreover, "hardly any symbol directly signifies the characters it signifies" (ibid.), while the icon is so apt at representing a quality directly that it may well draw no distinction at all between itself and its object: "[I]t is an affair of suchness only" (Peirce: 5.74). This is, in my view, the semiotic content of our first experiential encounters with reality, as well as the most common form of our experience of discourse, which we might call the naive experience of language, when we forget or simply do not know that we are dealing with signs and tend to confuse what we are reading or hearing (graphic signs and sound waves) with the objects of our perception.[19] Another good reason for calling *la langue* senseless is that symbols as phonological sequences are arbitrary and of a conventional nature, while our experience of *langage* is essentially qualitative.

It is true that the divide between symbols and icons is not total, since "every symbol must have, organically attached to it, its Indices of Reactions and its Icons of qualities" (Peirce 5.119). However, "whatever [a symbol] signifies," says Peirce (1976: 255), "it signifies by its power of determining another sign signifying the same character." It is difficult for a sign to have less content, less 'body', so to speak, than that attributed to the symbol in this definition. This is the second reason why I insist on stating that *la langue*, as such, is senseless. There is a very interesting opposition raised by Peirce (ibid.) between the efficiency of the iconic word 'buzz', an example of onomatopoeia, which determines our direct access to its meaning, and the symbolic phrase 'the sound of sawing', which, though probably more precise, overtly represents an indirect access to its meaning. His conclusion is that "[a] symbol cannot exert any real force, because it is a law" (ibid.: 250). There is a presentness and resemblance in icons or even mere iconic signs that is missing in the conventional mediation of symbols. Pure icons are apt at exhibiting the qualities they signify, hence the degenerate character of their relation to their objects. They cannot assert anything, nor can they give us the assurance of the existence of their objects. They can only be fragments of more complete signs. But they are perfect in putting their interpreter face to face with the character signified, which is what symbols cannot do, because they are "particularly remote from the Truth itself. They are abstracted.... They serve to bring reasonableness and law" (ibid.: 243). So, am I wrong in equating arbitrariness with nonsense? I think not, because only convention enables *la langue* to make sense, thanks to *relationis rationis*.

Conclusion

I have already stated that I do not intend to join the debate on the iconicity of language, due to what is meant by language as *langue*, not *langage* in the sense that I am trying to develop. I mean to show that essentially the phenomena of *langage* are, or are based on, feelings "comprising *all* that is immediately present."[20] "A feeling is a state of mind having its own *living* quality.... It is an element of consciousness."[21]

The function of habit and of the Thirdness of *la langue* is to make us "conscious that a connection between feelings is determined by a general rule" (Peirce: 6.20). We then grow "aware of being governed by a habit" (ibid.). Certainly, the consciousness of a habit constitutes a general conception, and this is why it seems so unnatural to distinguish between language and languages. I conceive of *langage* as an evolving mode of being, an experience that takes us from the shores of Firstness to those of Thirdness and back, a constant ebb and flow between quality, feeling, and obedience to the rules of convention.

University of Perpignan

Notes

1. Saussure (1979 [1972]: 112) states: "[N]ous avons d'abord distingué, au sein du phénomène total que représente le *langage*, deux facteurs: la *langue* et la *parole*. La langue est pour nous le langage moins la parole."
2. In a discussion of Saussure's views, Guillaume (1994: 35–36) claims that "L'équation saussurienne: langage = langue + parole justifiée dans les langues sémitiques à racines et traitement interne de la racine, cesse de l'être dans nos langues à radicaux et à traitement externe du radical. Il convient dans ces langues de lui substituer l'équation, universellement valable: langage = langue + discours. Un vaste champ d'investigation pour la grammaire comparée, qui la conduirait *à s'intéresser, plus qu'elle ne l'a fait jusqu'à présent, au mécanisme de causation du langage*, est celui de la mutation de la racine en radical" (emphasis added).
3. Consider the very title of B. Malmberg's book (1979), *Le Langage, signe de l'humain*.
4. Mostly orally, in the course of the weekly seminar of the Institut de Recherches en Sémiotique, Communication et Education (IRSCE), held in the University of Perpignan (France) since 1974.
5. See Peirce, "Regenerated Logic" (3.435): "Neither the predicate, nor the subjects, nor both together, can make an *assertion*. The assertion represents a compulsion, which experience, meaning *the course of life*, brings upon the deliverer to attach the predicate to the subjects as a sign of them taken in a particular way. This compulsion strikes him at a certain instant; and *he remains under it forever after*.... It is ... a permanent conditional force, or *law*. The deliverer thus *requires a kind of sign* which shall signify a law that *to objects of indices an icon appertains as sign of them* in a given way. Such a sign has been called a *symbol*. It is the *copula* of assertion" (emphasis added). See also Réthoré (1988a: e8–e10; and 1988b: 553–55).
6. As a matter of course, the vast majority of interpreters do not happen to be professional linguists.
7. Peirce, in "The Logic of Relatives" (3.459), claims that "[a] verb by itself signifies a mere dream, an imagination unattached to any particular occasion. It calls up in the mind an *icon*."
8. Peirce (3.419) calls them (logical) subjects: "The subjects are the indications of the things spoken of, the predicates, words that assert, question, or command whatever is intended," which implies not confusing them with grammatical subjects. We should also remember that he thought the concept of 'pro-demonstrative' far more preferable to that of 'noun': "... [T]he shallowness of syntax is manifest in its failing to recognise the impotence of mere words, and especially of common nouns, to fulfil the function of a grammatical subject. Words such as *this, that, lo, hallo, hi there*, have a direct, forceful action upon the nervous system, and compel the hearer to look about him; and so they, more than ordinary words, contribute towards indicating what the speech is about. But this a point that grammar and the grammarians ... are so far from seeing as to call demonstratives, such as *that* and *this*, pronouns—a literally preposterous designation, for nouns may more truly be called pro-demonstratives." For further reading, see also Peirce 3.459.
9. We know that nouns, in themselves, are symbols and cannot play the role of indices, though their determiners can. The determiners may belong to various parts of speech: articles, possessive or demonstrative determiners (generally

called adjectives in traditional grammars), quantifiers, restrictive relative clauses, etc.
10. Illustrations of the category of Firstness can be found in many passages of Peirce (1.350-2, 1.417, 8.329, 1.350, 1.361, 1.306, 1.310, 5.44). See also Réthoré (1988b: 268–74).
11. In note 5.
12. Peirce, "Regenerated Logic" (3.435, also published in *Monist* vol. 7: 19–40). See also Réthoré (1988b: 553ff).
13. It is certainly worth reading (or re-reading) "Questions Concerning Certain Faculties Claimed by Man," published by Peirce in *Journal of Speculative Philosophy* 2 (1868): 103–14; intended as Essay IV of the "Search for a Method" (1893), reproduced in *Collected Papers* (5.213-63), and edited and translated into French by Balat, Deledalle, and Deledalle-Rhodes (1993: 43–64).
14. I do not wish here to be taken to assume that speech always precedes writing.
15. In the case of disease or trauma (either physical or psychical), when they are serious enough to affect our language.
16. In a prior paper (Réthoré 2000a: 495), I quoted a comment made by R. Innis on J. Dewey (Innis 1998–99: 90). In his paper, Innis insisted on the fact that both the unity and totality of all experience were rooted in the quality of Firstness, with the result that experience and its object render quality manifest. I believe that this is how *langage* is made manifest, through signs of quality, i.e., qualisigns or icons.
17. In "Kaina Stoicheia" (1976: 237), Peirce stated that "[a] definition is the logical analysis of a predicate in general terms.... A definition does not assert that anything exists."
18. This is an analogy with a remark made by Peirce about sense-qualities, namely, a magenta color (6.198).
19. This is why I believe it is important to insist, after Peirce, on the semiotic difference between icons and iconic signs (see supra).
20. Peirce (6. 18) (emphasis added). I have chosen this definition to substantiate my conception of *langage* as being not merely verbal.
21. Ibid. (emphases added). These are the implied meanings of such phrases as 'the life of signs', or the world as a 'profusion of signs'.

Works Cited

Balat, M., G. Deledalle, and J. Deledalle-Rhodes. 1993. *Charles S. Peirce: A la Recherche d'une méthode*. Perpignan: Presses Universitaires de Perpignan.
Eimas, P.D. 1985. "The perception of speech in early infancy." *Science* 252: 34–40.
Guillaume, G. 1994. *Langage et science du langage*. Paris: Librairie Nizet; Québec: Presses de l'Université Laval.
Innis, R. 1998–99. "John Dewey et sa glose approfondie de la théorie peircienne de la qualité." In *Logique de l'icône, à partir de la théorie de C. S. Peirce*, ed. A. Jappy. Québec: Université du Québec à Chicoutoumi (Canada): *Protée, théories et pratiques sémiotiques* 26 (3): 89–98.
Jacques, F. 1979. *Dialogiques, Recherches logiques sur le dialogue*. Paris: P.U.F., 1979.

———. 1983. "La Mise en communauté de l'énonciation." *Langages* 70: 45–71.
Katz, J. 1981. *Language and Other Abstract Objects*. Oxford: Basil Blackwell.
Malmberg, M. 1979. *Le Langage: signe de l'humain*. Paris: Picard, coll. Empreinte.
Peirce, C.S. 1931–36 [1958]. *Collected Papers of Charles Sanders Peirce*. 8 vols. Vols. 1–6 ed. Charles Hartshorne and Paul Weiss. Vols. 7–8 ed. A. W. Burks. Cambridge, Mass.: Harvard University Press.
———. 1976. *The New Elements of Mathematics by Charles S. Peirce*. Edited by C. Eysele. Vol. 4. The Hague and Paris: Mouton Publishers.
Réthoré, J. 1988a. "La Proposition chez Peirce: sujet-prédicat. Et la copule?" Bruxelles: *Degrés* 54–55: e1–e11.
———. 1988b. *La Linguistique sémiotique de Charles S. Peirce: Propositions pour une grammaire phanéroscopique*. Ph.D. diss. A.N.R.T. Université de Lille III. ISSN: 0294-1767 (microfiches).
———. 1998. "L'Interprétation, fondement du langage et condition de toute signification." In *L'Interprétation*, ed. L. Hébert. Québec: Université du Québec à Chicoutoumi (Canada): *Protée, théories et pratiques sémiotiques* 26 (1): 19–27.
———. 2000a. "*Langage*, an Actual Partner to *discours* and *langue*." In *Semiotic Contributions in Honor of Vilmos Voigt's 60th Birthday*, ed. J. Bernard and G. Withalm. Berlin and New York: Mouton de Gruyter. *Semiotica* 128 (3/4): 487–97.
———. 2000b. "Le Domaine du langagier: langue ou langage? Le point de vue de la sémiotique." In *Linguistique sur corpus: Etudes et réflexions*, ed. M. Bilger. Perpignan: Presses Universitaires de Perpignan: *Cahiers de l'Université de Perpignan* 31: 227–38.
———. 2001. "The language of the English: The tones of a people." Toulouse: Presses Universitaires de Toulouse-Le Mirail: *Caliban*: 163–77.
Réthoré, J., and C. Paucsik-Tourné. 1998–99. "Quand le discours se veut langage d'un sujet plutôt qu'instance indifférente de la langue." In *Logique de l'icône;, à partir de la théorie de C. S. Peirce*, ed. A. Jappy. Québec: Université du Québec à Chicoutoumi (Canada): *Protée, théories et pratiques sémiotiques* 26 (3): 35–44.
Saussure, F. de. 1979 [1972]. *Cours de linguistique générale*. 2d ed. Critique préparée par Tullio de Mauro. Paris: Payothèque.
Wittgenstein, L. 1958. *Philosophical Investigations*. Trans. G.E.M. Anscombe. Oxford: Basil Blackwell.

Laura A. Janda

Cognitive "Hot Spots" in the Russian Case System

One of the lessons of the preceding Peirce seminar was the compatibility of Peircean semiotics with the framework of cognitive linguistics, as established in particular by Danaher (1999), Haley (1999), and Janda (1999). In this framework, meaning is derived from human perceptual and conceptual experience, and grammar is an essential part of the symbolic structure of language. Grammar evolves through the metaphorical and metonymical extension of meaning derived from concrete perceptual/conceptual experience, providing an abstract architecture that facilitates the joining of lexemes in complex symbolic units. Grammatical structure is ultimately an abstraction (via parable) of "small physical stories," such as the flow of energy from subject to object in a transitive construction (Turner 1996). Thus, all linguistic forms and structures bear meaning, and a given linguistic entity always bears its meaning, never being silenced or entirely emptied of content. Polysemy is the norm, enabling forms to be variously nuanced in different surroundings. True synonymy is, however, relatively rare, since different linguistic entities almost invariably call up slightly different construals and/or different aggregates of polysemous concepts.

This view of a tight relationship between perception and polysemous meanings (which themselves interact) is properly reminiscent of Peirce's famous "lake of consciousness," where perceptions striking the surface enter into skeletal sets, networks of meanings that float about, crossing each other's paths and occasionally bumping up against each other in the life of the mind.

This essay will examine the semantic networks of the Russian case system as an example of this type of semiotic phenomenon. In Russian, cases serve as syntactic cornerstones, determining the contours of grammatical constructions. Though the Russian cases are both abstract and polysemous, they are firmly grounded in perceptual experience of physical realia, such as relative location, movement, and salience. Together, the semantic networks of the Russian cases provide a rich expressive system, often allowing speakers to choose among two or more grammatical means to describe "the same" perception of reality. These points of ambiguity and overlap are the cognitive "hot spots" that we will examine in detail.

The Structure of Russian Case Semantics

Russian has six cases: the nominative, instrumental, accusative, dative, genitive, and locative. Together, these cases form an austere and efficient system, enabling speakers to describe all possible relationships of entities, both to each other and to events. Each case can be used to express both concrete physical relationships, as well as relationships in other domains, such as time, purpose, emotion, states of being, scalar values, etc. The various meanings of a given case constitute a skeletal set, a coherent semantic network in which all uses are clearly related to one another, rather than being an unmotivated random list. Although much of case usage is associated with various trigger words (usually prepositions or verbs, though nouns, adjectives, and even adverbs can participate), these collocations are best understood as well-motivated semantic associations. Cases never appear as automatic or semantically empty units, as arbitrary accidents of grammatical structure. Their meaning is always apparent, and a given trigger word is associated with a given case precisely because the meanings of the trigger word and of the case are compatible. Case meaning is therefore most appropriately treated as a significant semantic presence in all grammatical constructions.

The following is an overview of the gross structure of the Russian case system, listing the major submeanings of each case, with indications of their usage. This system of meanings is based on over 15 years of empirical research on the semantics of case in Russian and other Slavic languages, arrived at through analysis of large databases of authentic language. Both the results presented here on the language internal interactions of Russian and the results presented elsewhere on cross-linguistic comparisons (cf. Janda in press a, in press b, forthcoming; Janda and Clancy forthcoming) confirm the reality of this case system, since the behaviors we observe are not random, but are clearly motivated within such a system.

- **Nominative: a name** (naming, subject); **an identity** (predicate nominative)
- **Instrumental: a means** (means, instrument, path, agent); **a label** (predicate instrumental); **an adjunct** (preposition s); **a landmark** (prepositions of location)
- **Accusative: a destination** (movement, direct object, points in time); **a dimension** (durations, distances, amounts, comparisons); **an endpoint** (places and times a given distance away)
- **Dative: a receiver** (indirect object); **an experiencer** (benefit, harm, and modal uses); **a competitor** (matching forces, submission)
- **Genitive: a source** (withdrawal); **a goal** (approach); **a whole** (possession/'of', quantification); **a reference** (lack, comparison, near)
- **Locative: a place** (location in space, time, and other domains)

The dynamics of this system enable speakers to make choices in how they use it. Individually, each case is underdetermined, representing an aggregate of abstract, flexible meanings that can be extended via metaphor and metonymy. The relative lack of restrictions on case use gives speakers the agility they need to negotiate all situations, including novel ones (such as when an entirely new word or concept enters a language, requiring integration into grammatical constructions). Collectively, however, cases are overdetermined, presenting a system with expressive means beyond the bare minimum for communication. Frequently, perceptual/conceptual experiences that are "the same" (or very nearly so) can be expressed using more than one grammatical construction, entailing a choice among cases. The system thus supports overlapping and contiguous semantic expressions, and acknowledges the existence of ambiguity.

The Cognitive "Hot Spots"

We will focus specifically on instances in which the Russian case system presents speakers with alternative case constructions for synonymous expressive goals. As we shall see, these alternatives are not scattered at random across the case system, but are relatively restricted and systematic, constituting entrenched relationships among cases motivated by semantic similarities. These systematic relationships target semantically significant junctures in the grammatical landscape of case, namely, the places where potential ambiguity resides. In these spots, there is no one-to-one mapping of perceptual input and case use, or, indeed, the perceptual/conceptual experience may itself be ambiguous. The places where these ambiguities arise involve some basic concepts, such as location, trajectory, reference, control, agency, means, categorization, and causation. The case system acknowledges the fact that a given experience may be cognitively manipulated in multiple ways by providing alternative strategies in terms of case constructions. Ultimately, the vast majority of alternatives are not entirely synonymous: any case construction emphasizes some meanings while suppressing others; indeed, no linguistic expression captures the totality of a perceptual/conceptual experience. Such experiences are too richly textured to be fully comprehended and processed. Choices must always be made.

Three parameters can be used to construct a typology of inter-case relationships: (1) the number of cases involved, (2) the type of semantic relationship (contiguous, overlapping, virtually synonymous), and (3) the factors contributing to the semantic relationship (various kinds of construal, including metonymic reduction). While we will use all three parameters in this study, we will focus primarily on semantic relationships and what they mean for human cognitive systems.

In terms of the number of cases engaged in a semantic relationship, the most common relationship involves a 1 x 1 contrast, in which one case is used in one construction, but another one is used in another construction. An example is the following pair of constructions: *stradat' bessonnicej* [suffer **insomnia-INST**] vs. *stradat' ot bessonnicy* [suffer from **insomnia-GEN**], both of which mean 'suffer from **insomnia**'. Occasionally, we see a 1 x 1 x 1 contrast, in which there are three similar constructions, each using a different case. For example, compare the following three constructions: *U nego* **ogromnye sredstva** [At him-GEN **enormous** means-NOM] vs. *On raspolagaet ogromnymi sredstvami* [He-NOM has-at-disposal **enormous means-INST**] vs. *On imeet ogromnye sredstva* [He-NOM possesses **enormous means-ACC**], all of which mean 'He has **enormous means/great wealth**'. There are additionally some more complex types of contrast, which are relatively rarer. These contrasts involve grammatical constructions that are entirely different in their composition, and thus the contrast is a complex one. For example, we could class as 2 x 2 contrasts the following: *učit' kogo čemu* [teach **who-ACC what-DAT**] vs. *prepodavat' komu čto* [teach **who-DAT what-ACC**] 'teach **someone something**'; *Ja nuždajus' v den'gax* [**I-NOM** need in **money-LOC**] vs. *Den'gi mne nužny* [**Money-NOM me-DAT** needed-NOM] 'I need money'; *odarit' kogo čem* [give-present **who-ACC what-INST**] vs. *podarit' komu čto* [give-present **who-DAT what-ACC**] 'give **someone something**'. In the remainder of this essay we will focus on the 1 x 1 and 1 x 1 x 1 contrasts, since they offer the crispest, most unencumbered comparisons of case uses.

Synonymy is not a uniform phenomenon. Although all of the contrasts examined below juxtapose constructions that are in some sense synonymous, the semantic relationship between constructions varies, and we can distinguish three types of synonymy: contiguous, overlapping, and virtual. This is not an exhaustive inventory of types of synonymy, nor are the types themselves discrete. In some situations we encounter meanings that are contiguous or parallel, yet are distributed complementarily on the basis of some feature. For example, the prepositions *v* and *na* can be used with the accusative case to designate the destination of movement, and the preposition *k* can also be used with the dative case for the same purpose; all three prepositions can be glossed as 'to'. The distribution of these preposition + case constructions is determined primarily by animacy: animate destinations (usually people) require *k* + DAT, whereas inanimate destinations (usually places) use *v* or *na* + ACC. Although there is a strong parallelism between the two constructions, they are not entirely synonymous, since going 'to' a person is a somewhat different experience (it does not involve physically encroaching upon the person's body) from going 'to' a place (which does involve physical encroachment). In addition to contiguous synonymy, there is also overlapping synonymy, in which the situation described might seem to be "the same," using the same lexemes, but we get slightly different overlapping meanings from two different cases. An example of overlapping synonymy is the use of the accusative vs. genitive cases with a group of verbs denoting waiting and wanting. For example, we can say both *Boris ždet avtobus* [Boris-NOM waits **bus-ACC**] and *Boris ždet avtobusa* [Boris-NOM waits **bus-GEN**] to describe a scene where Boris is waiting for a bus. However, if we use the accusative case, we imply that Boris is waiting for a specific bus, whereas the genitive suggests that Boris just wants to get away and will take any bus that comes. There is plenty of semantic overlap between the two constructions, which differ only in the degree of specificity ascribed to Boris's intentions. In a few rare instances we encounter virtual synonymy, a situation in which it is quite difficult to establish any semantic difference between two case constructions. The adverbs *žal'/žalko* 'pity, sorry' can be used with either the accusative or the genitive case to say 'It's too bad about X', with no discernable difference in meaning. Similarly, the distinction between *izučat'* + ACC vs. *učit'sja* + DAT, both of which mean 'study', is minimal.

Construal plays an essential role in the competition between alternative case constructions. We will examine pairs and triplets of contrasting constructions that share a similar meaning and often also share lexical trigger words (or have very similar trigger words). Alternative constructions vary in the way they handle issues such as foregrounding, backgrounding, volition, blame, emotional involvement, etc. Although the objective reality may be the same (or nearly so), the speaker's construal plays a role in every utterance. Using what is known about the semantic structure of the Russian case system, it is possible for us to examine the construals motivating various case constructions in a coherent and systematic way. One very common source of case contrasts is metonymic reduction, that is, the relationship between a path and its endpoint. Often, it is possible to refer only to the final location of a path; in such instances, the endpoint stands metonymically for the whole path. This type of metonymic reduction is evident when we contrast English uses of *over*, for example, as in *Bill went over the hill* and *Sally lives over the hill*, where Sally's location is merely the endpoint of a movement whose entire trajectory is traversed by Bill.

Construals Involving the Nominative

The following tables illustrate how nominative: a name contrasts with dative: an experiencer, genitive: a reference, instrumental: a means, and accusative: a destination.

1. 'I want to sleep'	
N: name *Ja xoču spat'* [I-NOM want sleep]	D: exp *Mne xočetsja spat'* [Me-DAT wants-self sleep]

Nominative: a name vs. dative: an experiencer

The nominative subject of a verb, also interpretable here as the agent, is always de facto an experiencer of the action of the verb. Conversely, the distinguishing feature of the dative case is its potential subjecthood (Bachman 1980, Smith 1992, Janda 1993, Janda in press b), a fact that links the dative and nominative cases. The nominative case assigns a volitional role to the subject, whereas the dative case portrays the sleepy speaker as merely a passive experiencer of circumstance.

2. 'She is smarter **than her brother**'	
N: name *Ona umnee, čem* **brat** [She-NOM smarter, than **brother-NOM**]	G: ref *Ona umnee* **brata** [She-NOM smarter **brother-GEN**]
3. 'I won't be there'	
N: name *Ja ne budu tam* [I-NOM not be there]	G: ref *Menja tam ne budet* [**Me-GEN** there not be]
4. '**He** has enormous means'	
N: name *On imeet ogromnye sredstva* [**He-NOM** has enormous means-ACC]	G: ref *U* **nego** *ogromnye sredstva* [At **him-GEN** enormous means-NOM]

Nominative: a name vs. genitive: a reference

The subject of a sentence always has special salience, for it is a point of reference both for naming items and for predicates. The genitive case is also used to identify reference points. In the instance of the comparison, the nominative case simply names the brother, implying a parallel between the girl's intelligence and his. The genitive case, however, sets up the brother as a reference point on a scale of intelligence. Either negation can be treated exactly like a positive assertion by assigning the nominative case, or a speaker can emphasize the negation as separation from a reference point, as with the genitive case. The use of the genitive with negation carries an additional connotation of lack of access; whereas the nominative is a neutral statement, the genitive implies that 'I' will simply not be available and that the speaker does not intend to provide any further information. 'Have' can be expressed as a transitive verb with a nominative subject (he), or as existence at the possessor (him), which is a genitive reference point; because Russian is primarily a BE language, the latter construction is preferred.

5. 'He has **enormous means**'		
N: name *U nego ogromnye sredstva* [At him-GEN **enormous means-NOM**]	**I: means** *On raspolagaet ogromnymi sredstvami* [He-NOM enjoys **enormous means-INST**]	**A: dest** *On imeet ogromnye sredstva* [He-NOM has **enormous means-ACC**]

Nominative: a name vs. instrumental: a means vs. accusative: a destination

In addition to being the nominative subject of existence at the possessor and the accusative destination of 'having', a possessed item (enormous means) can also be understood as the means by which 'having' is experienced, using the instrumental case.

6. '**Who** operated on the patient'		
N: name *Kto bol'nogo operiroval* [**Who-NOM** patient-ACC operated]	**I: means** *Bol'noj byl operirovan kem* [Patient-NOM was operated **who-INST**]	**G: ref** *Bol'noj operirovalsja u kogo* [Patient-NOM operated-self at **who-GEN**]

Nominative: a name vs. instrumental: a means vs. genitive: a reference

An agent ('who') can be expressed as the nominative subject of an active verb. For passive verbs, there are two options: either the agent can be an instrumental means for achieving the verbal activity, or the agent can be a genitive point of reference, the location at which the activity takes place (similar to versions of 'have' above). With each case, the construal is slightly different. The nominative subject and instrumental agent bear a relationship typical for transitive vs.

passive constructions, and the -*sja* passive (which perhaps more resembles middle voice) is interpreted rather as a causative (cf. Toops 1987), suggesting that the patient had the operation done by a designated professional.

The following table illustrates how nominative: an identity (predicate nominative) contrasts with instrumental: a label and accusative: a destination.

7. 'He was/became **a soldier**'		
N: id *On byl soldat* [He-NOM was **soldier-NOM**]	**I: label** *On byl/stal soldatom* [He-NOM was/became **soldier-INST**]	**A: dest** *On postupil v soldaty* [He-NOM entered in **soldiers-ACC**]

Nominative: an identity vs. instrumental: a label vs. accusative: a destination

Whereas nominative: an identity sets up a simple equation X = Y, naming both X and Y on either side of the copular verb, instrumental: a label describes the category (Y, 'soldier') through which an item is manifested. The instrumental case emphasizes the unequal status of X and Y—X is a specific instance, but Y is the name of a category that X belongs in. The use of the accusative: a destination depends upon an understanding of states of being as locations that can be entered; stepping into the ranks of soldiers is metonymically understood as a reference to the entire act of becoming a soldier, and this construction emphasizes the fact that 'he' has joined a profession.

Construals Involving the Instrumental

The following tables illustrate how instrumental: a means contrasts with accusative: a destination, accusative: a dimension, genitive: a source, and genitive: a whole.

8. 'throw **stones**'	
I: means *brosat'sja kamnjami* [throw **stones-INST**]	**A: dest** *brosat' kamni* [throw **stones-ACC**]

Instrumental: a means vs. accusative: a destination

Either one can achieve an action by means of an item, using the item as a resource or instrument to carry out the action, or one can think of the activity as transitively affecting the item. The special construal of the instrumental amounts to a meaning such as 'use stones as projectiles; engage in the act of throwing using stones'.

9. 'live **an interesting life**, walk **across a field**; living **life** isn't **walking across a field**'	
I: means *žit' interesnoj žizn'ju, idti polem* [live **interesting life-INST**, walk **field-INST**]	**A: dim** *žizn' prožit' ne pole perejti* [**life-ACC** live-through not **field-ACC** walk-across]

Instrumental: a means vs. accusative: a dimension

One can move through time or space using an expanse of either domain—such as a field or a life—as a path, a means to go (instrumental), or one can simply traverse an expanse (accusative). Again, the instrumental requires the more marked construal, this time highlighting the fact that movement passes through some sort of conduit.

10. 'suffer **from insomnia**'	
I: means *stradat' bessonnicej* [suffer **insomnia-INST**]	**G: source** *stradat' ot bessonnicy* [suffer from **insomnia-GEN**]

Instrumental: a means vs. genitive: a source

Here the means by which suffering is manifested is understood as the cause of suffering, but there is another metaphor for causation, which involves understanding the cause as a source.

11. 'fill a glass **with water**; a glass full **of water**'	
I: means *napolnit' stakan vodoj* [fill glass-ACC **water-INST**]	**G: whole** *stakan polon vody* [glass-NOM full-NOM **water-GEN**]

Instrumental: a means vs. genitive: a whole

Manipulation of a substance can be understood as a manipulation for which the substance is the means by which the manipulation takes place; manipulation of a substance can alternatively focus on the amount manipulated, in which case we view that amount as a part of the whole, some of the substance.

The following table illustrates how instrumental: an adjunct contrasts with locative: a place.

12. 'He has money with **him**'	
I: adjunct *U nego den'gi s soboj* [At him-GEN money-NOM with **self-INST**]	**L: place** *U nego den'gi pri sebe* [At him-GEN money-NOM at **self-LOC**]

Instrumental: an adjunct vs. locative: a place

The presence of the money in a person's possession can be understood either as a relationship of togetherness between the money and the person, or as a relationship of proximal location.

The following table illustrates how instrumental: a landmark contrasts with genitive: a goal.

13. 'before we left'	
I: landm *pered tem, kak my uexali* [in-front-of **that-INST**, how we-NOM left]]	**G: goal** *do togo, kak my uexali* [to **that-GEN**, how we-NOM left]

Instrumental: a landmark vs. genitive: a goal

Prior existence can be interpreted as a static temporal location in front of an item, or as a movement toward the item. This is similar to metonymic reduction, for we have a relationship between a point and a trajectory. This relationship is partially motivated by the fact that time can be conceived of both as a static space that we move through and as something that moves along as we stand still.

Other contrasts discussed above:

5. [instrumental: a means vs. nominative: a name vs. accusative: a destination]
6. [instrumental: a means vs. nominative: a name vs. genitive: a reference]
7. [instrumental: a label vs. nominative: an identity vs. accusative: a destination]

Construals Involving the Accusative

The following tables illustrate how accusative: a destination contrasts with dative: a competitor, dative: a receiver, genitive: a goal, and genitive: a reference.

14. 'go to **someplace**'	
A: dest *idti v, na čto* (+ non-humans) [go (in)to, (on)to **what-ACC**]	**D: comp** *idti k komu* (+ humans) [go to **who-DAT**]
15. 'believe (in) **someone, something**'	
A: dest *verit' v kogo, vo čto* [believe in **who-ACC**, in **what-ACC**]	**D: comp** *verit' komu, čemu* [believe **who-DAT, what-DAT**]
16. 'study **math**'	
A: dest *izučat' matematiku* [study **math-ACC**]	**D: comp** *učit'sja matematike* [teach-self **math-DAT**]

Accusative: a destination vs. dative: a competitor

In all instances, we have a contrast between movement to a destination (including the metaphorical understanding of a transitive action as being transferred from the subject to the object—accusative) and submission to an item that exerts some kind of control, rather than being a mere destination (dative). The sense of directionality is strong for both the accusative and the dative, but the dative additionally emphasizes the fact that the destination has a force of its own.

17. 'Boris waits **for the/a bus**'	
A: dest *Boris ždet avtobus* [Boris-NOM waits **bus-ACC**]	**G: goal** *Boris ždet avtobusa* [Boris-NOM waits **bus-GEN**]
18. 'It's too bad about **the money**'	
A: dest *žal'/žalko den'gi* [pity **money-ACC**]	**G: goal** *žal'/žalko deneg* [pity **money-GEN**]

Accusative: a destination vs. genitive: a goal

Here we see the near equivalence of the direct object as the destination of an action (accusative) and the same item as the goal of an action (genitive). Goals and destinations are cognitively very similar concepts.

19. 'I don't see **the/a car**'	
A: dest *Ja ne vižu* **mašinu** [I-NOM not see **car-ACC**]	**G: ref** *Ja ne vižu* **mašiny** [I-NOM not see **car-GEN**]

Accusative: a destination vs. genitive: a reference

This distinction plays on the difference between a tangible, actual referent, which is the direct object (accusative), and something referred to but not actually accessed, as a genitive reference point perceptually separated from the speaker (genitive). In other words, both expressions can be used to describe not seeing a car, but when the accusative is used, a specific car is referenced and presumed to exist. The use of the genitive signals an absolute negation, used when there is no car at all in sight, specified or unspecified.

20. 'for **it/him**; a letter **for him**'		
A: dest *v, na, za, pro* **nego** [for **it/him-ACC**]	**G: goal** *do, dlja, radi* **nego**; *pis'mo dlja* **nego** [for **it/him-GEN**; letter-NOM for **him-GEN**]	**D: rec** *pis'mo emu* [letter-NOM **him-DAT**]

Accusative: a destination vs. genitive: a goal vs. dative: a receiver

In all instances we are dealing with the target of purpose, and all of these expressions share a sense of directedness toward an item. This is another example of how these three cases express directed movement: in a fairly neutral way with the accusative; emphasizing the salience of a goal (rather than just the whole path to the target) with the genitive; and highlighting the potential subjecthood of a receiver (who will presumably read the letter) with the dative.

The following tables illustrate how accusative: a dimension contrasts with dative: a competitor and locative: a place.

21. 'similar to, equal to **someone/something**'	
A: dim *poxože na kogo/čto, rostom s(o) kogo/čto* [similar onto **who/what-ACC**, size approximately **who/what-ACC**]	**D: comp** *podobnyj, roven komu/čemu* [similar, equal **who/what-DAT**]
22. 'sell mimosa for **two rubles** a kilo; for **one ruble** a kilo'	
A: dim *mimozu prodat' po dva rublja za odin kilogramm* [mimosa-ACC sell for **two rubles-ACC** for one kilogram-ACC]	**D: comp** *mimozu prodat' po odnomu rublju za odin kilogramm* [mimosa-ACC sell for **one ruble-DAT** for one kilogram-ACC]

Accusative: a dimension vs. dative: a competitor

Here we compare engagement of a dimension of an item (accusative) with submission to an item (dative). Involvement can be viewed as a mere transitive action or as an action that signals yielding to something.

23. 'talk about **oneself**'	
A: dim *govorit' pro sebja* [talk about **self-ACC**]	**L: place** *govorit' o sebe* [talk about **self-LOC**]

Accusative: a dimension vs. locative: a place

Activity can be understood either as being transferred to a given dimension or as existing at a location. This relationship is similar to metonymic reduction, since again we see a correlation between movement and location.

Other construals discussed above:

5. [accusative: a destination vs. instrumental: a means vs. nominative: a name]
7. [accusative: a destination vs. instrumental: a label vs. nominative: an identity]
8. [accusative: a destination vs. instrumental: a means]
9. [accusative: a dimension vs. instrumental: a means]

Construals Involving the Dative

The following table illustrates how dative: an experiencer contrasts with genitive: a whole.

24. 'He smashed **his father's** car'	
D: exp *On razbil **otcu** mašinu* [He-NOM smashed **father-DAT** car-ACC]	**G: whole** *On razbil mašinu **otca*** [He-NOM smashed car-ACC **father-GEN**]
25. 'the end **of something**'	
D: exp *konec čemu* [end-NOM **what-DAT**]	**G: whole** *konec čego* [end-NOM **what-GEN**]

Dative: an experiencer vs. genitive: a whole

Possession can be understood as either an experience (dative) or as a part-whole relationship (genitive). When the dative case is used, there is an implication that the possessor is having some kind of experience (often a negatively evaluated one, such as suffering or damage), whereas the use of the genitive is relatively neutral.

Other construals discussed above:

20. [dative: a receiver vs. accusative: a destination and genitive: a goal]
1. [dative: an experiencer vs. nominative: a name]
14, 15, 16. [dative: a competitor vs. accusative: a destination]
21, 22. [dative: a competitor vs. accusative: a dimension]

Construals Involving the Genitive

The following table illustrates how genitive: a whole contrasts with locative: a place. In both instances we are dealing with something that can be construed either as a part-whole relationship or as a location. The time elapsed during an operation can be understood as a feature of the operation, or the operation can be viewed as a temporal location for the activity of assisting. Items that are parts of physical objects can also be understood as being located on the larger entities that they belong to.

26. 'assist during **an operation**'	
G: whole *assistirovat' vo vremja operacii* [assist in time-ACC operation-GEN]	L: place *assistirovat' pri operacii* [assist at **operation-LOC**]
27. 'a branch **of a tree**, the fingers **of the left hand**'	
G: whole *vetka dereva, pal'cy levoj ruki* [branch-NOM **tree-GEN**, fingers-NOM **left hand-GEN**]	L: place *vetka na dereve, pal'cy na levoj ruke* [branch-NOM on **tree-LOC**, fingers-NOM on **left hand-LOC**]

Genitive: a whole vs. locative: a place

The following table illustrates how genitive: a reference contrasts with locative: a place.

28. 'be at **someone's place**; in, at **someplace**'	
G: ref *byt' u kogo* (+humans) [be at **who-GEN**]	L: place *byt' v, na čem* (+ non-humans) [be in, on **what-LOC**]
29. 'stand by **the road**'	
G: ref *stojat' u dorogi* [stand at **road-GEN**]	L: place *stojat' pri doroge* [stand at **road-LOC**]
30. 'receive salary after **the completion** of work'	
G: ref *polučit' zarplatu posle okončanija raboty* [receive salary-ACC after **ending-GEN** work-GEN]	L: place *polučit' zarplatu po okončanii raboty* [receive salary-ACC after **ending-LOC** work-GEN]

Genitive: a reference vs. locative: a place

All three contrasts involve the use of one item (marked as either genitive: a reference or locative: a place) to specify the position of another item. These contrasts are motivated by the fact that the use of reference points and positional landmarks are both good strategies for describing location.

Other construals discussed above:

10. [genitive: a source vs. instrumental: a means]
11. [genitive: a whole vs. instrumental: a means]
13. [genitive: a goal vs. instrumental: a landmark]
17, 18. [genitive: a goal vs. accusative: a destination]
2, 3, 4. [genitive: a reference vs. nominative: a name]
19. [genitive: a reference vs. accusative: a destination]
20. [genitive: a goal vs. accusative: a destination vs. dative: a receiver]
24, 25. [genitive: a whole vs. dative: an experiencer]
6. [nominative: a name vs. genitive: a reference vs. instrumental: a means]

Construals Involving the Locative

All other construals have already been discussed above:

12. [locative: a place vs. instrumental: an adjunct]
23. [locative: a place vs. accusative: a dimension]
26, 27. [locative: a place vs. genitive: a whole]
28, 29, 30. [locative: a place vs. genitive: a reference]

The following table summarizes the data presented above. Note, however, that all contrasts are presented multiple times in this table so that they can be seen from the perspective of each case (i.e., nominative: a name vs. dative: an experiencer as well as dative: an experiencer vs. nominative: a name).

Example	Contrast	Conceptual Domains Involved
1.	**N: a name** vs. D: an experiencer	personal vs. impersonal
2, 3, 4.	**N: a name** vs. G: a reference	comparatives, negation, possessor
5.	**N: a name** vs. I: a means vs. A: a destination	possession
6.	**N: a name** vs. I: a means vs. G: a reference	active vs. passive vs. causative/middle
7.	**N: an identity** vs. I: a label vs. A: a destination	states of being
5.	**I: a means** vs. N: a name vs. A: a destination	possession
6.	**I: a means** vs. N: a name vs. G: a reference	passive vs. active vs. causative/middle
8.	**I: a means** vs. A: a destination	resource vs. direct object

9.	**I: a means** vs. **A: a dimension**	paths in space and time
10.	**I: a means** vs. **G: a source**	causation
11.	**I: a means** vs. **G: a whole**	fill with (resource) vs. full of (quantity)
7.	**I: a label** vs. **N: an identity** vs. **A: a destination**	states of being
12.	**I: an adjunct** vs. **L: a place**	with vs. location
13.	**I: a landmark** vs. **G: a goal**	prior temporal location
5.	**A: a destination** vs. **N: a name** vs. **I: a means**	possession
7.	**A: a destination** vs. **N: an identity** vs. **I: a label**	states of being
14, 15, 16.	**A: a destination** vs. **D: a competitor**	destinations, believing, studying (mental yielding)
17, 18.	**A: a destination** vs. **G: a goal**	intentional goals
19.	**A: a destination** vs. **G: a reference**	negation
20.	**A: a destination** vs. **G: a goal** vs. **D: a receiver**	intentional goals/purpose
21, 22.	**A: a dimension** vs. **D: a competitor**	similarity, distributed amounts
23.	**A: a dimension** vs. **L: a place**	locus of verbal/mental activity
20.	**D: a receiver** vs. **A: a destination** vs. **G: a goal**	intentional goals/purpose
1.	**D: an experiencer** vs. **N: a name**	personal vs. impersonal
24, 25.	**D: an experiencer** vs. **G: a whole**	possession
14, 15, 16.	**D: a competitor** vs. **A: a destination**	destinations, believing, studying (mental yielding)
21, 22.	**D: a competitor** vs. **A: a dimension**	similarity, distributed amounts
10.	**G: a source** vs. **I: a means**	causation
13.	**G: a goal** vs. **I: a landmark**	prior temporal location
17, 18.	**G: a goal** vs. **A: a destination**	intentional goals
20.	**G: a goal** vs. **A: a destination** vs. **D: a receiver**	intentional goals/purpose
11.	**G: a whole** vs. **I: a means**	full of (quantity) vs. fill with (resource)
24, 25.	**G: a whole** vs. **D: an experiencer**	possession
26, 27.	**G: a whole** vs. **L: a place**	simultaneity, possession/part-whole
2, 3, 4.	**G: a reference** vs. **N: a name**	comparatives, negation, possession
6.	**G: a reference** vs. **N: a name** vs. **I: a means**	causative/middle vs. active vs. passive
19.	**G: a reference** vs. **A: a destination**	negation
28, 29, 30.	**G: a reference** vs. **L: a place**	location, time after
12.	**L: a place** vs. **I: an adjunct**	location vs. with

23.	**L: a place** vs. A: a dimension	locus of verbal/mental activity
26, 27.	**L: a place** vs. G: a whole	simultaneity, possession /part-whole
28, 29, 30.	**L: a place** vs. G: a reference	location, time after

The thirty sets of case contrasts presented in the tables are probably not an exhaustive inventory of this phenomenon, but they are highly representative of the behavior of case in the Russian language, and it is believed that they include all major systematic contrasts. Given the overall number of case meanings and possible combinations, the number of case contrasts found here is less than 15 percent of those that might theoretically exist. Further examples are unlikely to significantly alter this figure. We should also note that the majority of case contrasts are not merely isolated phenomena, but are instead endemic to Russian grammar, serving multiple purposes (see, for example, sets 2, 3, and 4, in which a contrast of nominative: a name vs. genitive: a reference provides alternative construals for comparison, negation, and the role of possessor). What we have is therefore a highly constrained phenomenon, one that is neither random nor arbitrary. As suggested above, it appears that case contrasts target cognitively significant junctures in the interpretation of perceptual input. We can now turn to a discussion of these junctures, which involve the following issues: the telling of grammatical stories, possession, control, purpose, time, and other domains (both spatial and abstract). Ultimately, all of these issues emerge from human perceptual experience, as argued below.

Grammatical Stories

1. personal vs. impersonal
6. active vs. passive vs. causative/middle
8. resource vs. direct object
3, 19. negation
10. causation
11. fill with (resource) vs. full of (quantity)

This group of contrasts manipulates syntactic roles to produce alternative grammatical stories to describe similar perceptual input. Contrast 1 provides two alternative stories for situations involving an undergoer and an event, interpreting the undergoer as either an active agent that produces the event, or as a passive experiencer of the event. Contrast 6 provides three alternative stories for situations involving an agent, an event, and a patient, interpreting the event as either a product of the agent, something produced by means of the agent, or something that happens at the location of the agent. Human perceptual experience abounds with both intransitive and transitive events, and the alternative grammatical stories allow these events to be viewed from various perspectives. Contrast 8 is very similar, interpreting an item used in an action as either an instrument for bringing about the action or as the patient of the action. The involvement of items in actions as either instruments or patients is another pervasive experience. Contrast 11 interprets a substance as either the means for filling or as the whole from which a part is used when something is full; manipulation and measurement of substances is likewise a basic human experience. Causation, the issue of contrast 10, interprets an item (the cause) as either a means or a source, reflecting the ambiguous human experience of causes. Contrasts 3 and 19 present negation as either parallel to positive assertion (nominative or accusative) or as distinct from it (genitive). When negation is distinct, this distinction is predicated upon the lack of perceptual access that the speaker has to the item negated, rather than the actual existence or non-existence of the item.

Possession

4. possessor
5. possession
24, 25. possession
27. possession/part-whole

The relationship of possession can be interpreted in various ways. The possessor (prototypically human) can be either the agent of possession or a landmark for the location of a possessed item (4, 5). The possessed item can be alternatively construed as the means by which the experience of possession is realized (cf. the use of the instrumental in 5). Another possibility is to view the possessor as the whole of which the possessed item is a part (cf. the use of the genitive in 24, 25, and 27). This interpretation contrasts with others that involve the construal of the possessor as an experiencer (strongly emphasizing the role of the human being in this relationship) or as merely a location. Possession is an abstract relationship, partly derived from and partly projected onto reality. The establishment of this relationship is a hallmark feature of human experience.

Control/Purpose

14, 15, 16. destinations, believing, studying (mental yielding)
17, 18. intentional goals
20. intentional goals/purpose

Interactions of control and intent rank nearly as high as possession in terms of both their significance for the human experience and their prominence in motivating case contrasts. All of these contrasts involve action (be it actual physical movement or abstract intention) directed toward targets, differentiated according to the control exerted by the target and/or the intent of the agent.

Time

9. paths in space and time
13. prior temporal location
26. simultaneity
30. time after

Time is one of the most ubiquitous features of human experience, and indeed our ability to mentally manipulate time (remembering the past, imagining the future) is one of the capacities that sets us apart as humans. We have no direct perceptual access to time, a mental construct deduced from changes perceived in ourselves and our environment. Languages tend to use space as a metaphor for time, but because the features of space and time do not match very well (space is three-dimensional, while time is at best one-dimensional, and defective at that; all points in space are equally accessible, and we can travel through space, while only one point in time is accessible, and we cannot travel at will; etc.), there are varying mental models of time, even within single languages. Sometimes we imagine time as if it were a two-dimensional space, and other times as it if were a one-dimensional time line. Within the model of the time line, we can imagine ourselves either as static, with time moving past, or as travelers moving along the time line. And we can face either in the direction of the future (looking ahead), or in the direction of the past (following our forebears, those who have gone before us). The case contrasts involving time provide various construals for expanses of time, duration, and times prior to and following. Contrast 9 allows us to view a stretch of time as either a two-dimensional space (accusative) or as a conduit through which activity passes (instrumental). Contrast 13 construes a prior time as either a fixed point in a time line where our orientation is toward the future (instrumental; meaning that a prior event is before, or literally in front of, an event that takes place later), or as motion toward a reference point, where orientation is unspecified (genitive). Contrast 26 allows us to understand duration as either a part of a process (genitive) or as a (temporal) location alongside an activity. Contrast 30 presents alternative construals for a point in time that is later than another, viewed either as a static reference point (genitive) or as a point perceived with an orientation toward the past, where a later event follows those that precede.

Other Domains

2. comparatives
7. states of being
12. with vs. location
21, 22. similarity, distributed amounts
23. locus of verbal/mental activity
28, 29. location

The remaining contrasts deal with a variety of physical and abstract domains. Contrasts 12, 28, and 29 prove that even concrete location is open to interpretation. For contrast 12, co-location can be interpreted as either accompaniment (possible because the referent is human) or proximal position. The human factor plays a deciding role in contrast 28, since the use of a locative preposition is not possible when one human being is located at another human being (requiring the second person to be a reference point marked with the genitive); physical encroachment on or in a place is possible only for non-human locations or non-human referents at a location (such as clothes or glasses). Contrast 29 involves no human factors, but simply interprets 'near' as a separation from a reference point (genitive) or a location at a place (locative). The other contrasts in this group variously interpret abstract domains in terms of spatial dimensions. As we have seen with time above, spatial metaphors of this type involve imperfect and ambiguous mappings. Comparatives (contrast 2) and distributed amounts (contrast 22) both involve amounts that can be alternatively construed as points along a scale (genitive) and points of control (dative), or treated as mere objects (nominative and accusative). States of being, similarity, and topics of conversation or thought are all conceivable as various kinds of mental spaces that human beings can understand and manipulate in multiple ways.

Conclusions: The Lessons of Semantic Relationships among Cases

The case contrasts observed in Russian grammar are a limited, non-random, well-motivated phenomenon that demonstrates the powerful, meaningful connections holding the case system together. These contrasts are also indicative of the relationship between perception and linguistic expression and the centrality of specifically human subjective experience in the symbolic repertoire of language. In Peircean terms, this is a compelling story of the interaction of Firstness (the raw ability to aggregate and manipulate case meanings), Secondness (the perceptual/conceptual experiences that ground case meanings), and Thirdness (the actual structuring of case meanings in networks). Firstness, being pure potential, does not force singular interpretations, but broadly enables multiple strategies. Secondness may itself present ambiguity. And Thirdness can vary in the way this ambiguity is absorbed into systems. There is an overlay of Thirdness throughout this phenomenon, since both Firstness and Secondness aim toward Thirdness and are influenced by it. And Thirdness is active at both a microlevel (the interactions of submeanings of a single case) and a macrolevel (the interactions of various case meanings in the contrasts presented here). These relationships, and indeed the final interpretant, are anything but static fixtures. Our uniquely human experiences and our uniquely human ability to objectify the nonconcrete (via ontological metaphor) animate the three Peircean categories in the ebb and flow of our uniquely human imagination.

University of North Carolina-Chapel Hill

Works Cited

Bachman, Ronald David. 1980. "The subject potential of the dative case in modern Russian." Unpublished Ph.D. diss. Ohio State University.

Danaher, David S. 1999. "Iteration and the Peircean habit." In *The Peirce Seminar Papers IV*, ed. Michael Shapiro, 563–88. New York/Oxford: Berghahn Books.

Haley, Michael C. 1999. "Metaphor, mind, and space: What Peirce can offer Lakoff." In *The Peirce Seminar Papers IV*, ed. Michael Shapiro, 417–40. New York/Oxford: Berghahn Books.

Janda, Laura A. 1993. *A Geography of Case Semantics: The Czech Dative and the Russian Instrumental*. Berlin/New York: Mouton de Gruyter.

———. 1999. "Peircean semiotics and cognitive linguistics: A case study of the Russian genitive." In *The Peirce Seminar Papers IV*, ed. Michael Shapiro, 441–66. New York/Oxford: Berghahn Books.

———. in press a. "Cases in collision, cases in collusion: The semantic space of case in Czech and Russian." In *Where One's Tongue Rules Well*, ed. Laura Janda, Steven Franks, and Ronald Feldstein. Columbus, OH: Slavica.

———. in press b. *The Case Book for Russian*. Columbus, OH: Slavica.

———. forthcoming. "The case for competing conceptual systems." To appear in *Cognitive Linguistics Today*, ed. Barbara Lewandowska-Tomaszczyk, 367–87.

Janda, Laura A., and Steven J. Clancy. forthcoming. *The Case Book for Czech*.

Smith, Michael B. 1992. "The role of image schemas in German grammar." *Leuvense Bijdragen* 81: 385–410.

Toops, Gary H. 1987. "Russian contextual causatives." *Slavic and East European Journal* 31: 595–611.

Turner, Mark. 1996. *The Literary Mind*. New York: Oxford University Press.

Victor A. Friedman

Interrogation and Nonconfirmativity: A Peircean Approach to the Intersection between Expressive Past and Present

0. Introduction

This paper continues the investigation begun in Friedman (1999) by examining the interaction of nonconfirmativity and interrogation. Jakobson (1957 [1971]) originally identified interrogation as a status category, i.e., one qualifying the narrated event, but Aronson (1977, 1991) has argued cogently for a redefinition of status as qualifying the relation of the speaker to the narrated event, a category that includes confirmativity and nonconfirmativity (see also Friedman 1977: 21–81).[1] The intersection of interrogation and nonconfirmativity raises interesting issues about the nature of assertion and responsibility (cf. Réthoré 1999). Moreover, the difference in the interaction of nonconfirmativity and interrogativity in Albanian, the Frasheriote Aromanian dialect of Bela di suprã, and Balkan Slavic/Turkish can be analyzed in terms of the role of interpretants in contact-induced linguistic change (cf. also Shapiro 1991: 22–41).[2]

The research for this article was aided by a grant for East European Studies from the American Council of Learned Societies with funding from the U.S. Department of State/Research and Training for Eastern Europe and the Independent States of the Former Soviet Union Act of 1983 (Title VIII) and by a grant from the National Endowment for the Humanities (reference: FA-36517-01).

What we find is that Aromanian stands midway between Albanian and Balkan Slavic/Turkish in this respect, and the impact of language contact on the linguistic code seems to index cultural impact and/or habit-change.

1. Nonconfirmativity

I shall begin with a brief review of the main points of Friedman (1999) in order to set the context. In that article I discussed the contrast between the following Albanian sentences:

(1a) *Qumështi është i verdhë*
(1b) *Qumështi qenka i verdhë*
    'The milk is yellow'

The difference between the plain indicative *është* 'is' in (1a) and the nonconfirmative indicative *qenka* 'is' in (1b) can be summarized by the following three nuances (contextual variant meanings) associated with nonconfirmative status:

1. surprise (admirative *sensu stricto*),[3] which is an emotive quality expressing a reaction of the speaker [first person], a kind of interjection that is spontaneous and immediate,[4] i.e., a kind of Firstness. Insofar as surprise is a quality of the speaker's emotional state of being unto itself, mediating only between the speaker and the object, *qenka* has an emotional dynamic interpretant (sympathetic mode, cf. Shapiro 1983: 65);
2. ironic doubt or disbelief (dubitative), which corresponds to the appellative or conative function of language because it involves replication and therefore requires the presence of a second person, whose statement is being refuted (cf. Haiman 1995: 338, "replication invalidates"), hence a type of Secondness, a force, a resistance to a statement, i.e., a categorical rejection, an energetic dynamic interpretant (percussive mode, Shapiro 1983: 65);
3. neutral report, deduction, or other mediated response (nonguarantive), which requires a third person, since in a closed addresser-addressee situation repetition without confirmation is refutation; for a nonguarantive to be uttered neutrally it must therefore refer to a third person or other conditioning factor and is thus cognitive rather than emotive

or appellative, involving objective evaluation rather than surprise or refutation, reflecting a type of Thirdness.[5] It involves a mental element—often, but not always, inference or report—and it mediates between the inherent acceptance of admirativity (surprise is caused by the speaker's willingness to confirm something unexpected) and the rejection of dubitativity by neither accepting nor rejecting but rather constating. It treats the information as of relative value; it has a logical dynamic interpretant (usual, Shapiro 1983: 65).

In its tripartite semantic nature, the Albanian nonconfirmative embodies within itself a kind of triadic semeiosis, thus illustrating the recursiveness of the semiotic process. By its very specification of speaker attitude, it partakes of Firstness, Secondness, and Thirdness, of (emotion in and of itself on the part of) the speaker, of (resistance of the speaker to) the addressee, and of a cognitive evaluation (but not guaranteeing) of something that is outside the speaker and the addressee. The sign mediated by these interpretants, within the Albanian grammatical system, is the former inverted perfect (e.g., third singular *ka qenë* literally 'has been' > *qenë ka* > *qenka* 'is'), which has ceased to be a perfect and has been completely transformed into a nonconfirmative present.

In Albanian, it was the entire process of postposing the auxiliary to the participle and then creating new paradigms once the meaning of the inverted perfect had shifted to a present that signified nonconfirmativity. The semiotic process was a complex interaction of morphosyntactic inversion and the creation of new interpretants for the new signs. The process moved from immediate to dynamic to final and from emotive to energetic to logical. The Frasheriote Arumanian speakers of Bela di suprã, however, upon coming into contact with Albanian, perceived the *-ka* of the third person singular present Albanian nonconfirmative as an iconic index of nonconfirmativity and created a new immediate interpretant out of the final interpretant of a single Albanian sign, which in its turn went through stages of becoming dynamic and final (cf. Andrews 1990: 44–80 and 1997).[6]

2. Interrogation

Let us now turn to interrogation as a sub-category of assertion as discussed in Réthoré (1999). Citing Peirce (2.291), Réthoré (1999:

223) points out that while Peirce often assimilated assertions to declaratives, he was also capable of distinguishing the latter as including the former as well as statements that were "doubtful or *mere* [emphasis added] interrogations." In this passage, Peirce is discussing the rise of the term *indicative* "or, as it should be called, *declarative* mood" (2.291). Later, Réthoré (1999: 224) cites Peirce (MS L 75b: 396, 1902): "The meaning of a sentence remains the same ... whether it be believed or doubted, asserted (by somebody's making himself responsible for it), commanded (by somebody's expressing that he holds another responsible for it), or just a question (when somebody expresses an attempt to induce another to make himself responsible for it)." As a request for information (i.e., attempting to make another take responsibility for an assertion), questions are traditionally divided between the so-called WH-question type, which demands more than simple confirmation or denial, and the Yes/No Question type, which is the type Réthoré (1999: 227) cites from Culioli (1985). From the point of view of assertion pragmatistically defined in Réthoré (1999), however, this distinction is not of relevance here. Our example will be a WH-question, but it could just as easily be of the Yes/No type.

A distinction that will be of relevance, however, is that between the question that signifies genuine interrogation and the so-called rhetorical question, which rejects a real or putative answer or attempts to force a declaration on the addressee. Since a rhetorical question may still attempt to make the addressee take responsibility for an assertion, in that sense it seems to partake of interrogativity, but it carries an additional nuance that is either dubitative as defined above, or *infelicitous* in Austin's (1962: 14) terminology. In other words, a rhetorical question is a declaration phrased (disguised) as a question. As we shall see below, this distinction is crucial to the grammars of the languages under consideration here, and suggests differences in the semiotic processes that affected their respective developments of nonconfirmativity.

In terms of the semiotics of punctuation (cf. Battistella 1993, 1999), assertions are indexed by three types of full stops: the exclamation point (which corresponds to the admirative and also the imperative), the period (which is neutral and also potentially nonguarantive), and the question mark (which by itself does not correspond to the dubitative, but does partake of Secondness in its addresser-addressee specificity). There is, however, a fourth sign of punctuation, namely, the combination of the exclamation point and the question mark. This is a sign of the rhetorical question, i.e., the question that combines admirativity and dubitativity and is not a question *sensu stricto*.[7]

3. Interrogation and Nonconfirmativity in Albanian

Consider the following situation involving a nonrhetorical Albanian question in the plain present indicative and in the nonconfirmative indicative. A man walks into a barber shop expecting to find the owner, a master barber, but instead no one is there but the owner's apprentice. The potential customer has two choices in inquiring after the man he is looking for:

(2a) *Ku është mjeshtri?*
(2b *Ku qenka mjeshtri?*
'Where is the boss?'

Question (2a) contains a neutral request for information, whereas, in the context given above, version (2b) could only convey surprise at not finding the boss in the shop and could not be dubitative or nonguarantive. An admirative question in this context is thus simultaneously a request for information (attempt to have the addressee take responsibility for an assertion) and an implicit assertion that the speaker had expected to find the boss in his shop. Sentence (2a), which is indicative *sensu stricto*, is a simple interrogative assertion. Sentence (2b), which employs nonconfirmative status and is thus still declarative in Peirce's sense (cf. 2.291, note 1), is contextually admirative and thus carries an added element of surprise, i.e., disappointed expectation. In opposition to sentence (1b), the context of sincere assertive interrogation of (2b)—this is not a rhetorical or repetitive question implying dubitativity (incredulity) to be discussed below—neutralizes the possibility of a nonguarantive interpretation.

If the barber comes out from behind a curtain at the back of the shop, and the customer realizes that the barber was in the building all along and simultaneously receives an answer to his question by seeing the barber, he has the following possibilities of response:[8]

(3a) *Ah, këtu je.*
(3b) *Ah, këtu qenke/paske qenë/qenkësh/paskësh qenë!*
'Ah, here you are'

Response (3a) is a simple acknowledgment that the barber's act of coming out from behind a curtain in the back of his shop is a sign (index or token) of his presence. Response (3b), however, contains a grammatically expressed tone (cf. Réthoré 2000, 2001) of the speaker's surprise that is absent from (3a). It thus adds a quality of Firstness to the Secondness of apprehending the sign of the barber's presence. At the same time, however, the grammar of Albanian permits the speaker to use, in addition to a present nonconfirmative, a perfect, imperfect, or pluperfect nonconfirmative (given in that order in [3b]) as a substitute for the present, to express his surprise at the present discovery of a pre-existing fact (cf. Friedman 1999: 524–25). The substitutions carry with them nuances of 'as it turns out, you have been here all along and I was unaware of it'. The choice itself can be iconic: the more remote the underlying time reference (from perfect as 'past event relevant in the present' through imperfect 'past durative event' to pluperfect 'past anterior event'), the stronger the tone of surprise at the moment of discovery, i.e., the more remote the speaker's expectation from the actual and pre-existing state.

4. Interrogation and Nonconfirmativity in Macedonian

Let us now turn to this same scenario in Macedonian. Upon entering the barber shop, the customer could only ask the question using a present indicative:

(4a) *Kade e majstorot?*
(4b) **Kade bil majstorot?*
　　'Where is the boss?'

However, when the master barber emerges from the back room, the customer could exclaim:

(5a) *A, tuka si.*
(5b) *A, tuka si bil!*
　　'Ah, here you are!'

Sentence (5a) is also present indicative, but sentence (5b) refers to the present discovery of a pre-existing state and is equivalent, in its effect, to the Albanian nonconfirmative of (3b).[9] Sentence (5b) uses an unmarked past that is nonconfirmative by virtue of its opposition to a marked confirmative.[10] Although the correct translation into English requires a present tense, the correct usage in Macedonian requires a past state that has come to the unexpected attention of the speaker at the moment of speech. It is thus not the case that the opposition present/past is neutralized in (5b), as has often been argued (e.g., Lunt 1952: 80); rather, the present recognition of a state that existed in the past is expressed by a past tense (perfect-related) form.[11]

5. Interrogation and Nonconfirmativity in Aromanian

In the Frasheriote Aromanian dialect of Bela di suprã, the non-confirmative can be used felicitously in (6b) but not in (6a):

(6a) *Iu iesti/*fuska maistorlu?*
 'Where is the boss?'
(6b) *Ah, tini iesht/fuska acia!*
 'Ah, here you are!'

The Aromanian displays a borrowed Albanian morphology with a Balkan Slavic/Turkish semantic restriction. That is, the particle -*ka*, borrowed from Albanian as an indexical legisign whose final interpretant is nonconfirmativity, has the same type of restrictions as the Slavic *l*-participle in interrogative assertions. These restrictions constitute a different "cumulation of dynamic interpretants over time" (Shapiro 1991: 33).

6. Interrogation and Dubitativity

Before pursuing this line of thought, let us consider the one context that would permit an Aromanian nonconfirmative and a Balkan Slavic/Turkish (old) perfect with (apparently) present meaning, i.e., with the translation 'is' in English. Such a context occurs if the question is not being asked as a request for information, i.e., if the question is not a question but rather a dubitative exclamation, in other words, a rejection of a previous statement (answer). Thus, for example, if the customer upon entering the shop had inquired of the apprentice after the whereabouts of the master and the apprentice had answered something that the customer knew to be untrue, the customer could grammatically exclaim:

(7a) *Abe, iu fuska maistorlu?!* (Aromanian)
(7b) *Abe, kade bil majstorot?!* (Macedonian)
(7c) *Abe, usta neredeymiş?!* (Turkish)
 'Wha-a-a, *where* is the boss [did you say]?!'

In the Albanian of (2b), the question is pragmatically sincere, although also emotive and expressing surprise.[12] In Balkan Slavic and Turkish, however, the nonconfirmative cannot be used in a question that requests information concerning the present. If, however, the utterance is dubitative and thus actually refers to a previous statement, i.e., has some element of pastness that is purely appellative in its Secondness, a nonconfirmative is acceptable. In this respect, the Aromanian patterns with the Macedonian and Turkish, although the origin of its nonconfirmative is Albanian. In a Peircean sense, the rhetorical question is still an assertion, but it is an assertion with a declarative intent. Its dynamic interpretant is thus quite different from that of the interrogative question.

7. Interrogation, Nonconfirmativity, and Interpretants

From the viewpoint of the theory of interpretants in its application to language learning as elucidated by Andrews (1990: 44–80)—albeit here in a multilingual rather than a classroom environment and with implications for language change at a more collective (general structural, historical) rather than individual level—the contrasting of nonconfirmative interrogation in Albanian, Aromanian, and Balkan Slavic/Turkish shows a habit-change in which the final logical interpretants of nonconfirmativity have different ultimate logical interpretants (cf. Shapiro 1983: 67). I would argue that this difference relates to the history of acquisition and contact, for which Shapiro (1991: 40) cites the following relevant passage from Peirce (5.489): "It is not to be supposed that upon every presentation of a sign capable of producing a logical interpretant, such interpretant is actually produced. The occasion may be either too early or too late. If it is too early, the semeiosis will not be carried so far, the other interpretants sufficing for the rude functions for which the sign is used. On the other hand, the occasion will come too late if the interpreter be already familiar with the logical interpretant, since then it will be recalled to his mind by a process which affords no hint of how it was originally produced." Although Labov's data demonstrate that the variational phenomena leading to language change occur in adolescence and that a given speaker's language varies over time, thus indicating that language acquisition per se is not always "the matrix of language change" (Shapiro 1993: 41), it is certainly also the case that contact phenomena are both acquisitional and language changing. In the case of the three different interactions of nonconfirmativity and interrogativity, we have three different cases of what had been, at an earlier stage, emergent grammar (Andersen 1973).[13] In each case an ultimate logical interpretant has been brought to a new pattern by final causation (cf. Shapiro 1993: 41).

In Friedman (1999: 516), I noted that the explicit observation of grammaticalized nonconfirmativity by native grammarians of the Balkan (Indo-European) languages goes no further back than the late nineteenth and early twentieth centuries. In the case of Turkish, however, this type of observation was made in the eleventh century by the first native grammarian (Dankoff 1982: 412), and, as a grammatical phenomenon, it is attested in the oldest Turkic texts of the eighth century (Tekin 1968: 192–93). Given that during this period the attested languages of the Balkans (Greek, Latin, and, later, Slavic) did not have such categories and that their development in the later stages of Balkan Slavic and some Balkan Romance took place, if at all, during the Ottoman period, the role of contact with Turkish in these developments must be viewed as at least potential.[14] At the same time, the fact that status developed most systemically in Albanian and Balkan Slavic as a whole, in Balkan Romance only partially,[15] and not at all in Greek might be linked to Turkish as a sign (token or index) of prestige, especially urban prestige, in competition with prestige factors of the languages with which it was in contact.[16] In Friedrich's (1975: 208–10) terms, the bilingual speaker (interpretant) would thus link cultural code and linguistic code.

In comparing the Albanian and Balkan Slavic phenomena, Ylli (1989) makes the point that the Albanian nonconfirmative always has an element of doubt (*sensu largo*) that can be lacking in the Balkan Slavic/Turkish uses of their respective former perfects. When interrogation is contrasted to declaration, however, we find that in Balkan Slavic/Turkish—in opposition to Albanian—it is only with dubitative meaning that a nonconfirmative question with apparent present reference can be asked. Interrogation thus tests belief and at the same time is diagnostic of temporal reference. The peculiar combination of Albanian morphology and Balkan Slavic/Turkish restriction found in the Frasheriote Aromanian of Bela di suprã reflects a conceptual intermediacy resulting, it would seem, from temporal posteriority (cf. Peirce 5.489). Peirce's view of language combined with textual and grammatical evidence gives us a basis for two relative chronologies. It is arguable that diachronically the order of transmission was Turkish

[> Balkan Slavic >] Albanian > Aromanian (cf. Shapiro 1991: 33). In terms of social relations as indexed by grammatical change, however, and also in terms of the development of interpretants, Aromanian is located between Albanian and Turkish/Balkan Slavic.

In some of her recent work, Réthoré (2000, 2001) has raised points that are directly relevant to the development of nonconfirmativity in the Balkan languages. The diagrams in Réthoré (2001: 175–77), which in the context of her work represent three different models of interpretation, can be taken to represent—in our Balkan context—a diachronic model of the development of nonconfirmativity from *otherness* (two speakers using a language foreign to both) through *dissimilarity* (two speakers who are politically related to but do not belong to the dominant collective regardless of their competence in its language) to *resemblance* or *identity* (two speakers who are natives). The matrix language here begins as Turkish but then shifts to Balkan Slavic or Albanian and finally to Aromanian. By referring the signs of Turkish to the closest possible corresponding legisigns in Balkan Slavic or Albanian (and then by the recursion of this same process from those languages in Aromanian), speakers change habits and create new categories. Moreover, these categories relate to Réthoré's (2000, 2001) recent discussion of *tone*. Especially in their admirative and dubitative functions, nonconfirmatives actualize tone as a token of Secondness and thus render the phonological as grammatical.

The theory of the role of interpretants in language acquisition proposed by Andrews (1990: 44–80) and extended to contact-induced change in Friedman (1999) is crucial in understanding the play among factors that produced the current set of linguistic relations. In this sense, Albanian, Aromanian, and Balkan Slavic/Turkish taken together form a triad. Albanian has a marked nonconfirmative; Balkan Slavic and Turkish have a marked confirmative, and their respective nonconfirmatives exist only in opposition to it;[17] while Aromanian has a marked nonconfirmative, like its Albanian source, but a usage that bears restrictions of Balkan Slavic and Turkish.

Balkan Slavic/Turkish nonconfirmative usages are strategies that evolved from perfects without ever becoming completely restructured (cf. the discussion of Peirce 5.489 above). Albanian followed a similar evolution but with complete restructuring coordinated with the failure to develop a marked confirmative. It is worth noting, in connection with Jappy (this volume) that the Albanian case exemplifies a grammatical item arising out of another grammatical item, i.e., out of syntactic and not lexical material. Moreover, the assignment of meaning to word order in Albanian can be taken as a kind of iconicity or perhaps even a metaphoric hypoicon (cf. Peirce 2.277, cited in Jappy, this volume), insofar as the removal of the possessive auxiliary to a position after the main verb reflects a removal or distancing of the speaker's present or past willingness to confirm the statement.[18] Aromanian borrowed the Albanian nonconfirmative marker, but now deploys it in a manner similar to that of Balkan Slavic/Turkish in interrogation. Shapiro (1991: 119) makes the point with regard to logical interpretants that "the form of meaning is markedness." In its position between Albanian and Balkan Slavic/Turkish, Aromanian shows a type of marked nonconfirmativity combining the morphological sinsign of the Albanian with a Balkan Slavic/Turkish argument. This reflects the external history of the Frasheriote Aromanians of Bela di suprã, who came to southwestern Macedonia from the plains of Myzeqe in central Albania. It is only in the dynamic infelicity of the dubitative that the three become as one.

University of Chicago

Notes

1. Aronson (1977, 1991) does not directly address the question of where he will assign interrogativity in his revised system, although he hints (Aronson 1991: 115) that it would be treated as a nonshifting designator, akin to 'aspect' or 'mood' in his terms. The exact assignment need not concern us here, although the questions it raises should be addressed in the future.
2. In this essay, I shall be using the term 'Balkan Slavic' as a convenient shorthand for 'Macedonian and Bulgarian'. In other contexts, the two languages must be treated separately and/or the southernmost dialects of Serbian (the so-called 'Torlak' or 'Prizren-Timok' dialects) must also be included, but these issues are not relevant to the matters considered here.
3. The traditional term 'admirative' was first used in the Albanian grammar of Dozon (1879: 226–27), who introduced the French *admiratif* on the basis of Kristoforidhi's Greek *aposdókētoi* 'unexpected'.
4. I also made the point that while surprise is the result of a stimulus and thus enters into indexicality (CP 2.254–65, 2.274–302), and thus Secondness (Parmentier 1994: 17), as a linguistic expression it obviously embodies all of the various relevant elements of the sign relation. In terms of the trichotomy of person within language, however, surprise does not require the existence of another person in order to function as surprise. The speaker is sufficient.

5. An example of another conditioning factor is, for example, a person reciting an account of something he or she may have been witness to but does not remember clearly (or at all). In such cases, there is still a sense of third-party intervention, regardless of the actual source.
6. The Aromanian equivalents of the Albanian sentences (1a and 1b) are *Laptile iesti galbin* and *Laptile fuska galbin*. It is worth noting that the origin of the Aromanian admirative in expressions of surprise (Firstness) is indicated by the fact that when Marjan Markovik´ and I discovered it while doing field work in 1992, a context of surprise was the first in which it occurred in spontaneous usage. Similarly, in Albanian, 'surprise' was the first meaning to be perceived among the earliest grammarians describing Albanian, cf. note 3 above.
7. It is worth noting that the exclamation point and question mark can be combined with each other, but neither can combine normally with a single period. Similarly, the meanings of admirativity and dubitativity can be combined felicitously, but neither is compatible in and of itself with the neutral nonguarantive.
8. I am assuming a situation in which the customer is a regular patron and therefore on familiar (second singular) terms with the barber. The use of second plural forms would bring in different types of social indexicality that are not relevant for our considerations here.
9. See Friedman (2000) for details.
10. The nonconfirmative or unmarked past continues an originally perfect construction (auxiliary 'be' + past resultative participle in *-l*), which became the unmarked past elsewhere in Slavic. The old synthetic preterits (aorist/imperfect), like the Turkish past tense in *-di*, are markedly confirmative, i.e., specify the speaker's vouching for the truth of the statement, often—but not always—because the event described was witnessed. (The Macedonian sentence *No potoa* **se slučija** *raboti za koi ne znaev* 'But then things **happened** that I didn't know about'—which uses a synthetic preterit (aorist) and was said by a speaker aware of the fact that the things in question *did* happen—demonstrates that confirmation and not witnessing is the basic meaning [see Friedman 1977: 21–51]).
11. The facts illustrated by sentences (4a), (4b), (5a), and (5b) are, ceteris paribus and mutatis mutandis, the same for Bulgarian and Turkish. Similar expressions are found in Scandinavian languages and, via calquing, also when Scandinavians speak English, e.g., upon first tasting a good glass of wine—"That was a nice wine!"—despite the fact that most of the wine remains to be drunk.
12. If, however, (2b) were uttered with dubitative intent and intonation (again, quite probably with a lexical marker of emphatic vocativity such as *abe*), then the effect would be the same as in (7a,b,c), and, moreover, the paradigm choices available would be the same as illustrated in (3b).
13. The connection between nonconfirmativity and abduction is discussed by Guentchéva (1990: 48).
14. I noted in Friedman (1999: 526) the debate concerning contact versus native development on the basis of universal principles. The two points of view, however, are not mutually exclusive. Linguistic creativity (cf. Friedrich 1975: 235–36) in the context of multilingualism can combine them both. With regard to Albanian, it is worth noting that the synthetic inverted perfect does not always appear to have the current nonconfirmative meaning in the earliest continuous texts, which all date from after the Ottoman conquest (as do the earliest such texts in Romanian).

15. In South Danubian Balkan Romance, i.e., Aromanian and Megleno-Romanian, the Frasheriote Aromanian phenomenon is limited to a single dialect, and in Megleno-Romanian the nonconfirmative use of an inverted perfect is probably related to contact with Balkan Slavic (cf. Friedman 1994 and 2001). The presumptive mood of Daco-Romanian (North Danubian Romance) is semantically related in its functions, but markedly modal in its construction (cf. Friedman 1998).
16. I have in mind here the prestige that Greek and Latin retained in the face of the Turkish conquest as languages of the city and of religion. Although Slavic, too, was spoken in cities and used in liturgies, it was always in competition with Greek and/or Latin until the time of the arrival of the Turks, after which it was in retreat as a liturgical language in the South Balkans until the nineteenth century. It is worth noting that the Greek third singular present *lé[e]i* 'one says' is used as a kind of particle expressing what appears to be a complex of meanings related to nonconfirmativity. Most examples of this use of *lé[e]i* resemble reportative particles such as Russian *mol* or Bulgarian *kaj*, which, in the appropriate context, can be dubitative. But *lé[e]i* is also used in emphatic affirmation that has a sort of admirative quality:

(i) —*Ítan kaló to fagitó?*—*Kaló, léi!*
—Was the meal good?,—Very good! (Kriarás 1995)

(I am indebted to César Montoliu for bringing this usage and examples of it to my attention.)
17. I am excluding the issue of Balkan Slavic and Turkish pluperfects and modal constructions (*sensu largo*), which need not concern us here.
18. Much the same phenomenon is observable in Megleno-Romanian (cf. Friedman 1994) in which the inversion of the perfect, e.g., *ău fost > fost-ău* 'he/she/it has been/was', also reflects a distancing of the speaker from the events described, rendering them as reported, surprising, doubted, or disbelieved.

Works Cited

Andersen, H. 1973. "Abductive and deductive change." *Language* 49: 765–93.
Andrews, E. 1990. *Markedness Theory: The Union of Asymmetry and Semiosis in Languages*. Durham: Duke University Press.
———. 1997. "The semiotics of catastrophe in linguistic change." In *Semiotics around the World: Synthesis in Diversity*, vol. 1, ed. I.R. and G.F. Carr, 178–82. Berlin: Mouton de Gruyter.
Aronson, H.I. 1977. "Interrelationships between aspect and mood in Bulgarian." *Folia Slavica* 1 (1): 19–32.
———. 1991. "Towards a typology of verbal categories." In *New Vistas in Grammar: Invariance and Variation*, ed. L.R. Waugh and S. Rudy, 111–31. Amsterdam: Benjamins.
Austin, J.L. 1962. *How to Do Things with Words*. Cambridge, Mass.: Harvard University Press.

Batistella, E. 1993. "Notes on the sign structure of English punctuation." In *The Peirce Seminar Papers*, vol. 1, ed. M. Shapiro, 7–30. Providence: Berghahn Books.
———. 1999. "A Peircean approach to the apostrophe." In *The Peirce Seminar Papers*, vol. 4, ed. M. Shapiro, 87–110. New York: Berghahn Books.
Culioli, A. 1985. *Notes du séminaire de DEA 1983–1984*. Poitiers: University of Poitiers.
Dankoff, R. with J. Kelly, ed. and trans. 1982. Mahmud al-Kāšġarī *Compendium of the Turkic Dialects (Dīwān Luġāt at-Turk.)* (Turkish Sources 7). Part 1. Cambridge, Mass.: Harvard University Press.
Dozon, Auguste. 1879. *Manuel de la langue chkipe ou albanaise*. Paris: Société asiatique de Paris.
Friedman, V.A. 1977. *The Grammatical Categories of the Macedonian Indicative*. Columbus: Slavica.
———. 1994. "Surprise! Surprise! Aromanian has had an admirative!" *Indiana Slavic Studies* 7: 79–89.
———. 1998. "The grammatical expression of presumption and related concepts in Balkan Slavic and Balkan Romance." In *American Contributions to the 12th International Congress of Slavists*, ed. A. Timberlake and M. Flier, 390–405. Columbus: Slavica.
———. 1999. "Peirce, Albanians, and Vlahs: Semiotics and status in the Balkan *Sprachbund*." In *The Peirce Seminar Papers*, vol. 4, ed. M. Shapiro, 515–29. New York: Berghahn Books.
———. 2000. "Confirmative/nonconfirmative in Balkan Slavic, Balkan Romance, and Albanian, with additional observations on Turkish, Romani, Georgian, and Lak." In *Evidentials in Turkic, Iranian and Neighbouring Languages*, ed. L. Johanson and B. Utas, 329–66. Berlin: Mouton de Gruyter.
———. 2001. "The Vlah minority in Macedonia: Language, identity, dialectology, and standardization." In *Selected Papers in Slavic, Balkan, and Balkan Studies* (Slavica Helsingiensa 21), ed. J. Nuorluoto, M. Leiwo, and J. Halla-aho, 26–50. Helsinki: University of Helsinki.
Friedrich, P. 1975. "The lexical symbol and its relative non-arbitrariness." In *Linguistics and Anthropology: In Honor of C. F. Voegelin*, ed. M.D. Kinkade, K.L. Hale, and O. Werner, 199–247. Lisse: Peter de Ridder.
Guentchéva, Z. 1990. "Valeur inférentielle et valeur 'admirative' en bulgare." *Sâpostavitelno ezikoznanie* 15 (4/5): 47–52.
Haiman, J. 1995. "Moods and metamessages: Alienation as mood." In *Modality in Grammar and Discourse*, ed. J. Bybee and S. Fleischman, 329–45. Amsterdam: Benjamins.
Jakobson, R. 1957 [1971]. *Shifters, Verbal Categories, and the Russian Verb*. Cambridge, Mass.: Harvard University Department of Slavic Languages and Literatures (reprinted in *Selected Writings*, vol. 2: *Word and Language*, 130–7. The Hague: Mouton).
Kriarás, E. 1995. *Neo Elliniko Leksiko*. Athens: Ekdoti Athēnon
Lunt H. 1952. *A Grammar of the Macedonian Literary Language*. Skopje: Državno knigoizdatelstvo.
Parmentier, R.J. 1994. *Foundations of Peircean Semiotics*. Bloomington: Indiana University Press.
Peirce, C.S. 1931–58. *Collected Papers of Charles Sanders Peirce, I–VIII*. Cambridge, Mass.: Harvard University Press.

Réthoré, J. 1999. "A critical view of assertion from the perspective of Peircean pragmatics." In *The Peirce Seminar Papers*, vol. 4, ed. M. Shapiro, 223–42. New York: Berghahn Books.

———. 2000. "*Langage*, an actual partner to *discours* and *langue*." *Semiotica* 128 (3/4): 487–97.

———. 2001. "The Language of the English: The tones of a people." *Anglophonia/ Caliban* 9: 163–77.

Shapiro, Michael. 1983. *The Sense of Grammar: Grammar as Semiotic*. Bloomington: Indiana University Press.

———. 1991 *The Sense of Change: Language as History*. Bloomington: Indiana University Press.

Tekin, T. 1968. *A Grammar of Orkhon Turkic*. Bloomington: Indiana University Press.

Ylli, Xh. 1989. "Habitorja e shqipes dhe mënyra ritreguese (preizkazno naklonenie) e bullgarishtes." *Studime filologjike* 43 [26] (2): 47–56.

Jørgen Dines Johansen

Reading as Iconization

1.0 Literature

Words are the prime example of symbolic signs, and languages are predominantly symbolic sign systems. However, it is easily shown that languages need the iconic and indexical dimensions to function. The online text itself does contain iconic and indexical indications, but largely these dimensions have to be reconstructed by the interpreter, who must use both memory and imagination to fill in the proper conceptual content and relationships. When we are talking about a familiar universe, such a filling in is done automatically and most often unconsciously. Of course, this process may rise to the level of consciousness when, for instance, we attempt to remind others and ourselves of the specific features of something. Furthermore, we are aware of recognizing objects and relationships in the world from only a verbal description.

The same is true of universes that do not exist independently of their verbal descriptions. In order to make sense of a fictional universe of discourse, the reader has, as pointed out by Ingarden (1965 [1931]) and Iser (1978), to supplement what is not mentioned but is presupposed. In the translation of the symbolic signs of the text into iconic ones, there is, however, an indefinite number of equally valid ways of realizing what is indicated but not specified in the text. Intersemiotic translation always uses the stock of knowledge of the translator in question, and the phenomenologists of experience are right in stressing that there is a "private component" to every stock of knowledge (see Schutz and Luckmann 1973: 112). Thus, when a character or scene is imagined, there will be widely different solutions determined by the experiences and imaginary force of the individual reader, yet those solutions may still be within the possibilities delimited by the significations of the linguistic text. Such intersemiotic translation is effectuated in public by the director, the scene painter, the stage master, and the actors, who together transform the symbolic signs of the drama into iconic and indexical signs to fill the empty stage for an audience—and everybody knows the power of a staging to spoil or create wonders of a text. And such realizations of the text—its transmutations, as Jakobson calls this form of translation—are active in furthering the emotional engagement of the reader. The reason is that to iconize literary texts most often means to call up images related to memories and fantasies that are drive-cathected because they are related to the intimate and emotional life of the recipient.

1.1 Three ways of iconizing the literary text

Since according to Peircean semiotics there are three types of iconic signs—images, diagrams, and metaphors—there should also be three ways to iconize the text during reading. And indeed there are. The three ways are: first, identification and recognition of the elements or parts represented in the text, i.e., imaginative iconization or imaginization, linked with the production of mental images triggered by the literary text; second, the structuring of what is represented as a network of relationships, i.e., diagrammatic structuration; and third, the relating of elements and relationships of the universe represented in the text to other conceptual structures, i.e., allegorization.

1.1.1 Imaginization

Imaginization has to do with the use of imagination in linking the symbolic signs of the text with iconic ones. In fact, some readers claim to equate the experience of reading a novel, for example, to that of going to the cinema, since the text becomes realized as a movie on their internal screen. It must be stressed, however, that although vision is very powerful, imaginative iconization covers the different modes of perception. With regard to literature, this is especially important because the realization of both sound images and rhythm and the linking of these with emotions play an important role in reading poetry. Furthermore, when the iconized text deals with representations of lifeworld and human interaction, enjoyment, and suffering, it becomes invested with fragments of the readers' personal knowledge. This is why there is, it seems to me, a double, and prima facie self-contradictory, reason why people often react passionately to literature. On the one hand, readers are thrilled by visions or stories that are definitely coming to them from the outside and bringing something novel that enlarges their minds. On the other hand, in relating to the fictional universe they necessarily bring in their own memories and fantasies, and consequently also the love and the hate, and the triumphs and humiliations they have gone through.

Of course, imaginization may lead to bad readings, irresponsible and self-indulgent readings that go against the significations of the text. I must admit, however, that I don't see how we can put an end to it.[1] I am also confident that expert readers do the same thing. Indeed, they *should* read in this way, because if they don't, they will miss an important way of experiencing the text and be blind to one of literature's main functions. Expert readers, however, are trained to follow the instructions of the text, i.e., they are sensitive to its semantics and cultural context, so that many of their associations, memories, and fantasies will be disregarded right away because they are immediately deemed incompatible with the text.

To view the literary text as a set of instructions for different ways of iconization may be useful. Despite the fact that iconization is not restricted to vision, let us inquire a little further into the pictorial mode of imaginative iconization. First of all, it should be pointed out that literature favors imaginization because attention is directed not outwards from the text to the lifeworld of the readers but inwards. The verbal representation is not compared and matched with perception; rather, its instructions are matched with the imagined iconic representation it calls forth.

As to the instructions, literary texts differ widely in the number, in the wealth of details, and in the criteria of selection of such clues for iconization. Some movements (for instance, both romanticism and realism, though in different ways) offer rich instructions for the imaginative iconization of the readers; others (classicism, for example) are less generous. In any case, even a text that offers many instructions on how to iconize it leaves an indefinite—practically speaking, an infinite—number of decisions to the reader. Thus, literature calls for creative collaboration.

Obviously, this creative process may be fully conscious. However, the different schools of psychology do agree that most mental processes are unconscious. Consequently, it seems likely that what may call forth—in addition to the text's instructions—conscious and emotionally charged images, based on memory and fantasy, also has an impact on similar unconscious processes.

Hence, imaginization may partly explain the force of literature because reading creates or recalls images linked with memories and fantasies that are personal and private. Obviously, since these processes are more or less opaque even to the imagining subject, this aspect of iconization seems little accessible for scholarly study. However, even if the precise nature of the images of individual readers is largely inaccessible, or at least accessible only through interviews (maybe supported by tests), it may be possible to investigate types of images related to verbal descriptions of scenes and actions.

First of all, the text itself to a certain extent delimits what can and what cannot count as valid imaginative transmutations, or an iconic exemplification, of it. A famous scene from *Madame Bovary* may illustrate this:

> They gradually began to talk more frequently of matters outside their love, and in the letters that Emma wrote him she spoke of flowers, poetry, the moon and the stars, naïve resources of a waning passion striving to keep itself alive by all external aids. She was constantly promising herself a profound happiness on her next trip; then she confessed to herself that she had felt nothing extraordinary. This disappointment quickly gave way to a new hope, and Emma returned to him more avid and enflamed than before. She undressed brutally, ripping off the thin laces of her corset so violently that they would whistle round her hips like a gliding snake. She went on tiptoe, barefooted, to see once more that the door was locked, then with one movement, she would let her clothes fall at once to the ground; — then, pale and serious, without a word, she would throw herself against his breast with a long shudder.
> Yet there was upon that brow covered with cold drops, on those stammering lips, in those wild eyes, in the grip of those arms, something strange, vague and sinister that seemed to Léon to be subtly gliding between them to force them apart. (Flaubert 1965 [1857]: 205)

When *Madame Bovary* was accused of offending against public morals, this scene was cited by the prosecutor as admirable from the point of view of art, but execrable from the point of view of morality. And even today it may be considered outspoken, even graphic. This example exemplifies that there is, first, a certain order of events that has to be respected. For instance, Emma drops her clothes after she has assured herself that the door is locked; it is the last act described, before she throws herself at Leon's breast. Second, certain details are highlighted in the verbal description; the synaesthetic description of the thin laces being ripped off the corset is important. Third, a representation, which may count as an iconic exemplification of a linguistic text, has not only to be true to the order of events and significant details, it must also conform to the mood and emotional tenor of the text. In this case, any iconic representation that portrayed Emma as an unworried person, happily and carelessly enjoying sensual pleasures, would be invalid. Fourth, however, there is very much that is not specified at all: What dress is Emma wearing? How does she look in the nude? It would be a fair guess that Léon is already in bed when Emma throws "herself against his breast with a long shudder," but in fact the text does not say so; he may just as well be standing.

Secondly, analysis of imaginization will use the knowledge that many objects, scenes, and actions and interactions have a limited set of typical realizations to fill in what is presupposed but not mentioned. There is a certain number of ways that things are usually done and are usually conceived, because within a given culture the members share a cultural competence. Within cognitive philosophy and semantics, especially in the work of Lakoff and Mark Johnson, the integration of perception and conceptual knowledge is taken for granted. Lakoff (1987: 455) claims "that our perception and our mental images are structured by image schemas and that the schemas associated with lexical items are capable of fitting the schemas that structure our perceptions and images. On this hypothesis, we do not have pure unstructured perceptions and images. Perceptions and images are not merely pictorial. In perceiving and forming images, we impose a great deal of image-schematic structure. It is this image-schematic structure that allows us to fit language to our perceptions and rich images." Mark Johnson (1987: 208) distinguishes between two conceptual levels, that of basic level concepts and that of image-schemata: "(a) The *basic level*, at which we distinguish elephants from giraffes ... and at which we distinguish walking from running, and standing from sitting. This is the level of understanding that we have evolved to permit us to function passably well in our environment.... (b) The *image-schematic level,* which gives general form to our understanding in terms of structures such as CONTAINER, PATH, CYCLE, LINK, BALANCE, etc. This is the level that defines form itself, and allows us to make sense of the relation among diverse experiences." In this view, it is possible to describe typical mental imagery, or at least pertinent features of it, because it is linked both with species-specific image-schemata and with common experiences and conceptual structures within a culture. Furthermore, a stock of clichés, for instance, pictorial, will exist that iconological studies may show to be common to the members of a culture, or to communities within it.

Imaginization is certainly subjective and personal, and it is precisely the fact that it uses personal and private experiences that gives it its emotional force. However, one should not confuse subjectivity—not even the personal—with uniqueness. On the contrary, subjectivity is based on properties that we share as a species, properties related to age and sex, cultural properties, and properties characteristic of the communities to which we belong. And this is true of mental imagery and fantasies as well. While two readers may very rarely exemplify a symbolic representation with identical images, the images may well be similar. Discussions of book illustrations and movies based on works of literature show that most people have vague, but nevertheless resistant, mental images of scenes and characters that allow them to launch an articulate criticism at other iconic exemplifications.

Because, in reading literature, the verbal structure comes first, the linguistic text is seen as a set of instructions for imaginizing. However, most neuroscientists hold what has been called the dual-code theory of mental representation, which states that there are two representational systems, verbal and nonverbal, that may operate independently but normally interact in an adult human being. They are also located differently in the brain (e.g., the distinction between the left and the right hemispheres), and they operate on different principles because verbal processing is strictly sequential, while mental imagery is spatial and more holistic although images are scanned. Consciousness, according to Antonio Damasio, for instance, is not necessarily correlated with language: core consciousness and core self are nonverbal.

> Curiously, the very nature of language argues against it having a primary role in consciousness. Words and sentences denote entities, actions, events, and relationships. Words and sentences translate concepts, and concepts consist of the nonlanguage idea of what things,

actions, events and relationships are. Of necessity, concepts precede words and sentences in both the evolution of the species and the daily experience of each and every one of us. The words and sentences of healthy and sane humans do not come out of nowhere, cannot be the de novo translation of nothing before them....

One could argue, in fact, that the consistent content of the *verbal* narrative of consciousness—regardless of the vagaries of its form—permits one to deduce the presence of the equally consistent nonverbal, imagined narrative that I am proposing as the foundation of consciousness. (Damasio 2000: 185–86)

Thus, Damasio sees language as a translation of something prior that is of nonverbal nature, and he points out that people suffering from global aphasia are both conscious and able to communicate with others. Damasio also holds that language is immensely important, but this is because of its "ability to translate, with precision, thoughts into words and sentences, and words and sentences into thoughts; in the ability to classify knowledge rapidly and economically under the protective umbrella of a word; and in the ability to express imaginary constructions or distant abstractions with an efficient simple word" (ibid.: 111). To Damasio, the mind in general is characterized by the processing of mental images, and to him, the flow of images constitutes thought.

Finally, according to Damasio and other neuroscientists, concepts are distributed in many places in the brain according to sensory modality. Using the concept "hammer" as an example, Damasio explains: "Although the memory of separate aspects of our interactions with hammers are kept in separate parts of the brain, in dormant fashion, those different parts are coordinated in terms of their circuitries such that the dormant and implicit records can be turned into explicit albeit sketchy images, rapidly and in close temporal proximity. The availability of all those images allows us, in turn, to create a verbal description of the entity and that serves as a base for the definition" (ibid.: 221). The point of this sketchy, to say the least, excursion into neurobiology is the last part of what has just been quoted from Damasio. Here it is claimed that verbal definitions are built on the interrelatedness of a large number of images that are founded on an experiential relationship with the object in question. Hence, it is implied not only that nonverbal mental images precede verbal ones, as Damasio has stated elsewhere, but also that, asked for a verbal definition, a person will activate nonverbal mental imagery in order to be able to offer one. Damasio adds that this recall of images is executed swiftly and effortlessly.

In this view, then, it seems that an interaction between verbal and nonverbal will always be necessary in order to understand the contents of a text, or, as Damasio puts it, a translation from concepts to words and sentences, and vice versa. If this is true, there will always exist some relationship between word/sentence and clusters of mental images, as illustrated in figure 1. However, we may surmise that the activation of the dormant and implicit records of images may remain unconscious. If this is the case, then imaginizing while reading literature means making conscious and elaborating on what is at any rate going on unconsciously.

There is, however, also another point, because in spite of claims made by some readers, it is hard to believe that anyone can experience a whole novel, such as *War and Peace*, as a movie, if this

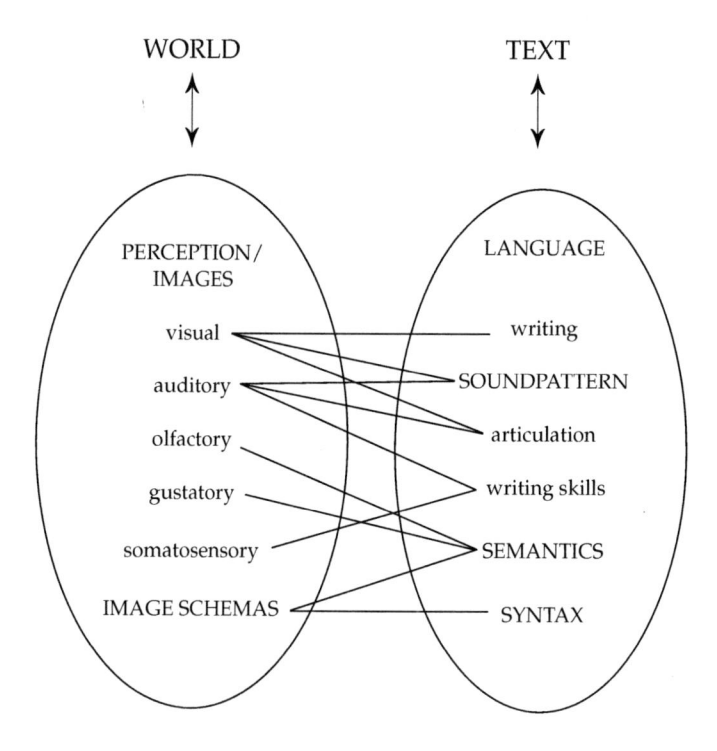

```
            WORLD                    TEXT
              ↕                        ↕

      ┌──────────────┐         ┌──────────────┐
      │ PERCEPTION/  │         │  LANGUAGE    │
      │   IMAGES     │         │              │
      │   visual     │─────────│  writing     │
      │   auditory   │─────────│ SOUNDPATTERN │
      │   olfactory  │         │  articulation│
      │   gustatory  │         │ writing skills│
      │ somatosensory│         │  SEMANTICS   │
      │ IMAGE SCHEMAS│         │   SYNTAX     │
      └──────────────┘         └──────────────┘
```

FIGURE 1

assertion is meant literally. And as the example from *Madame Bovary* shows, the amount of work demanded for consciously filling in what is not mentioned in the text itself would be stunning (although, of course, there are different levels of perceiving and imaginizing). Anyway, other readers experience only fragments of the text, tableaux, and scenes with the mind's eye—and texts give instructions for the imaginization of only parts of a scene, for imaginizing certain details while leaving it to readers to create pictorial unity (or unity within other perceptual modes). Hence, even if image processing is constantly proceeding on an unconscious level, only fragments thereof need to become conscious. For many readers the dominant way of experiencing a literary text is not as a continuous flow of images, as an inner movie theater; rather, it is diagrammatic. This bring us to the second way of iconizing the text.

1.1.2 Diagrammatization

Diagrammatization is abstractive, systematic, and concerned with the totality of the text. Concretely, some readers are less concerned with realizing images than with keeping track of the semantic attributes of the text elements; they see transformations and reversals as something abstract that affects the relations between the different parts of the text. They somehow look at the text as an algebraic structure, albeit a very peculiar kind of algebra.

It is a dogma of Peircean semiotics that signification presupposes the dynamic interaction between the iconic, indexical, and symbolic dimensions of signs, and to this dogma I myself subscribe. However, even if signification, in the last analysis, presupposes the possibility of intersemiotic translation, the different sign systems of human communication, and especially language, may possess a relative autonomy, in the sense that understanding is possible without any conscious translation into other sign systems, e.g., from symbolic into iconic signs. During conversation or reading, we simply do not translate all parts of the text into still or moving pictures, and nevertheless we understand it. We need not consciously activate all semiotic connections in the mind to make sense of a text. We do need, however, to keep track of relations and transformations on the given semiotic level. For instance, Blake's little poem

> What is it men in women do require?–
> The lineaments of gratified desire.

What is it women do in men require?–
The lineaments of gratified desire.
   (Blake 1971: 167)

may certainly make us remember the expression of gratified desire of one or several partners at one or several occasions, i.e., it may trigger a number of individual mental images. In many readers, however, this will not happen at all, or it may at least not be the first and principal effect of reading it. Instead, the reader may first notice its parallelism, i.e., the almost identical wording of the two parts, the repetition of the rime, and its repeated question/answer structure. Second, at least on the face of it, the poem may be interpreted as stating two universal affirmative propositions: (1) every man wants to make certain that he gratifies the desire of his female partner, and (2) every woman wants to make certain that she gratifies the desire of her male partner. Such a reading is concerned with proportion and reciprocity: in the particular respect treated by the poem, man is to woman as woman is to man. The point of the poem is not at all to give instructions that may trigger vivid images. It is piece of gnomic poetry, a riddle that attempts to establish what is universally (or shouldn't we rather say wished for to be universally) true. Instead of provoking mental images, the poem is preoccupied with sound because its sound shape supports its meaning and significance. Its formal and material properties are designed to convince or persuade the readers about its truth. And to understand it, we only need to know the meaning of the words and recognize their concatenation.

In fact, the poem seems to use an image-schema rather than being about basic level images. Among the image-schemata mentioned by Mark Johnson is one called MATCHING. Because each of the two relationships mentioned in the poem are reciprocal, and together they are symmetrical, it seems to me that this poem offers an example of matching.

In longer and more complex texts, whether poetry or prose, we simply need, at least unconsciously, to make diagrams of relations and transformations at different text levels. Such activities are systematized within the study of literature, especially within the semiotic tradition from Russian formalism to the cognitive study of literature. But this effort is really an effort of discovering text properties, not of inventing them or adding to the text. In contradistinction to imaginative iconization, which clearly adds an iconic exemplification to the text (in much the same way a director embeds the written text within an iconic exemplification), the diagrammatization of the text claims to lay bare what is already there. It is not a claim that a given particular diagram of the text is the only possible one, not even at the level in question, but a claim that it is a valid representation of textual relations that may be pointed out in the text. For instance, the two great folklorists Vladimir Propp (1968) and Bengt Holbek (1986, who builds on Köngas Maranda) each made thorough studies of the folktale, but they ended up with very different diagrams of its narrative structure. In my opinion, both diagrammatizations are valid because they structure the tales according to well-defined criteria and recognizable text elements. However, the criteria differ; they do not contradict each other—they just focus on different relationships. The essential difference is that Propp analyzes the tales from the point of view of the initially active hero, whereas Holbek see the folktale as featuring two heroes (a hero and a heroine) who are taking turns in being active and passive. Although, personally I find Holbek's model superior because it is able to integrate and explain more basic oppositions than the one by Propp, preferring one model to the other depends on what seems relevant to the aims of one's own studies.

Thus, diagrammatization works with relations rather than entities, both on the level of language and on the level of images. It takes place on the level of image-schemata: (1) as syntax, in an extended sense, within the verbal system, and (2) as relations between objects within the nonverbal system. However, linguistic significations must also include basic level material in order to represent a lifeworld or a fictional universe of discourse. Concerning the relationship between images and words, diagrammatization seems to favor words and to work with lexical meanings without calling forth rich imagery. If, however, lexical meanings ultimately are redeemed by some kind of imagery, what happens to linguistic semantics? In figure 2, as regards language, only semantics has been focused on. The question is whether linguistic semantics is more than a kind of relay station that transmits the linguistic input to a plurality of nonlinguistic mental patterns. In other words, is there a relatively autonomous level of signification related to language?

Obviously, the problem has not escaped the linguists from Saussure onwards. One answer, proposed by Hjelmslev, is to distinguish between both form and substance and expression and content. Linguistic semantics, in this view, is the study of content

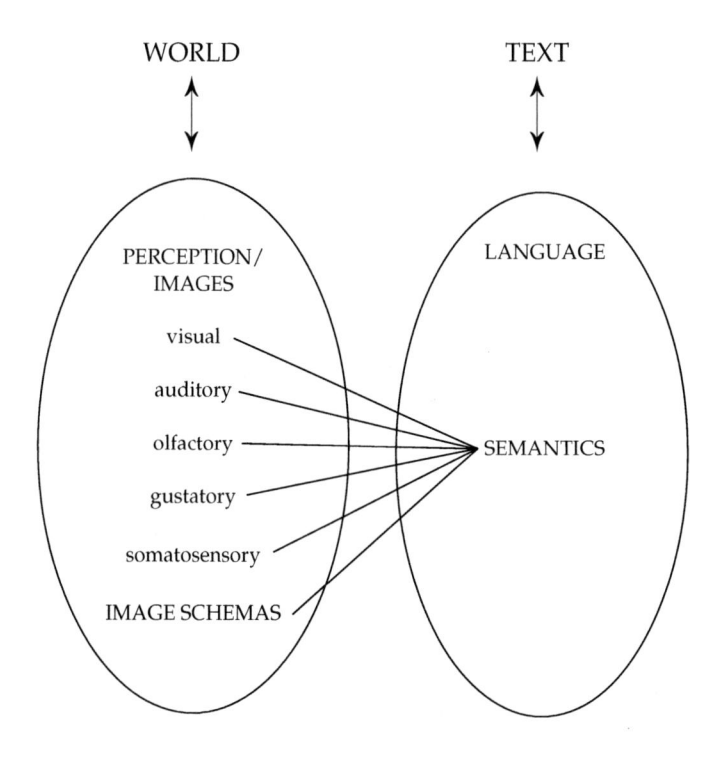

```
         WORLD                    TEXT
           ↕                        ↕

   ⎛                ⎞        ⎛            ⎞
   ⎜  PERCEPTION/   ⎟        ⎜  LANGUAGE  ⎟
   ⎜    IMAGES      ⎟        ⎜            ⎟
   ⎜                ⎟        ⎜            ⎟
   ⎜    visual ─╮   ⎟        ⎜            ⎟
   ⎜   auditory ─╮  ⎟        ⎜            ⎟
   ⎜   olfactory ───┼──→ SEMANTICS       ⎟
   ⎜   gustatory ─╯ ⎟        ⎜            ⎟
   ⎜ somatosensory ╯⎟        ⎜            ⎟
   ⎜ IMAGE SCHEMAS  ⎟        ⎜            ⎟
   ⎝                ⎠        ⎝            ⎠
```

FIGURE 2

form, that is, the way in which a given language parses the substance, the amorphous continuum the world is supposed to have consisted of before the formative influence of language. The classical example is also given by Hjelmslev, namely, that of the partition tree/wood/forest in Danish, German, and French:

> This congruence within one and the same zone of purport turns up everywhere. Compare also, for example, the following correspondences between Danish, German, and French:

		Baum	arbre
træ		Holz	bois
skov		Wald	
			forêt

We may conclude from this fact that in one of the two entities that are functives of the sign function, namely the content, the sign function institutes a form, the *content-form,* which from the point of view of the purport is arbitrary and which can be explained only by the sign function and is obviously solidarity with it. In this sense, Saussure is clearly correct in distinguishing between form and substance. (Hjelmslev 1953: 33–34)

Hjelmslev, it seems to me, is not stating his case for semantics as the study of the content form of language very well, not to mention its importance. The so-called content-form is, as he justly remarks, arbitrary and, I would like to add, a mere matter of usage, at least on the level of lexical semantics. What his example really shows is the lack of congruence between words and concepts. The Danes, like the Germans, French, and English, do distinguish between tree meaning a material, i.e., wood, and tree meaning an individual specimen of some species of trees, i.e., tree. They know very well when to go to the *trælasthandel* (timber merchant), and when to go to the *planteskole* (forest nursery). It just so happens that both "tree as a material" and "tree as a plant" are called by the same expression in Danish *træ*. I would further venture to hold that, in contradistinction to the content-form of lexical semantics, as exemplified by Hjelmslev, conceptual distinctions are hardly arbitrary. In this case, the distinction between material and specimen seems grounded in and motivated by our interaction with the environment in the experiential universe, and it is indifferent to the so-called content-form of different languages.

A radical response to the non-isomorphic relationship between concepts and linguistic entities would be to remove semantics as a part of linguistics proper, on the grounds that linguistic content cannot be studied independently of conceptual structures that are the outcome of the interrelation of mental images. This proposal is, in fact, not unfamiliar to linguistics itself. However, removing semantics from linguistics would be disastrous because neither phonology nor syntax can be studied without presupposing semantic distinctions. Furthermore, some linguists, in my opinion rightly, point out that semantics itself is dependent on pragmatics.

A less radical response would be to grant that in the different natural languages, semantic, in contradistinction to conceptual, distinctions do play a role in thinking because they function as labels that will trigger the coordination of mental images. This, however, may not be the whole story because we may share the labels without fully sharing the mental images that they trigger, i.e., without sharing the full range of conceptual distinctions. The word "woman" may, indeed, give rise to different images in different people. However, the same people who construct different mental images of the word "woman" may agree on its propositional content, or its semantic markers: a woman is an adult human being possessing female sexual characteristics, or formulated as semantic markers: + human + adult + femininity. Furthermore, there may be an agreement on a vague level of such points as to what constitutes womanhood while the specific purport may be controversial. In this case, for instance, the middle-sized world, to which our language is tuned according to Mark Johnson, may privilege anatomy, simply because it is visible and tangible while other differences on micro-levels are unnoticed or neglected (e.g., hormonal or cerebral differences between the sexes). In the final analysis, such questions have to do with the distinction between dictionary and encyclopedia (see, for instance, Eco 1986, 1990, and 1992). In practice, this distinction is hard to sustain, although dictionary definitions are often thought to be differential and negative ("woman" is defined by opposition to "man," i.e., + human + adult + femininity vs. + human + adult + masculinity), whereas encyclopedic definitions are positive and explanatory, and such definitions are most often narratives.

My point is not to deny the relevance of linguistic semantics, but rather to indicate that the place and scope of semantics and language have changed since Hjelmslev could triumphantly state:

> [I]t is wrong to believe that the concept is prior to the word or that thought is prior to language. On the contrary, the concept presupposes the word, thought presupposes language as its necessary foundation.
> Consequently, language is indeed not only the *expression* of thought. Language is a *basis* for thought. In relation to thought language is primary. Without articulate language articulate thought could not exist. Language articulates thought, segments it, and specifies its concepts. Without language we could only divide the world into individuals, we would not be able to comprise the individuals into classes. (Hjelmslev 1936: 32)

Today, the relationship between thought and language is deemed more complex. It seems that linguistics has to find its place, not as the only science basic to the study of thought, but as a member of a set of related sciences preoccupied with the study of signification and cognition, such as, for instance, semiotics, neuroscience, cognitive psychology, and metaphor studies.

Returning to the relationship between images and diagrams, there is a limit to privileging the tangible and perceptible aspects evoked by linguistic signs, namely, the fact that not all such signs do evoke images, or they will only evoke them contingently. The words "virtue," "wisdom," "courage," "temperance," and "justice" do not easily evoke mental images. And the argument that mental images are not evoked by words in isolation, but only by propositions is not valid: "Wisdom, courage, temperance, and justice constitute the philosophical virtues according to Plato" is certainly a proposition, but it doesn't do much better with regard to images than the isolated words. Again, it is possible to relate well the properties of these concepts and their opposites to each other by using diagrams. In fact, I suppose that it is by virtue of such a diagrammatic relationship that they manage to signify at all. I think, however, that in order to relate them to images, what one might call a narrative mediator between concept and image is required: "A temperate man does not eat and drink excessively or indulge excessively in erotic pleasures." However, at least in this case, the other words of this truncated narrative, "eat," "drink," and "erotic pleasures," certainly offer opportunities for imaginizing. The lack of image formation with regard to many words and propositions confirms the analysis of the poem by Blake. The point is not that meaning is possible without reference to bodily experiences—I don't think that it is. The point is rather (1) that the link between linguistic meaning and bodily experience need not be immediate, and (2) that bodily experience itself is governed by schemata.

Another argument in favor of at least a certain relative autonomy of semantics is the important advantage in relying only on the linguistic level of meaning formation, namely, that it speeds up the process of understanding. While reading Blake's poem, we may consciously disregard any image on the basic level, only attending to the isomorphic nature of the semantico-syntactic structures. That we are dealing with (significant) form itself, as Mark Johnson would say, is a fact of which we may not be aware at all.

Hence, diagrammatization is a process whose contribution to text understanding consists in the progressive linking of parts in the unfolding of the text. Novel meanings are created not by virtue of modification of basic level mental images, but rather through the novel juxtaposition and combination of ready-made linguistic meanings. For instance, Holbek (1986) is not redefining the conception of the young male or the young female or the meaning of active vs. passive; rather, he is offering a novel interpretation by noticing how these traditionally defined entities are combined differently in the course of the tale.

1.1.3 Allegorization

Finally, the metaphoric reading means to continuously allegorize the text. To allegorize means to speak otherwise than one seems to speak, and thus allegorical interpretation means looking for a second meaning.[2] In addition to the *sensus litteralis*, the common signification of words and the reference to historical facts, the interpreter is searching for a *sensus plenior* to reveal a more profound meaning that is not apparent. Many of the more or less systematized allegorical readings of the classical texts and of the Bible during antiquity and the Middle Ages have become infamous. However, allegorical reading is a kind of abstractive and applicative enterprise that attempts to tune the text to what were, or are, currently considered important aesthetic, moral, or epistemological issues. Thus, Paul writes to the Galatians:

> For it is written that Abraham had two sons, the one by a bondmaid, the other by a freewoman.
> But he *who was* of the bondwoman was born after the flesh; but he of the freewoman *was* by promise.
> Which things are an allegory: for these are the two covenants; the one from the mount Sinai, which gendereth to bondage, which is Agar.
> For this Agar is mount Sinai in Arabia, and answereth to Jerusalem which now is, and is in bondage with her children.
> But Jerusalem which is above is free, which is the mother of us all. (4.22-26)

The underlying structural device of this little passage is analogy, and it is already rather complex. It uses oppositions and identifications: Isaac is opposed to Ishmael as Sarah is to Hagar, and Isaac is identified with the New Covenant, as Ishmael is identified with the Old. Furthermore, Hagar is identified with Mount Sinai, which is identified with the Jerusalem of this world, and the latter is opposed to the Jerusalem above. Thus, there are transcategorical linkings of different domains; persons, i.e., mothers and sons; locations, i.e., landscape and city; and contractual relationships between man and a Supreme Being. But this is not the whole point. The current interest of this allegory is, according to Paul, that the Galatian brothers are, like Isaac, the children of promise, and that they should stand fast in their Christian freedom and not "entangle again with the yoke of bondage." Thus, an application is added that itself adds another analogy to the semantic tissue, namely, as Ishmael is to Isaac, so are the gentiles to the Galatians.

Since allegory is a species of metaphor,[3] it is no wonder that allegorizing is a process that starts in the text itself. In fact, there seems to be an allegorical side to most, maybe all, literary texts, and some genres, such as the fable, make it a main feature. But that allegories need not be didactic is evident from Anachreon's very short but complete allegory: "Pray, why do you look askance at me, my Thracian filly, and shun me so resolutely as though I knew nothing of my art? I would have you to know I could bridle you right well and take rein and ride you about the turning-post of the course. But instead you graze in the meadows and frisk and frolic to your heart's content; for you have no clever breaker to ride you" (84 in *Lyra graeca* 1944: 181). But what is this little poem about? Interestingly, it contains no clues whatsoever as to its allegorical nature. Why is it also about a nubile maiden (a fact already stressed by the appended commentary in the *Lyra graeca*), not only about a filly? The answer may be that the poem's basic analogy, that rider is to horse as man is to woman (very far from Blake´s non-allegorical proportion woman : man :: man : woman), already explores pre-existing cultural stereotypes: sexual intercourse is like riding and to make a newlywed woman obedient is like domesticating and breaking in a precious animal (and Alcman has a direct comparison of maidens and horses). Furthermore, without the allegory, although it is certainly objectionable, the poem would become not void of meaning but less interesting.

The thirst for metaphorical iconization, i.e., allegorization, is part of our general quest for meaning. In many cases, the second meaning is thought guaranteed by some kind of absolute authority, for instance, in case it is claimed to reveal what is meant and willed by a godhead (the famous transcendental signified). Nevertheless, even when knowledge is considered fallible,[4] transcategorical linking is seen as something precious despite the fact that it is well known that a difference persists between the elements belonging to the different categories (see below). There are, it seems to me, two reasons for this appreciation of the second meaning. First, the linking of two or more domains means that the principal domain (often called the target domain) is understood in the light of the other(s). The objectionable metaphor in Anachreon's poem, by giving a glimpse of how probably most Greek men then looked at women, offers valid, albeit grim, information about sexual and marital relationships of that time. Precisely because it is highly ideologically and emotionally charged, it tells us something significant about their attitudes. Hence, metaphorically, i.e., analogically, created meaning is valuable from both a cognitive and an emotional point of view.

Secondly, even if second meanings do not reveal unassailable truths, they are felt to enrich the text in question simply by creating connections. The indication that what is represented is not only itself but simultaneously also a sign of something else endows texts, lifeworlds, and human beings with a complexity that is most often conceived of as a profundity because it is felt that new dimensions are added to the phenomena. Kafka's *The Trial* is not only about Joseph K.'s falling victim to the weird courts operating in the attics of the city. It is also about a person succumbing to his cruel superego, or about the mechanisms of dictatorship, or about man's relation with a cruel father-god, i.e., in addition to the *sensus litteralis* there is another sense, the *sensus plenior*, or even more such senses.

Finally, in allegorization there is a quest for the generic. The bondwoman Hagar and her son Ishmael are individual beings, but they are taken to represent the Old Covenant. Joseph K., too, is an individual person, but allegorized he may represent the son unsuccessfully trying to break away from the law of the father. When we allegorize a text, we are not trying to connect it with personal memories or fantasies; rather, we are attempting to tie it up with culturally shared patterns of interpretation. Paul's reading of *Genesis 16–21* attempts to project a Christian reading onto an Old Testament text, and in doing so he applies the most general and the most important interpretive principle he knows. Hence, allegorization embodies general relationships or principles in a concrete case; thereby, in addition to being a phenomenon, state of affairs, or action in its own right, what is represented becomes an example of what is generally believed to be the case.

2.0 Conclusion: Reading as Iconization

Even if in different readers one mode of iconizing the text may become predominant, the concrete reading process will switch between these levels. Sometimes the reading provokes a vivid image or a series of images—whether visual, auditory, olfactory, or of taste and touch—or weak feelings of pleasure or pain. Sometimes the text is experienced as a diagram, an equation, or a parallelogram of forces. And sometimes it is taken to exemplify states of affairs or mind in the lifeworld contemporary with that of the text or with that of the reader. All three ways of reading are not only valuable, they are necessary since the very process of understanding literature calls for them all. If nothing in the text's representation of settings, props, and actions can be recognized to correspond to what can be retrieved as memory or fantasy images; if elements and parts cannot be related to each other; and if the issues of the text cannot be typified and mapped onto situations, dilemmas, and conflicts in the lifeworld, then the text will remain black marks on the paper.

The interplay between the three kinds of iconization will determine the nature and pace of the reading process. Obviously, whether the reader actualizes the rhythm and sound pattern of the text or produces visual imagery from description and dialogue, it means dwelling on smaller segments of the text and thus breaking up the journey to look at self-created sights (or to listen to sounds). Reading diagrammatically means an effort to knit together the different parts of what is represented in the chain of signs. In this case, the meaning of any segment of the text will depend upon its role and place in the text's process of connecting and transforming. Such a reading will tend to have a certain drive that urges on the reader to solve its riddles by knowing the end and, from this position, surveying it as a network of spatial relations, a kind of semantic skeleton. The allegorical reading, like the imaginative, also slows down the reading process because it is an attempt to relate textual patterns of meaning to another text that seems to belong to its immediate interpretants but which, nevertheless, has to be produced by the reader. In spite of the difficulties just mentioned, the ability and necessity to switch between these modes of iconization will guarantee a good deal of common ground between the readings of members within the same culture.

Depending on genre, period, and movement, literary texts differ in whether they give priority to imaginization, diagrammatization, or allegorization. Some texts, gnomic poetry, for instance, favor the diagrammatic and allegoric, while realistic narrative favors imaginative iconization and pretends that allegorization, as a species of metaphor, does not matter at all—an illusion, of course. However, although such differences are important, the efficiency and value of literature is to a large extent dependent on its simultaneous cultivation of all three modes of iconization. It makes it possible to dwell on the imaginative possibilities offered by the text, and to experience it as representing a nearly, but not totally, coherent universe within which developments and transformations almost have a logic of their own. Finally, it may point to an almost perfect matching between elements and structures of the text and a second pattern of signification.

In all three cases, however, there are openings, alternative ways of patterning, and partial mismatches. With regard to imaginative iconization, i.e., the translation of symbolic into iconic sign, only something, but certainly not everything, is prescribed (cf. a director's staging of a play). Diagrammatization clearly offers alternatives on different levels: one can choose between different systems of representation (e.g., geometric or arithmetic representation and between curves and columns). Furthermore, diagrams are based on interpretations, and thus alternative interpretations, i.e., alternative linkings of elements, will produce different diagrams. Allegorization, i.e., metaphoric iconization, is by the very nature of its process bound to reveal mismatches, differences, and incompatibilities.

University of Southern Denmark, Odense

Notes

1. Eco's distinction between "interpretation" and "use" and semantic and critical interpretation may turn out to be less than waterproof (see Eco 1990: 44–63, see also Eco 1986 and 1992).
2. Or for a second, third, and fourth meaning, as in the famous fourfold interpretation of the scriptures in the Middle Ages: literal, allegorical, tropological, and anagogic.
3. Because transcategorical linking is common to metaphor, allegory, and symbol, I find it impossible to distinguish clearly between them. I would venture to say that an analogy is a proportion between usually three or four elements as, for instance, an arithmetic analogy (such as a - b = b - c; e.g., $8 - 6 = 6 - 4 \rightarrow 2 = 2$). A metaphor is a semantically interpreted analogy that links elements from categorically different domains (e.g., Peter, the Apostle, is called the Rock, and in whichever way this is interpreted, a person is described as a specimen of inorganic nature). A symbol, it seems to me, is a metaphor that has gained a certain generality, either within a limited text corpus (e.g., within that of an individual

author) or within a culture at large. Finally, an allegory may be defined as a more or less extended and a more or less consistent network of metaphors.
4. Furthermore, truth as a correspondence between propositions and reality is conceived not as something beyond discussion, but as something that has to be investigated and defended by arguments.

Works Cited

Anachreon, see *Lyra graeca*
Blake, William. 1971. *The Complete Poems.* Edited by W.H. Stevenson. London: Longman.
Damasio, Antonio. 2000. *The Feeling of What Happens.* London: Vintage.
Eco, Umberto. 1984. *Semiotics and the Philosophy of Language.* Bloomington: Indiana University Press.
———. 1990. *The Limits of Interpretation.* Bloomington: Indiana University Press.
———. 1992. *Interpretation and Overinterpretation.* With Richard Rorty, Jonathan Culler, and Christine Brooke-Rose. Edited by Stefan Collini. Cambridge: Cambridge University Press.
Flaubert, Gustave. 1965 [1857]. *Madame Bovary.* Translated by E. Marx Eveling and P. de Man. New York: W.W. Norton.
Hjelmslev, Louis. 1936. "On the Principles of Phonematics." In *Proceedings of the 2nd International Congress of Phonology, 1935.* Cambridge GB: 49–54. Reprinted in L. Hjelmslev. 1973. *Essais linguistiques II.* Traveaux du Cercle Linguistique de Copenhague 14: 157–62. Copenhagen.
———. 1953 [1943]. *Prolegonema to a Theory of Language.* Baltimore: Waverly Press.
Holbek, Bengt. 1986. *Interpretation of Fairy Tales.* Helsinki: Academia Scientarum Finnica. FF Communications No. 239.
Ingarden, Roman. 1965 [1931]. *Das literarische Kunstwerk.* Tübingen: Max Niemeyer Verlag.
Iser, W. 1978. *The Act of Reading.* Baltimore: Johns Hopkins University Press.
Johnson, Mark. 1987. *The Body in the Mind: The Bodily Basis of Meaning, Imagination, and Reason.* Chicago: University of Chicago Press.
Lakoff, George. 1987. *Women, Fire, and Dangerous Things: What Categories Reveal about the Mind.* Chicago: University of Chicago Press.
Lyra graeca I–III. 1944 [1922–27]. Translated and edited by J.M. Edmons. Cambridge, Mass./London: Harvard University Press, Heinemann: Loeb.
Peirce, Charles S. 1931–58. *Collected Papers of Charles Sanders Peirce.* 8 vols. Edited by Charles Hartshorne, Paul Weiss, and A.W. Burks. Cambridge, Mass.: Harvard University Press.
———. Unpublished manuscripts. Numbered and paginated by the Institute for Studies in Pragmatism. Lubbock: Texas Tech University.
Propp, V. 1968 [1928]. *Morphology of the Folktale.* Austin: University of Texas Press.
Schutz, Alfred, and Thomas Luckmann. 1973. *The Structures of the Life-World.* Evanston, Ill.: Northwestern University Press.

Previous Volumes

THE PEIRCE SEMINAR PAPERS
Essays in Semiotic Analysis

Editor: Michael Shapiro, Professor of Slavic and Semiotic Studies, Brown University

"An excellent collection reflecting the ever-widening appeal and potential of Peirce's logic of signs." — **Peirce Project Newsletter**

VOLUME 2

Contents:

David Savan in Memoriam (1916 – 1992), *Michael Shapiro*

The Interface of Iconicity and Interpretants, *Edna Andrews*

Collaterality and Genetic Linguistics, *Raimo Anttila*

Le représentamen, le fondement, le signe et l'abduction, *Jean Fisette*

David Savan and the Last Signs of Peirce, *James Jakób Liszka*

The Pragmaticist Theory of Human Cognition and the Conception of Common-Sense, *Dan Nesher*

Another Culture, *Peter H. Salus*

C. S. Peirce and American Semiotics, *David Savan*

The Trinity as Semiotic, *Marianne Shapiro*

On Hermeticism in Semiotics, *T. L. Short*

1994. 264 pages
ISBN 1-57181-060-9 hardback

VOLUME 4

"To anyone interested in the cognitive bases of language and/or the theoretical foundations of linguistics, this book has a great deal to offer."
— **Language**

1999. 700 pages, bibliog.
ISBN 1-57181-732-8 hardback

www.berghahnbooks.com

Of Related Interest

RELATIVE POINTS OF VIEW
Linguistic Representations of Culture

Edited by **Magda Stroinska**

The relationship between language and various kinds of non-linguistic behavior has been of great fascination for many of those working in the fields of cultural anthropology, linguistics, and philosophy, or, broadly understood, cultural studies. The authors in this volume explore this relationship in a number of cultures and social contexts and discuss the problem of linguistic relativism and its application to several areas of social interaction across cultures. The authors deal with such questions as how language and culture intersect resulting in different points of view on reality that are all equally authentic and rooted in experience. The question of the influence of language and culture on our perceptino of physical and social reality is re-examined for such domains as politics, commerce, working with people, religion, and gender relations.

Contents: Space and Time in Natural Language - Politicians on Drugs: Functions of Political Metaphor across Culture - Rendering Metaphor in Reported Speech - Between Relativism and Truth: Jean Baudrillard, the Sokal Affair, and the Use of Scientific Terminology across Cultural Boundaries - Nationalism and Culture: Some Reflections on the Construction of National Languages - Language, Culture, and Gender Identities: Examining Arguments about Marriage - Management, Culture, and Discourse in International Business - Emotion and Labor in Cultural Comparison - From "Ulla Ulla" to "Cosmic Linguistics": On Alien Language and Culture in Science Fiction - Intercultural Competence: Theories into Practice

Magda Stroinska teaches in the Department of Modern Languages, McMaster University.

2000, 256 pages, bibliog., index
ISBN 1-57181-202-4 hardback
ISBN 1-57181-340-3 paperback
Volume 5, *Polygons: Cultural Diversities and Intersections*

www.berghahnbooks.com